e-mail Directory of
Publishers and Booksellers in India

Second Revised and Enlarged Edition

DIRECTORY

e-mail Directory of Publishers and Booksellers in India

Second Revised and Enlarged Edition

Compiled by
Amita Gupta
Ashish Kumar

ATLANTIC
PUBLISHERS & DISTRIBUTORS (P) LTD

Published by

ATLANTIC

PUBLISHERS & DISTRIBUTORS (P) LTD

7/22, Ansari Road, Darya Ganj,
New Delhi-110002
Phones : +91-11-23273880, 23275880, 23280451
Fax : +91-11-23285873
Web : www.atlanticbooks.com
E-mail : info@atlanticbooks.com

Branch Office
5, Nallathambi Street, Wallajah Road,
Chennai-600002
Phones : +91-44-64611085, 32413319
E-mail : chennai@atlanticbooks.com

ISBN 978-81-269-1070-0

Rs. 195.00

Printed in India at Nice Printing Press, A-33/3A, Site-IV, Industrial Area, Sahibabad, Ghaziabad, U.P.

PREFACE

We are glad to place in the hands of the readers the revised, updated and enlarged edition of *E-mail Directory of Publishers and Booksellers in India*. It will be highly useful to publishers and booksellers in India. Besides, the *Directory* will be useful to a large number of companies dealing in products and services used by the Publishing & Bookselling Industry, for example, Paper-Manufacturers & Distributors; Computers—Software & Hardware; Packaging Machinery & Materials; Printers & Binders; EPABX-Manufacturers & Distributors; and dealers in Office Furniture and Equipment, Photocopy Machines and Supplies, Slotted Angle Racks, etc. It will also be beneficial to librarians in procurement of books.

Postal transmission of information takes time; that is why it is called 'snail mail'. In contrast, electronic transmission has made possible instant transmission which is also less costly than the other modes. In the modern age, where things are moving very fast, promptness is required in every field of work. The electronic transmission is far more certain and instant in providing service. Keeping in mind the demand of the modern world, the present *Directory* has been compiled. It will ably serve the needs of all those connected, directly or indirectly, with publishing and book selling trade.

An effort has been made to make the *Directory* as accurate as possible. In spite of this, the compilers and the publisher do not accept responsibility for any mistake which still creeps in.

We shall be grateful if e-mail address changes in the *Directory* are brought to our notice so that they can be corrected in the next edition to provide maximum benefit to the users.

AMITA GUPTA
ASHISH KUMAR

CONTENTS

A

A. MUKHERJEE & CO. PVT. LTD., Kolkata
✆ 22302256, Fax: 91-33-22313080
▮ 9330857871/9830361557
✉ amcpltd@yahoo.co.in, bibekbaidya@gmail.com

A. SAGAR BOOK HOUSE, Delhi
✆ (O) 22427658, 22469169 (R) 23281065
✉ asagarbh@yahoo.com

A&A PERIODICAL SUBSCRIPTION AGENCY (P) LTD., New Delhi
✆ 23240257, Fax: 91-11-23240273
✉ aasub.delb.vsnl.net.in

A.A. BOOK GALLERY, Coimbatore
✆ 2304650, 5358713
▮ 9842277764, 9842222764, 9842207764
✉ aabookshop@rediffmail.com

A.B. BOOK AGENCY, Bangalore
✆ 3317189, Fax: 3348390
✉ abba@bgl.vsnl.net.in

A.B.C. PUBLISHERS & DISTRIBUTORS, New Delhi
✆ 23278399, Fax: 91-11-23283380
✉ abcpd@rediffmail.com

A.H. WHEELER & CO. LTD., Allahabad
✆ (O) 23312629, 23318357 (R) 26858306
Fax: 23724798
✉ wheelerbooks@mantraonline.com

A.I.E.TS. COM. PVT. LTD., New Delhi
✆ 26691021, 26691713
✉ aiets@rediffmail.com

A.I.T.B.S. PUBLISHERS, Delhi
✆ 22549313, Fax: 91-11-22543416
✉ aitbs@vsnal.com

A.K. AGENCIES, Mumbai
✆ (O) 28737347 (R) 28661249
✉ agrawalajay@indya.com

A.K. EXPORTS, Mumbai
✆ 26327007
✉ akexports@rediffmail.com

A.P.C. BOOKS, New Delhi
✆ 28752604, Fax: 91-11-28756921
✉ apcmedicalbooks@yahoo.co.in

A.P.C. PUBLICATIONS (P) LTD., New Delhi
✆ 23517879, 23624945, Fax: 23513456
✉ apc@apcbooks.com

A.P.H. PUBLISHING CORPORATION, Delhi
✆ 23285807, Fax: 23274050
✉ aphbooks@vsnl.net

A TO Z BOOKS, Delhi
✆ 23869513
✉ rkdc@mantraonline.com

A.V.I. BOOKS, Guwahati
✉ avibooks2003@rediffmail.com

A.V.I. BOOKS (P) LTD., New Delhi
✆ (O) 23271887, 23259151 (R) 26484854
▮ 9811325467, Fax: 23262021
✉ avibooks@rediffmail.com

AACHARYA SHRI ENTERPRISES, Delhi
✆ 31042570, Fax: 22424057
✉ acharyashri@bol.net.in

AADHAR PRAKASHAN PRIVATE LIMITED, Panchkula
✆ 2566952, 5048541, Fax: 91-172-2570725
✉ aadhar_prakashan@yahoo.com

AAKAR BOOKS, Delhi
✆ (O) 22795505 (R) 22716654, Fax: 91-11-22795641
✉ aakarbooks@gmail.com

AAKARSHAN COMPUTER SYSTEMS PVT. LTD., New Delhi
✆ 26840453, 26827005, Fax: 91-11-26839133 — acs_b56@hotmail.com

AAKIF BOOK DEPOT, New Delhi
✆ 23257189, Fax: 23265480 — aakif@del3.vsnl.net.in

AALEKH PRAKASHAN, Delhi
✆ 22277625, 22290582, Fax: 22290582 — alekh@mantraonline.com

AAPKI SAMASYA HAMARA SAMADHAN, Delhi
✆ 23278761, 22170794 — arihant-int@vsnl.com

AARTI PRAKASHAN, New Delhi
✆ 26441516, 26485210, Fax: 91-11-26418721 — aartiprakashan@hotmail.com

AARUSHI BOOKS, New Delhi
▮ 9118085090, Fax: 91-11-23326744 — aarushibooks@hotmail.com

AAVISHKAR PUBLISHERS & DISTRIBUTORS, Jaipur
✆ 2578159, Fax: 91-141-2568159 — aavishkarbooks@hotmail.com

ABHIJEET PUBLICATIONS, Delhi
✆ 65698474 — abhijeetpublication@gmail.com

ABHIMANI PUBLICATIONS, Bangalore
abhimani@bgl.vsnl.net.in

ABHINAV PUBLICATIONS, New Delhi
✆ (O) 26566387, 26562784, 26524658
(R) 26560932, 26866112, Fax: 26857009 — shakti@nde.vsnl.net.in

ABHISHEK PRAKASHAN, Delhi
✆ 65640278 — abhpub@hotmail.com

ABHISHEK PUBLICATIONS, Chandigarh
✆ 5003768, Fax: 91-172-2707562 — abhpub@yahoo.com

ACADEMIA BOOKS, Kharagpur
✆ 03222-779254 — acad173@netscape.net

ACADEMIC BOOK CENTRE, Bikaner
✆ 0151-2526898, Fax: 2209388 — yash_pub@yahoo.com

ACADEMIC BOOK HOUSE, Mumbai
✆ 24142587 — kg_krishan@vsnl.net

ACADEMIC BOOKS DIVISION
(STERLING PUBLISHERS PVT. LTD.), New Delhi
✆ 26387070/7071, Fax: 91-11-26383788 — ghai@ned.vsnl.net.in

ACADEMIC BOOKS INTERNATIONAL, Jaipur
abishukla@yahoo.com

ACADEMIC BOOKS & PERODICALS, New Delhi
✆ 26487655 ▮ 9811143335 — abpsunil@yahoo.co.in

ACADEMIC EXCELLENCE, Delhi
✆ 22445526, 22453953 — books@indianacademicpublisher.com

ACADEMIC FOUNDATION, Ghaziabad
✆ 42621793, 42611015, Fax: 4611016 — academic@vsnl.com

ACADEMIC FOUNDATION, New Delhi
✆ 23245001-04, Fax: 23245005 — academic@vsnl.com

ACADEMIC (INDIA) PUBLISHERS (REGD.), New Delhi
✆ (O) 25742171, 25812181 (R) 25764880
Fax: 25722671 — angelaip@del3.vsnl.net.in

ACADEMIC PRESS (THE), Gurgaon
✆ 2322779, 2322005, Fax: 91-2324782 — ind-doc-sea@satyam.net.in, academic@hotmail.com

ACADEMIC PUBLISHERS, Kolkata
✆ (O) 22414857 (R) 23500559, Fax: 22413702 — acabooks@cal.vsnl.net.in

ACADEMIC PUBLISHERS, Kolkata
✆ 22571071, Fax: 91-33-22413702 — info@acabooks.net

ACADEMIC PUBLISHING LTD., Delhi
Fax: 22249614 — pkgupta@giasdlw.vsnl.net.in

ACADEMY OF INDIAN NUMISMATICS AND SIGILLOGRAPHY, Indore
✆ 2493931, Fax: 2532796 — skaca_numisigind@indiatimes.com

ACCUPRESSURE HEALTH CARE SYSTEMS, Delhi
✆ 23991804 — acs_syscm@yahoo.com

ACOUSTICS ENGINEERS, Pune
✆ 25534693, Fax: 25533453 — acen@vsnl.com

ACTIVAIR AIRFREIGHT INDIA (P) LTD., New Delhi
✆ 24602293, Fax: 24646482, 24628014 — activair@vsnl.com

ADAM PUBLISHERS & DISTRIBUTORS, New Delhi
✆ 23284740, 23282550, Fax: 23267510 — apd@bol.net.in

ADARSH ENTERPRISES, New Delhi
✆ 23246131, 23246132, Fax: 23246130 — adarshbooks@vsnl.com

ADHAAR PRAKASHAN PVT. LTD., Panchkula
✆ 2566952, 2567004, Fax: 91-172-2570725 — adhaar@sancharnet.in

ADHYATMA VIJNANA PRAKASHAN, Bahadurgarh
✆ 91-1276-243646, 243656, Fax: 91-1276-210344 — adhyatmavijnana@rediffmail.com

ADHYAYAN PUBLISHERS AND DISTRIBUTORS, New Delhi
✆ 23263018, 23277156, Fax: 91-11-23280028 — adhyayanpublishers@yahoo.com

ADITYA BOOKS PVT. LTD., New Delhi
✆ (O) 51724129-30, 29841409, 29849132
(R) 26922991 ▮ 9810773223
Fax: 51724167, 29841116 — abooks@vsnl.net.in

ADITYA MEDICAL BOOK DISTRIBUTORS, Lucknow
✆ 2231724, 2233416, Fax: 2229164 — adityamedical@msm.com

ADITYA MEDICAL PUBLISHERS, New Delhi
✆ 23243088, Fax: 91-522-2629164 — adityamedical@msn.com

ADITYA PRAKASHAN, Delhi
✆ 27245584, 27420564, Fax: 23282047 — bibimpex@giasd101.vsnl.net.in

ADVAITA ASHRAMA, Kolkata
✆ 22164000 — mail@advaitaasharma.org

ADVANCE STUDY CENTRE, Guwahati
✆ 2546533, 2525736, Fax: 0361-2660291 — lahkar1@sify.com

ADVENT BOOKS, New Delhi
✆ (O) 011-55450290 (R) 25455731
Fax: 011-25161868 — advent_books@hotmail.com

AERO EXPORTS, Delhi
✆ 23274339, 26222766, Fax: 23263567 — gagans@vsnl.com, sgagans@nde.vsnl.net.in

AFFILIATED EAST-WEST PRESS (P) LTD., New Delhi
✆ 23315398, Fax: 23260538 — affiliat@vsnl.com, affiliat@nda.vsnl.net.in

AFRO-ASIAN BOOK COUNCIL, New Delhi
✆ 23258865, Fax: 91-11-23267437 — afro@aabcouncil.org

AGARWAL BOOK STORE, Jamshedpur
✆ 439906, Fax: 424849 — abs@tatanagar.com

AGROBIOS (INDIA), Jodhpur
✆ 2643993, Fax: 91-291-2642319 — agrobios@sify.com

AGRO BOTANICAL PUBLISHERS, Bikaner
✆ 2522523, Fax: 0151-2526756 — agrobios@sify.com

AGROSCIENCES BOOK CENTRE , New Delhi
✆ 23242905, 23243058 ▮ 9810003188
Fax: 23243058 — abc_jain@123india.com

AGROTECH PUBLISHING ACADEMY, Udaipur
✆ 0294-2465635 — agrotechbooks@rediffmail.com

AHUJA BOOK COMPANY PVT. LTD., New Delhi
✆ 23276564, 23245859, Fax: 91-11-23281514 — info@ahujabooks.com

AJAI BOOK DISTRIBUTORS, New Delhi
✆ 24646404, 24615224, Fax: 24615224 — abddelhi49@yahoo.co.in

AJANTA BOOKS INTERNATIONAL (PUNJABI), Delhi
✆ (O) 23926182 (R) 27415016, Fax: 27415016 — ajandabi@ndf.vsnl.net.in

AJAY BOOK DISTRIBUTORS, Delhi
✆ 22043229, Fax: 91-11-22043229 — abd_books@yahoo.co.in

AJAY BOOK SERVICE PUBLISHERS & DISTRIBUTORS, New Delhi
✆ 23287655, Fax: 91-11-23279443 — info@ajaybookservice.com

AJAY PARMAR & CO., New Delhi
✆ 23284894, Fax: 91-11-23281819 — aparmar@vsnl.com

AJAY PRINTERS & PUBLISHERS, Roorkee
✆ 273140, 274740 — mehta@ndb.vsnl.net.in

AKALANK PUBLICATIONS, Delhi
✆ (O) 23915064, 32215064 (R) 23976292
Fax: 91-11-23986793 — info@akalank.com

AKANSHA PUBLISHING HOUSE, New Delhi
✆ 23263193, Fax: 91-11-23263193 — ektabooks@yahoo.com

AKASH BHARTI COMPUTECH, New Delhi
✆ 27949224 ▮ 9891463330 — professorfunny@yahoo.com

AKHAND JYOTI SANSTHAN/GAYATRI PARIVAR, Mathura
✆ 2403940, Fax: 2412273 — ajsansthan@awgp.org

AKHIL BHARATIYA MARATHI PRAKASHAK SANGH, Pune
✆ 91-20-25654949 — jyotsnaprakashan@vsnl.com

AKHIL VISHWA GAYATRI PARIWAR, Kanpur
✆ 91-512-2461754, Fax: 91-512-2409163 — vishwagayatri@rediffmail.com

AKSHAR PUBLICATIONS, Tripura (West)
✆ 2307500, Fax: 91-381-2323468 — rana-agt@yahoo.co.in

AKSHARA, Hyderabad
✆ 040-23543906, 23540568 — akshara@hd2.dot.net.in

AKS-O-AAWAZ, New Delhi
9899478610 — aksoaawaz@yahoo.com

ALAKANANDA PRACHURANALU, Vijayawada
2476966, Fax: 91-866-2476652 — viwabooks@vsnl.in

AL-BALAGH PUBLICATIONS, New Delhi
26914592 — abpublications@gmail.com

AL DARUSSALAFIAH, Mumbai
23088989, 23082737, Fax: 23065710 — salafiah@hotmail.com

AL-HASANT BOOKS (P) LTD., New Delhi
23271845, Fax: 91-11-41563256 — m_alhasanat@rediffmail.com

ALEKH PRAKASHAN, Delhi
22381582, 32911582, Fax: 91-11-223811582 — alekhprakashan@gmail.com

ALEKH PRAKASHAN, Delhi
(O) 22290582, 31062289 (R) 22293196 — alekh@mantraonline.com

ALEKH SAMVAD, Delhi
32911582, Fax: 91-11-22382582 — alekhsamvad@gmail.com

ALFA PUBLISHERS, New Delhi
91-11-23275092 — alfapublications@yahoo.co.in

ALKA PUBLICATIONS, Mumbai
22624439, Fax: 91-22-22632585 — manojlakhani@vsnl.net

ALL INDIA CONFEDERATION OF THE BLIND, New Delhi
27054082, Fax: 91-11-27050915 — aicbdelhi@yahoo.com

ALL INDIA MANAGEMENT ASSOCIATION, New Delhi
24634026, Fax: 24626689 — adcms@aima-ind.org

ALL INDIA NATURE CURE FEDERATION, Delhi
27482211, 27481710, Fax: 27477576 — bb_goel@indiatimes.com

ALL INDIA PUBLISHERS & DISTRIBUTORS (REGD.), Chennai
28233004, 55250321, Fax: 28204911 — aipdraj@vsnl.com, aipdrajdelhi@vsnl.net

ALL INDIA SOCIETY FOR ELECTRONICS & COMPUTER TECHNOLOGY, Bhopal
3293214, Fax: 91-755-2429096 — aisect_bpl@sancharnet.in

ALL INDIA TRAVELLER BOOKSELLER (REGD. A.I.T.B.S.), Delhi
22549313, 22460494, 22054798
Fax: 22543416, 22218401 — aitbs@ndf.vsnl.net.in

ALL INDIA URDU PUBLISHERS & BOOKSELLERS ASSOCIATION, New Delhi
23257189, Fax: 91-11-23265480 — aakif@del3.vsnl.net.in

ALLIANCE BOOK SUPPLIERS (PVT.) LTD., Delhi
22811856, 22288583, 22817533, Fax: 22812619 — abspl@vsnl.com, sdhar@nde.vsnl.net.in

ALLIANCE FRANÇAISE DE DELHI, New Delhi
43500200, Fax: 91-11-43500228, 43500229 — front_desk@afdelhi.org

ALLIANCE PUBLISHERS, Noida
(O) 2539073, 2401752, 2401753, 2580920
(R) 2430068, 2430314, Fax: 2584159, 2663699 — alliancepublishers@aisnoida.com, info@alliancepublishers.com

ALLIED BOOK CENTRE, Dehradun
9837066875 (R) 2650945, Fax: 0135-2656554 — abc_rediffmail.com

ALLIED BOOKS CENTRE, Jodhpur
✆ 264[illegible]993 — agrabios@vsnl.com

ALLIED CHAMBERS (INDIA) LTD., New Delhi
✆ 23239001, 23233001, Fax: 23235967 — aplnd@del2.vsnl.net.in

ALLIED PUBLISHERS LIMITED, Mumbai
✆ 22626476, 22617926, 22617924, Fax: 22617926 — alliedpl@bom4.vsnl.com

ALLIED PUBLISHERS PVT. LTD., New Delhi
✆ (O) 23239001, 23233002 (R) 24358751
Fax: 91-11-23235967 ▮ 9810054233 — alliedpublishers@eth.net

ALMOE DIGITAL SOLUTIONS (P) LTD., Bangalore
✆ 40468686, Fax: 91-80-40468687 — sumeet@almoe.com

ALTER MEDIA, Thrissur
✆ 0487-2422974 — altmedia@md4.vsnl.net.in

AMAN ISHARA, New Delhi
✆ 23265371, Fax: 91-11-23286630 — amanishara@yahoo.com

AMAN PRAKASHAN, Delhi
✆ 27015013, 27018426 — amanprakashan87@mantraonline.com

AMAR BOOK SELLERS, New Delhi
✆ 23324142, 23324153, Fax: 22434436 — amarbook@satyam.net.in

AMAR GRANTH PUBLICATIONS, Delhi
✆ 27252362, Fax: 27252362 — amargp@ndf.vsnl.net.in

AMARSATYA PRAKASHAN, Delhi
✆ 22050766 — amarsatya-prk@yahoo.com

AMAZAN BOOKS, New Delhi
✆ 23245111, Fax: 91-11-23245444 — uniqueselar@hotmail.com

AMAZON HOUSE OF BOOK & MUSIC, Aurangabad
✆ 0240-722928, 335220 — sharayuamazon@ip.eth.net

AMBAR PRAKASHAN, New Delhi
✆ 23625528, 23522997, 23670067, Fax: 23676058 — pitambar@bol.net.in

AMBANI BOOK DISTRIBUTORS, Rajkot
▮ 9824511244, Fax: 0281-2221254 — ambanibooks@yahoo.co.in

AMBIKA BOOK AGENCY, Jaipur
✆ 0141-2304921 — vikram.agri1@usa.net

AMERICAN INFN. RESOURCE CENTRE, New Delhi
✆ 23316841, Fax: 23329499 — libdel@pd.state.gov

AMICUS BOOKS, Kashmir
✆ 2427227, 2420493, 2426457, Fax: 0194-2427227 — amicusbooks@yahoo.com

AMIT BOOK DISTRIBUTOR, New Delhi
✆ 65164316, Fax: 91-11-27062968 — amit_abd@yahoo.com

AMIT BOOKS/AMIT PRAKASHAN, New Delhi
✆ 26452255, 26489507, Fax: 26478458 — amitprakashan@yahoo.co.in

AMIT PUBLISHERS & DISTRIBUTORS, New Delhi
✆ 65396510, 43560006, Fax: 91-11-23281136 — sb_amitpub@yahoo.com

**AMNESTY INTERNATIONAL (INDIA) FOUNDATION/
DAANISH,** New Delhi
✆ 26854763, Fax: 91-11-26510202 — mukul1961@yahoo.co.in

AMRIT BOOKS, New Delhi
✆ 51611861-65, Fax: 91-11-51611866 — sales@diamondpublications.com

AMUDHA NILAYAM LIMITED, Chennai
✆ 28261343, 28261790, Fax: 28257158 — japonica@rediffmail.com

ANADA PRAKASHAN PVT. LTD., Ahmedabad
✆ (O) 22139900, 22169956 (R) 25464118, 25468235 — anadaadi@sancharnet.in
Fax: 91-79-22139900

ANAMAYA PUBLISHERS, New Delhi
✆ 29523205, Fax: 91-11-29523205 — anamayapub@vsnl.net

ANAND ASSOCIATES, New Delhi
✆ 26123365, Fax: 91-11-22723067 — thrupti@vsnl.com

ANAND ASSOCIATES, Mumbai
✆ 22723065-66, Fax: 22723067 — thrupti@vsnl.com

ANANDA PUBLISHERS PVT. LTD., Kolkata
✆ 224214352, 224213417, Fax: 22193856 — ananda@cal3.vsnl.net.in

ANANDA SANGHA, Gurgaon
✆ 0124-5059550 — ananda@anandaindia.org

ANDREAS-PUNNOOSE FOUNDATION, Kottayam
✆ 2430470, Fax: 91-481-2320041 — kppunnoose@gmail.com

ANE BOOKS, New Delhi
✆ (O) 23276843-44 (R) 27011631, Fax: 011-23276863 — anebooks@vsnl.com

ANGEL PUBLISHING HOUSE, New Delhi
✆ 25772171, 25742171 — angelaip@del3.vsnl.net.in

ANGOOR PRAKASHAN, Delhi
✆ 91-11-65426615 — angoorprakashan@yahoo.in

ANIL BOOK CORNER, New Delhi
✆ 23713223 — abcplaza@yahoo.com

ANJUMAN TARAQQI URDU (HIND), New Delhi
✆ 23237210, 23236299, Fax: 91-11-23239547 — urduadabndli@bol.net.in

ANKIT INFORMATICS (P) LTD., New Delhi
✆ (O) 22468417, 22019574 (R) 22457606 — ankinfo@yahoo.com
Fax: 91-11-22019574

ANMOL PUBLICATIONS PVT. LTD., New Delhi
✆ 23261597, 23255577, 23278000, Fax: 23280289 — anmolpublications@vsnl.com

ANNAI NILAYAM, Sivakasi
✆ 04562-20683 — annai_nm@angelfire.com

ANTARCTICA GRAPHICS PVT. LTD., Kolkata
✆ 23502173, 23510564, Fax: 23507658 — anta.graphic@gems.vsnl.net.in

ANTIKA PRAKASHAN, Ghaziabad
✆ 91-120-6475212 — aantika1999@yahoo.co.in

ANUBHAV PRAKASHAN, Ghaziabad
✆ 2630699, 2635277 — anubhavprakashan@gmail.com

ANUBHUTI PRAKASHAN, Allahabad
✆ (O) 0532-2466870, 3152109 (R) 2466870 — am26j@rediffmail.com

ANUPRIYA PUBLISHING HOUSE, Jaipur
✆ 0141-2521627, 2524039 — mmgoyalg@satyam.net.in, anupriya_pub@yahoo.com

ANURADHA PUBLICATIONS, Chennai
✆ 24360134, Fax: 91-44-24357410 — anuradhaags@vsnl.net

ANURAG TRUST, Lucknow
✆ 91-522-2786782, 91-11-26895809 — anurag_trust@rediffmail.com

ANWESHA, Guwahati
✆ 2664662 — anweshaguwa@sify.com

APARNA BOOKS & PERIODICALS, Mysore
✆ 0821-2412258 — aparnabooks@vsnl.com

APEX PUBLISHING HOUSE, New Delhi
✆ 23512722, 31068948, Fax: 91-11-23622726 — apexhouse@rediffmail.com

APPLE BOOKS, New Delhi
✆ (O) 23289282 (R) 27125707 ▮ 9811010262 — applebooks@now-india.net.in

APPLE PUBLISHING INTERNATIONAL PVT LTD, Chennai
✆ 26224690, Fax: 91-44-26211085 — infor@applebooks.org

APPLIED MEDIA, New Delhi
✆ 25707820, 25708940 ▮ 9868157782 — appliedmedia@vsnl.com
Fax: 25707820

APPLIED MEDIA, Mumbai
✆ 22-26100406, Fax: 26115237 — applied@nda.vsnl.net.in

AR-RAHMAN PUBLICATIONS, Delhi
✆ 23266198 ▮ 9899031430, Fax: 23257196 — triveni@ndf.vsnl.net.in

ARAVALI BOOKS INTERNATIONAL (P) LTD., New Delhi
✆ 26388830-32, 26389736-38, Fax: 26388829 — aravali@nde.vsnl.net.in

ARCHAEOLOGICAL SURVEY OF INDIA, New Delhi
✆ 23019108, 23015283, Fax: 23010953 — asi@del3.vsnl.net.in

ARCHANA PUBLICATIONS (P) LTD., New Delhi
✆ 25698295, 25742276, 25767516 — booksforall@bookhiveindia.com

ARCHIES LTD., New Delhi
✆ 41410000, Fax: 91-11-41410060 — cb@archiesonline.com

AREEB PUBLICATIONS, New Delhi
✆ 23282550, 23284740, Fax: 91-11-23267510 — apd@bol.net.in

ARIDHI HI-TECH INDUSTRIES LTD., Mumbai
✆ 22873257, 22844117, Fax: 22870330 — aridhi@vsnl.com

ARIES BOOKS INTERNATIONAL, Chennai
✆ 24952605 — aries@md3.vsnl.in

ARIHANT PRAKASHAN, Meerut
✆ 2401479, 2512970, Fax: 91-121-2401648 — info@arihantprakashan.com

ARNOLD PUBLISHERS, New Delhi
✆ 23270718, Fax: 91-11-23267224 — arnoldind@mantraonline.com

AROGYADHAM RASTRIYA PARIVARIK SAWASTHYA PATRIKA, Muzaffar Nagar
✆ 2408226, 2401031, Fax: 2420476 — arogyadham@vsnl.com

AROO PUBLICATIONS PVT LTD, New Delhi
✆ 64140001, Fax: 91-11-23245011 — aroopublications@hotmail.com

ARORA BOOK COMPANY, New Delhi
✆ 23257092, 23257964, Fax: 91-11-23257964 — sumit311@hotmail.com

ARPANA ASHRAM, Karnal
✆ 2380801-03, Fax: 2380810 — at@arpana.org

ARSEE PUBLISHERS, Delhi
✆ 91-11-65966481, 23280657 — arseepublishers@rediffmail.com

ART BOOK CENTER, Ahmedabad
✆ (O) 26582130 (R) 26750361, Fax: 79-26306376 — artbookcenter_2000@yahoo.com

ARUN BROTHERS, Mumbai
arunbros@vsnl.com

ARUN PUBLISHING HOUSE (P) LTD., Chandigarh
✆ 2702318, Fax: 2702189 — arunpublishing@hotmail.com, nebaaph@sancharnet.in

ARUNODAYA PRAKASHAN, New Delhi
✆ 91-11-23275710 — vaniprakashan@gmail.com

ARVIND BOOK DISTRIBUTORS, New Delhi
✆ (O) 25107455, 25107456 (R) 25190992
Fax: 91-11-25467782 — arvindm@vsnl.net.in

ARVIND PRAKASHAN, Udaipur
✆ 2412758, Fax: 91-294-2413563 — arvindprakashan@hotmail.com

ARVIND PRAKASHAN PVT. LTD., Meerut
✆ 2520263, 2533607, Fax: 91-121-2521607 — arvind@surevin.net

ARYA BOOK DEPOT, New Delhi
✆ 28751221/23, Fax: 91-11-28756324 — aryabookdepot@yahoo.com

ARYA (MEDI) PUBLISHING HOUSE, New Delhi
✆ 23274004, 23277444 ▮ 9810195696 — amph@mantraonline.com

ARYA PRAKASHAN, Delhi
✆ 91-11-23233280 — sanjeevaryaprakashan@rediffmail.com

ARYA PUBLISHING HOUSE, New Delhi
✆ (O) 25767012 (R) 25766144, 25751410
Fax: 91-11-25716921 — aryabookdepot@yahoo.com

ARYAN BOOKS INTERNATIONAL, New Delhi
✆ 23287589, 23255799, Fax: 91-11-23270385 — aryanbooks@vsnl.com

ARYAN PUBLISHING CO. (P) LTD., Kolkata
✆ 91-033-22375278, 22121690, Fax: 22120278 — aryan2@cal3.vsnl.net.in

ARYAS' BOOK CENTRE, Udaipur
✆ (O) 2526060 (R) 2584669, Fax: 2523086 — aryabooks@datainfosys.net

ASCENT PUBLICATIONS, Delhi
✆ 91-11-23847953 — ascentlawpub@yahoo.com

ASHA PRAKASHAN GRAHA, New Delhi
✆ 28750159, Fax: 91-11-28756324 — aryabookdepot@yahoo.com

ASHBHA BOOK HOUSE, Delhi
✆ 22445595, 22713103, Fax: 91-11-22713103 — ashbhabooks2002@yahoo.com

ASHISH BOOKS MARKETING SERVICES, New Delhi
✆ 26944293 ▮ 9818975698, Fax: 91-11-26954200 — bisht_abms@rediffmail.com

ASHOK BOOK CENTRE, Vijayawada
✆ 0866-2476966, 2472096, Fax: 2476652 — abcbooks@md3.vsnl.net.in

ASHOK DILWALI, New Delhi
✆ 23324446, Fax: 91-11-23328731 — kinsey@del2.vsnl.net.in

ASHOKA BOOK DEPOT, Delhi
✆ 27032416, 23288391 — ashoka@indianbookfair.com

ASHOKA PUBLISHING HOUSE, Delhi
✆ 27858255, Fax: 91-11-27858355 — mail@goldenseriesbooks.com

ASIA LAW HOUSE, Hyderabad
✆ (O) 24742324, 24608000 (R) 23540517
Fax: 24564007
✉ asialaw@satyam.net.in

ASIAN BOOK CENTRE, New Delhi
✆ (O) 26518359 (R) 26189402, Fax: 91-11-26961034
✉ rameshsondhi@yahoo.com

ASIAN BOOK HOUSE, Kashmir
✆ 0194-2426989, 2428235 (R) 2427595
✉ abh32@rediffmail.com

ASIAN BOOKS PVT. LTD., New Delhi
✆ 23282098, 23271887, 23287577, 23259151-71-81
Fax: 91-11-23262021
✉ rtaneja@asianbooksindia.com

ASIAN EDUCATIONAL SERVICES, New Delhi
✆ (O) 26560187, 26568594 (R) 26480728
Fax: 91-11-26852805, 26855499
✉ asian37@vsnl.com

ASIAN EDUCATIONAL SERVICES, New Delhi
✆ 26491586, Fax: 91-11-26494946
✉ aes@aes.ind.in

ASIAN TRADING CORPORATION, Bangalore
✆ 548744, 5490444, Fax: 5479444
✉ mail@atcbook.net

ASIATECH PUBLISHERS INC., Delhi
✆ (O) 91-11-22724601
✉ asiatech@pb.com

ASM PRESS/NELSON THORNES, Chennai
✆ 24346244, 24346266, Fax: 24346529
✉ itpsesha@giasmd01.vsnl.net.in

ASSISSI PRINTING AND PUBLISHING HOUSE, Changanacherry
✆ 2420188, 2429188, Fax: 04824-2420466
✉ assissi@giasmd01.vsnl.net.in,
scaria@assissipublishers.com

ASSOCIATED BOOKSELLERS, Agra
▮ 9897877556, Fax: 91-562-4008061
✉ vikram_jain2000@yahoo.com

ASSOCIATED SUBSCRIPTION AND INFORMATION SERVICES (INDIA) PVT. LTD., Chennai
✆ (O) 24454500, 24421229 (R) 24413792
Fax: 044-24910910, 24918747
✉ asissb@md3.vsnl.net.in

ASSOCIATION OF INDIAN UNIVERSITIES, New Delhi
✆ 23230059, Fax: 91-11-23232131
✉ publicationsales@aiuweb.org

ATLANTIC PUBLISHERS & DISTRIBUTORS (P) LTD., New Delhi
✆ 23273880, 23275880, 23280451
Fax: 91-11-23285873
✉ info@atlanticbooks.com,
manish@atlanticbooks.com

ATLAS BOOKS & PERIODICALS, Delhi
✆ (O) 27154313 (R) 27040781
✉ atlasbooks@yahoo.com

ATMA RAM & SONS, Delhi
✆ 91-11-23946466, 23973082
✉ atmarambooks@hotmail.com

ATMONNATI PRAKASHAN, Allahabad
✆ 2645716, 2645757, Fax: 2645757
✉ atmonnati@hotmail.com

AUGUSTAN PUBLISHERS & DISTRIBUTORS, New Delhi
✆ 26193514, 26169374, 26175481, Fax: 26184046
✉ basi@del3.vsnl.net.in

AUREOLE PUBLISHING PVT. LTD., Noida
✆ 4346022, Fax: 91-120-4346025
✉ customerservice@aureole.com

AUREOLE PUBLISHING PVT. LTD., Noida
✆ 91-120-2531807, 2534301, 2440053
Fax: 91-120-2531807
✉ vineet@aureole.co.in,
aureole_pub@vsnl.net

AUTHORSPRESS, Delhi
✆ 22436299, 22460145, 26851905, Fax: 22460145 — authorspress@yahoo.com

AVANTGARDE PRESS, Kolkata
✆ 4664094, 4100500 — ipslind@cal2.vsnl.net.in

AVI BOOKS PVT. LTD., New Delhi
✆ 23287577, Fax: 91-11-23262021 — avibooks@rediffmail.com

AVICHAL PUBLISHING COMPANY, New Delhi
✆ 28752745, 28755383, Fax: 91-11-28756921 — aryabookdepot@yahoo.com

AYURVED-VIKAS, Ghaziabad
✆ 24777901-925 (Ext. 2108), Fax: 24777935 — shastrias@dabur.com

B

B. BROS. & CO., Kolkata
bbrothersco@yahoo.com

B. CHATTAR SINGH JIWAN SINGH, Amritsar
✆ 2542346, 2547974, 2557973, Fax: 2542346 — contact@csjs.com, csjssales@hotmail.com

B. JAIN PUBLISHERS PVT. LTD., New Delhi
✆ 23580800, 51698991
Fax: 91-11-23580471, 51698993 — info@bjain.com

B.B.P. PUBLICATIONS PVT. LTD., Meerut
✆ 0121-2663699, 2667799
Fax: 2663699, 2667799 — bbpmrt@vsnl.net

B.C. EXPORTS (INDIA)/BUTALA PUBLICATIONS, New Delhi
✆ 23626782, 23527048, Fax: 91-11-23626782 — bcexpo@vsnl.net

B.C.I. PUBLICATIONS, Bangalore
✆ 22219184, 25084623, 25716993
Fax: 91-080-25084632/5712077 — bcipub@vsnl.com

B.D.P. EDUCATIONAL BOOKS PVT. LTD., Delhi
✆ 27947795, Fax: 91-11-27944625 — bdpc@yahoo.com

B.I. CHURCHILL LIBINGSTONE, New Delhi
✆ 23325313-17, Fax: 91-11-23323138 — bigroup@del3.vsnl.net.in

B.I. PUBLICATIONS PVT. LTD., New Delhi
✆ 23325313 (4-5-6-7), Fax: 91-11-23323138 — bigroup@del3.vsnl.net.in

B.K. BOOK AGENCY, Kolkata
✆ 25681274, 22486604
Fax: 91-33-22486604, 22481620 — bkba@vsnl.net

B.P.B. MULTIMEDIA, New Delhi
✆ 23267741, 23325760, Fax: 91-11-23262008 — bpb@vsnl.net

B.P.B. PUBLICATIONS (P) LTD., New Delhi
✆ (O) 23325760, 23723393, 23254990-91
(R) 23969355, Fax: 91-11-23266427 — bpb@vsnl.com

B.P.I. (INDIA) PVT. LTD., Mumbai ✆ 23808817, 23808819, Fax: 23872625	bpipl@vsnl.com
B.R. INTERNATIONAL PUBLISHERS/B.R. WORLD OF BOOKS, Delhi ✆ 22212894, 22227885	br_intel@rediffmail.com
B.R. PAPERBACK/B.R. PUBLISHING CORPORATION, New Delhi ✆ 23259196, Fax: 91-11-23263035	brpc@vsnl.com
B.R. RHYTHMS, Delhi ✆ 27432112	info@brbhythms.com
B.R. WORLD OF BOOKS, New Delhi ✆ 23259648, Fax: 91-11-23263035	brpc@bsnl.com
B.S. PUBLICATIONS, Hydrabad ✆ 23445600-1, Fax: 91-11-23445611	contactus@bspublications.net
B.S. SHARMA & BROTHERS PUBLISHER & DISTRIBUTORS, Agra ✆ 0562-3104192, 2526779	bssharmapublishers@rediffmail.com
B.S.B. INFO CENTRE PVT. LTD., New Delhi ✆ 24611991, 24634222, 51646667 Fax: 91-11-24627172	standard@del3.vsnl.net.in, bsb@nda.vsnl.net.in
BABA ENTERPRISES (REGD.), Srinagar ✆ 2474500, Fax: 2475929	imraubaba1@yahoo.com
BABA POCKET BOOKS, New Delhi ✆ 65164316, Fax: 91-11-27062968	amit_abd@yahoo.com
BAGCHI & BAGCHI, Nagpur ✆ 22265244, Fax: 22266240	bagchis@nagpur.dot.net.in
BAHAI PUBLISHING TRUST OF INDIA, New Delhi ✆ 26819391, 26818990, Fax: 91-11-26812703	bptindia@del3.vsnl.net.in
BAHRI BROTHERS, Delhi ✆ 23861740, 23866291, Fax: 91-11-23868488	bahribrs@ndb.vsnl.net.in
BAHRI PUBLICATIONS, New Delhi ✆ 26445710, 26448606, Fax: 91-11-26448606	bahrius@del6.vsnl.net.in, bahrius@vsnl.com
BAHRI SONS (BOOKSELLERS & STATIONERS), New Delhi ✆ (O) 24694855, 24694610 (R) 26196234, 26101053 Fax: 91-11-24618637	bahrisons@vsnl.com
BAHUJAN DIVERSITY MISSION, New Delhi ✆ 91-11-65948667	diversitymission@yahoo.com
BALAJI BOOK DISTRIBUTORS, Faridabad ✆ 0129-5278504	balajibooks@sify.com
BALANI INFOTECH PVT. LTD., New Delhi ✆ 46573379, Fax: 91-11-41724167	balani@vsnl.net
BALIT PUBLICATIONS PVT. LTD., New Delhi ✆ (O) 26529459, 26511459 (R) 95124-2324263 Fax: 91-11-26855465	kanuj@vsnl.com
BALMEX LAWRIE & CO. LTD., New Delhi ✆ 26463628, Fax: 91-11-26467383	srivastava@balmexlawrie.net
BANARAS HINDU UNIVERSITY, Varanasi ✆ 2368598, Fax: 91-542-2368598	pppcellbhu@gmail.com
BANASTHALI BOOK CENTRE, Rajasthan ✆ (O) 01438-228377 (R) 01438-222227	navjeewannew@yahoo.com

BANI PRAKASH PVT. LTD., Guwahati
✆ 545030, Fax: 454751 — devchoudurygp@rediffmail.com

BANSAL BROTHERS, Dehradun
✆ (O) 2654615 (R) 2520703 ▮ 9897351136
Fax: 2659316 — bansalbrothers1@rediffmail.com

BANYAN TREE BOOKS PVT LTD., New Delhi
✆ 23274463, 23288769, Fax: 91-11-23278144 — info@banyantreebooks.com

BARODA BOOK CORPORATION, Baroda
✆ 2358736, Fax: 91-265-334920 — bbcorp@satyam.net.in

BARWARA BOOK HOUSE, Jaipur
Fax: 2223042 — sudharamchandani@hotmail.com

BATRA BOOK SERVICE, New Delhi
✆ (O) 23360129, 23365374 (R) 23545654
Fax: 91-11-23638484 — batrabooks@mantramail.com

BAUDDHABHARATI, Varanasi
✆ 91-542-3298044 — bauddhabhrti@satyam.net.in

BENNETT COLEMAN & CO. LTD., New Delhi
✆ 91-11-42512162 — jaideep.chakravorty@timesgroup.com

BETHANY PUBLICATIONS, Kottayam
✆ 2571515, 2578494, Fax: 0481-2571057 — bethanyg@vsnl.com

BETTER BOOK SERVICE PUBLISHERS & DISTRIBUTORS, Delhi
✆ 22775630, 22773282, 35602800, 35801198
Fax: 91-11-22773282 — dks@nda.vsnl.net.in

BETTER YOURSELF BOOKS, Mumbai
✆ 26510023, 26408557, 26403312
Fax: 26510925, 26454425 — marketing@stpaulbyb.com

BHAGWADVANI PRAKASHAN, Lucknow
✆ 0522-26340923 — thesatyamandir@yahoo.com

BHAKTIVEDANTA INSTITUTE, Kolkata
✆ 25009018, Fax: 91-33-25009018 — info@binstitute.org

BHAKT MANDLI NAI DILLI, New Delhi
✆ 56223494 ▮ 9868026219, Fax: 91-11-25587139 — newkoncepts@yahoo.com

BHALANI BOOK DEPOT, Mumbai
✆ 24148941, 24150803, Fax: 022-24145846 — bhalani@bom3.vsnl.net.in

BHALANI MEDICAL BOOK HOUSE, Mumbai
✆ 24137650, 24171660 (R) 24145027
Fax: 022-24138041 — bhalani@vsnl.com

BHALANI PERIODICALS AGENCY, Mumbai
✆ 24131569, 24180481, Fax: 022-24131569 — hetal@bom3.vsnl.net.in

BHARAT BOOK BUREAU, Mumbai
✆/Fax: 91-22-27579131/27578668 — chettiar@.giasbm01.vsnl.net.in, info@bharatbook.com

BHARAT BOOK CENTRE, Lucknow
✆ 91-522-2230381, 2200959 — bharatbookcentre@yahoo.com

BHARAT BOOK DEPOT, Bhagalpur
✆ 2420429 — bbbdbooks@sancharnet.in

BHARAT EDUCATIONAL STORES/BHARAT GRAPHICS, New Delhi
✆ 25723493, 25767576, 32363597
Fax: 91-121-2654212 — hk8000@yahoo.com

BHARAT EDUCATIONAL STORES/PIONEER EDUCATIONAL AIDS, New Delhi
✆ 23543179, Fax: 91-121-4002776 — hk8000@yahoo.com

BHARAT GYAN VIGYAN SAMITHI, New Delhi
✆ 26569943, Fax: 91-11-26569773 — bgvs_delhi@yahoo.co.in

BHARAT LAW HOUSE, Jaipur
✆ 236388, 2362216 — bharatlawhouse@yahoo.com

BHARAT LAW HOUSE (P) LTD., New Delhi
✆ (O) 27910001, 27910002, 27910003
(R) 27012323, 27016884, Fax: 91-11-27910004 — blh@nda.vsnl.net.in

BHARAT PUBLISHING HOUSE, New Delhi
✆ (O) 25757081, 23670067 (R) 25817796
Fax: 91-11-23676058 — pitambar@bol.net.in

BHARAT SCIENTIFIC SYNDICATE, Delhi
✆ (O) 27454322 (R) 9810215495 — bhanu262@rediffmail.com

BHARAT SECURITIES, New Delhi
✆ 25163321 — bharatsecurities@hotmail.com

BHARATI BHAWAN, New Delhi
✆ 23286557 — bbpddel@airtelbroadband.net

BHARATI BHAWAN (PUBLISHERS & DISTRIBUTORS), Patna
✆ 2670325, 2689717, 2671356, Fax: 2670010 — bbpdpat@vsnl.net.in, bbpdpat@sancharnet.in

BHARATIYA BHANDAR PUSTAKALAYA, New Delhi
✆ 51611861-65, Fax: 51611866 — sales@diamondpublications.com

BHARATIYA JNANPITH, New Delhi
✆ 24626467, Fax: 91-11-24654197 — sales@jnanpith.net

BHARATIYA KALA PRAKASHAN, Delhi
✆ 32967505, Fax: 91-11-27393083 — bkp3421@yahoo.co.in

BHARATIYA SAHITYA BHAVANA, New Delhi
✆ (O) 23280585 (R) 25102109
9811163639, 9868178633 — pragati1@ndf.vsnl.net.in

BHARATIYA VIDYA BHAVAN, New Delhi
✆ 23387595, Fax: 91-11-23382003 — bhavidya@del2.vsnl.net.in

BHARATIYA VIDYA BHAVAN, Mumbai
✆ 24950916, 24968466, Fax: 23630058 — brbhavan@bom7.vsnl.net.in

BHARATIYA VIDYA PRAKASHAN, Delhi
✆ 23851570, 23850944 — bvpbooks@hotmail.com

BHATKAL BOOK INTERNATIONAL, Mumbai
✆ 24941656, Fax: 022-24938049 — bhatkal.sen@axcess.net.in

BHATKAL BOOKS INTERNATIONAL, New Delhi
✆ 23265245, 23280068, 2630381, Fax: 23279203 — vansdel@nda.vsnl.net.in

BHATT BOOKS DISTRIBUTORS, Mumbai
✆ 28116435 — bhattbooks@usa.net

BHATT BROTHERS, Uttarakhand
✆ 01374-274232, 223977 ▮ 9412077677 — madhubhatt@sancharnet.in, bhattsrikrishna@yahoo.in

BHAVANA BOOKS & PRINTS, New Delhi
✆ 23415198, 23415205, Fax: 51517091 — rajanarya@vsnl.com

BHAVANA EDITION, Thiruvananthapuram ✆ 2467157	bhavana_ed@rediffmail.com
BHAVANA PRAKASHAN, Delhi ✆ 22756734, 22754663	bhavna_pub@rediffmail.com
BIBILIOCLUB.COM, New Delhi	info@bibilioclub.com
BIBLIA IMPEX PVT. LTD., New Delhi ✆ 23262515, 23278034, Fax: 91-11-23282047	bibimpex@nda.vsnl.net.in
BIBLIOMATICS, Manipal ✆ 2572186, Fax: 2573062	embese@sanchrnet.in
BIBLIOPHILE SOUTH ASIA/PROMILLA & CO. PUBLISHERS, New Delhi ✆ 65284748, Fax: 91-11-26961462	ashokbutani@gmail.com
BINNY PUBLISHING HOUSE, Delhi ✆ 23250635	kaushalgoyal@yahoo.com
BIOTECH BOOKS, New Delhi ✆ (O) 23245578, 23244987 (R) 27382765 Fax: 91-11-27382329	biotechbooks@yahoo.co.in
BIOTEK BOOK COMPANY, Delhi ✆ 27385809	biotek@ndb.vsnl.net.in
BIO-VISUAL PRODUCTS, New Delhi ✆ 23537644 ▮ 9319320015, Fax: 91-11-23537644	info@bio-visual.com
BIO-VISUAL PRODUCTS, Hyderabad ✆ 24760088, 65524946 ▮ 9391231100 Fax: 040-24760077	biovisual@satyam.net.in
BISHEN SINGH MAHENDRA PAL SINGH, Dehradun ✆ 2655748, Fax: 0135-2650107	bsmps@vsnl.net.in, smps@del2.vsnl.net.in
BISWA BANGIYA PRAKASHAN, Kolkata ▮ 9830012947, Fax: 91-33-22906591	bbp_cal@indiatimes.com
BLACK ROSE PUBLICATIONS, Delhi ✆ 65271509	vinodkalia@hotmail.com
BLACKIE & SON (CALCUTTA) PVT. LTD., New Delhi ✆ 23672082, Fax: 91-11-23677446	schand@vsnl.com, schandco@giasd101.vsnl.net.in
BLACKWELL PUBLISHING LTD., New Delhi ✆ 26293624, 26293841, Fax: 91-11-26477033	bslsesha@giasdl01.vsnl.net.in
BLACKWELL SCIENCE LTD., Chennai ✆ 24346244, 24346266, Fax: 24346529	itpsesha@giasmd01.vsnl.net.in
BOARD OF ISLAMIC PUBLICATIONS, New Delhi ✆ 26311423, Fax: 91-11-26820975	radiance@del3.vsnl.net.in
BODHI BOOKS, Kozhikode ✆ (O) 0495-2365874 (R) 0495-2374051	bodhibooks@hotmail.com
BOOK CENTRE, Visakhapatnam ✆ 0891-2562684, 2747759	bookcentre@eth.net
BOOK CHANNEL, Mumbai ✆ 22663337, 22662328, Fax: 022-22663281	bookchannel@vsnl.com
BOOK CIRCLE, New Delhi ✆ 23264444, Fax: 91-11-23263050	heritage@nad.vsnl.net.in

BOOK FAITH INDIA, New Delhi
✆ 23285722, Telefax: 23285081 — pilgrim@del2.vsnl.net.in

BOOK GALLERY, Gurgaon
✆ 2324782, Fax: 91-124-2324782 — bookgallery@gmail.com

BOOK HILL (INDIA), New Delhi
✆ 23585291, 23582785, Fax: 91-11-23587922 — bookhillindia@rediffmail.com, bookhill@indiatimes.com

BOOK LAND, Delhi
✆ 23912210 (R) 22154208, Fax: 91-11-23919045 — worldview@vsnl.com

BOOK LAND, Guwahati
✆ 2520617, 2637772 — bookland@satyam.net.in

BOOK LAND INTERNATIONAL (P) LTD., Mumbai
✆ 28643640, 28643674
Fax: 91-22-28619394 — bookland@vsnl.com

BOOK LINE (THE), New Delhi
(O) 56056760 (R) 25283394 ▮ 9810691567 — sales@thebooklineonline.com, tb18@hotmail.com

BOOK LINKS CORPORATION, Hyderabad
✆ 27567068, 27611582 — books@booklinkscorp.com, booklinks@usa.net

BOOK MARKETING SERVICES (INDIA) PVT. LTD., Chennai
✆ 28480220, Fax: 28480222 — jai@xlweb.com

BOOK MARY (THE), New Delhi
debashisnandy@rediffmail.com

BOOKMATE AGENCY, New Delhi
▮ 9818534566, Fax: 011-25054188 — bookmate_agency@rediffmail.com

BOOK N CD, Jodhpur
✆ 9414131894, Fax: 91-291-2441964 — email@bookncd.com

BOOK N CDS SYNDICATE, New Delhi
✆ 35340557, 32361740 — booksncds@yahoo.co.in

BOOK PALACE, New Delhi
✆ 23277655, 23287586, 23257494,
Fax: 91-11-23276646 — bookpalacepublishers@yahoo.com

BOOK PARADISE, Bangalore
✆ 26637466, Fax: 226639954 — jai@blr.vsnl.net.in

BOOK PARADISE (THE), Gurgaon
✆ 2322330, 2327543, Fax: 2327543 — bookparadise@hotmail.com

BOOK PLAZA, Ahmedabad
✆ 079-6430386, Telefax: 079-6440763 — bookplaza1@sanchanrnet.in, bookplaza@yahoo.co.in

BOOK REVIEW LITERARY TRUST (THE), New Delhi
✆ 26492031, Fax: 91-11-2355500 — thebookreview@hotmail.com, prchari@vsnl.net

BOOK ROUTE, New Delhi
✆ 22751804 ▮ 9811331694 — abidi7@now-india.net.in

BOOK SEA, Hyderabad
✆ 24757526 — bookseay@yahoo.com

BOOK SEARCH, New Delhi
✆ 29813206, 32334772, Fax: 91-11-29813206 — ifusion@bol.net.in

BOOK SELECTION CENTRE, Hyderabad
✆ 24750909, 24753218, Fax: 24752054 — bschyd@hd2.dot.net.in

BOOK SERVICE SYNDICATE, Bangalore
✆ 26686532, Fax: 26686286 — haren_bss@vsnl.com, haren@bgl.vsnl.net.in

BOOK SHELF, Ahmedabad
✆ 079-26441826, 26563707 — bookshelf@wilnetonline.net

BOOK SHOP (THE), Ludhiana
✆ 2404728, 2407142, Fax: 2403856 — shawls@shingora.net

BOOK SHOP (THE), Bhubaneshwar
✆ (O) 2531568 (R) 2575071, Fax: 0674-2544090 — thebooks@sify.com
▮ 9861028585

BOOK SUPPLY BUERAU, New Delhi
✆ 24611991, 24634222, Fax: 91-11-24627172 — standard@del3.vsnl.net.in, bsb@nda.vsnl.net.in

BOOK SYNDICATE (THE), Hyderabad
✆ 24755951, 24756722, Fax: 24756271 — booksynd@hd2.dot.net.in

BOOK SYNDICATE PVT. LTD., Kolkata
✆ (O) 23543123, 23500549, 22410922, 23507158 — bs_pl@sify.com
(R) 24661854, 23349648, Fax: 23503881

BOOK TEMPLE, New Delhi
✆ 22910377 — booktemple@rediffmail.com

BOOK VENTURE PUBLISHERS, Chennai
✆ 044-24344519, Fax: 044-24342009 — k.k.cheenu@ppl.sprintrpg.ems.vsnl.net.in, ksm@md2.vsnl.net.in

BOOK VISION, Srinagar
✆ 2424282, 2423208, Fax: 91-194-2424282 — bookvision@rediffmail.com

BOOK WALA, Amroha
✆ 05922-250277, 259167 ▮ 9837028782 — amrohaeducation@mickyonline.com

BOOK WORLD, New Delhi
✆ 23320128, 23353223, Fax: 91-11-23721188 — fln@del2.vsnl.net.in

BOOK WORLD, Goa
✆ 2421857, Fax: 0832-5643606 — books@goatelecom.com

BOOK WORLD ENTERPRISES, Mumbai
✆ 22015331, 22068538, Fax: 22059934 — bookworld@vsnl.com, bookworl@bom.7.vsnl.net.in

BOOK WORLD INDIA, New Delhi
✆ 23258766, 23258774, Telefax: 91-11-23258774 — bwindia@vsnl.com

BOOK WORM (THE), New Delhi
✆ 23322260, 23311140, Fax: 91-11-23723440 — bookworm@del2.vsnl.net.in, bookworm@vsnl.com

BOOK WORM, Goa
confident@sancharnet.in

BOOK ZONE—THE ASSISSI, Kottayam
✆ 2429188, 2420188, Fax: 2420466 — suman@assissipublishers.com

BOOKHIVE (INDIA), New Delhi
✆ 25778295, 6582518 ▮ 9811700512 — bookhire@yahoo.com

BOOKIONICS, Hyderabad
✆ 24753654, 25751134, Fax: 24756271 — bookionics@yahoo.com

BOOKLINE, Kolkata
✆ 22440903, 22454238, Fax: 91-33-22454238 — bookline@cal3.vsnl.net.in

BOOKMAN ASSOCIATES, Dimapur
✆ 230364, 233565, Fax: 233216 — bookmanassociates_dmr@rediffmail.com

BOOKMAN INDIA, Muzaffarnagar
✆ 2407870, 2400954, Fax: 2404925 — bmipph@hotmail.com

BOOKMART PUBLISHERS, New Delhi
bookmart@vsnl.com

BOOKMATRIX, Delhi
✆ 47091404, Fax: 91-11-47091473 — info@bookmatrix.com

BOOKS & BYTES INDIA PVT. LTD., New Delhi
✆ (O) 26672163, 26689383 (R) 29543849
Fax: 91-11-26689562 — books_bytes@mantraonline.com, books_bytes@hotmail.com

BOOKS & GIFTS SHOPPERS PARADISE, Guwahati
✆/Fax: 2633860 — jainmanojp_in@yahoo.com

BOOKS & PERIODICALS AGENCY, New Delhi
✆ 25786046, 25755096 — bpage@del2.vsnl.net.in

BOOKS-DEN, Bhopal
✆ (O) 2538564 (R) 2766520 — vikasjaitley@usa.net

BOOKS4U.IN, Agra
✆ 2856550, Fax: 91-562-2854582 — contact@books4u.in

BOOKS FOR ALL, Delhi
✆ 27401672, Fax: 91-11-23264368 — ipp@nde.vsnl.net.in

BOOKS FOR CHANGE, Bangalore
✆ 25321747, 25580346, Fax: 25586284 — bfc@actionaidindia.org

BOOKS INTERNATIONAL, New Delhi
✆ 42143438, Fax: 91-11-42143438 — lalwani_books@yahoo.com

BOOKS INTERNATIONAL, Lucknow
✆ 2376960, 2335846 — bookinter1@satyam.net.in

BOOKS INTERNATIONAL, Bangalore
✆ 080-6642273 — bookinti@bgl.vsnl.net.in

BOOKS N CDS SYNDICATE, Delhi
✆ 25285278, 25272401, Fax: 25276386, 25265397 — booksncds@yahoo.co.in

BOOKS SUPPLY BUREAU, New Delhi
✆ 24611991, 24628182, 24634222
Fax: 91-11-24627172 — standard@del3.vsnl.net.in, bsb@nda.vsnl.net.in

BOOKS TODAY, New Delhi
✆ 23352233, Fax: 91-11-23712998 — ashoke@indiatodaybookclub.com

BOOKSELL AGENCIES, Mumbai
✆ 26281138, Fax: 26211658 — booksellagencies@hotmail.com

BOOKSLINE, Mumbai
✆ 25213976 — ashokan66@yahoo.co.uk, booksline@vsnl.net

BOOKSLINE, Hyderabad
✆ 55578506 — supriyabha@indiatimes.com

BOOKSTOP AT CHARNOCK CITY, Kolkata
✆ 23581086, Fax: 033-23349908 — bright@gist1giasc101.vsnl.net.in

BOOKWELL, Delhi
✆ 27251283, Fax: 91-11-23281315 — bkwell@nde.vsnl.net.in

BOOKWELL PUBLICATIONS, New Delhi
✆ 23268786, Fax: 91-11-23281315 — bookwell@vsnl.net

BOTANICAL SURVEY OF INDIA, Kolkata
✆23584240, Fax: 91-33-23346040 — bsipubl@yahoo.com

BOUDHBHARATI, Varanasi
✆ 2210094 — bauddhabhrti@satyam.net.in

BRAIN MAPPING ACADEMY, Hyderabad
✆ 66135169, Fax: 91-11-24542215 — bmahyd@rediffmail.com

BRAIN TREE, Hyderabad
✆ 27644110 — braintreeindia@rediff.com

BRAND VISION (INDIA) PVT. LTD., Mumbai
✆ 56366662-63, 56314454 ▮ 9892192706
Fax: 22837214 — sniklje@usp-age.com

BREPO SYSTEM INDIA PVT. LTD., Delhi
✆ 27432104, 27432629, Fax: 91-11-27451555 — brepo@vsnl.com

BRIGHT GROUP OF PUBLICATIONS, New Delhi
✆ 23283226, 23282226, Fax: 91-11-23269227 — editorial@brightpublications.com, sales@brightpublications.com

BRIGHT SPORTS, New Delhi
✆ 55303278, Fax: 91-11-23327884 — tildelhi@vsnl.net

BRIJBASI ART PRESS LTD., Noida
✆ 2423846/47/48, Fax: 91-120-2420324 — brijbasi@airtelbroadband.in

BRILLIANT EDUCATIONAL AIDS, New Delhi
✆ 26611073 ▮ 9811092425 — umaparikh24@hotmail.com

BRITISH COUNCIL DIVISION, New Delhi
✆ 23711401, Fax: 91-11-23710717 — info@in.britishcouncil.org

BRITISH LIBRARY, Hyderabad
✆ 23230774, Fax: 23298273 — bl.hyderabad@in.britishcouncil.org

BROWSER: THE BOOKSHOP, Chandigarh
✆ 607680 — thebrowser@glide.net.in

BULSAR BOOK STORE, Valsad
✆ (O) 254077, 222377 (R) 241027, 253909 — bbs_valsad@yahoo.com

BURGUNDY INFOTECH, New Delhi
✆ 24354513/617, Fax: 91-11-24356489 — info@burgundyinfotech, sales@burgundyinfotech.com

BUSINESS HORIZONS, New Delhi
▮ 9212061554, Fax: 91-11-41637296 — info@businesshorizons.com

BUTALA PUBLICATIONS, New Delhi
✆ 23515310, Fax: 91-11-23514825 — butala@del.3.vsnl.net.in

BUTTERWORTH-HEINEMANN, New Delhi
✆ 23282580, 23279256, Fax: 91-11-23282650 — bh_india@id.eth.net, bh_india@satyam.net.in

BUTTERWORTHS INDIA, New Delhi
✆ 23739614, 23739616, 23326454,
Fax: 91-11-23326456 — info@bworthsindia.com

BUZME KHIZRE RAH, New Delhi
✆ 26844816, Fax: 91-11-26822414 — abbaszaidi84@rediffmail.com

BYWORD EDITORIAL CONSULTANTS, New Delhi
✆ 26180427, 51658883, Fax: 51658456 — byword@vsnl.com

■ ■ ■

C

C.B.S. PUBLISHERS & DISTRIBUTORS, New Delhi
✆ (O) 23271632, 23289259 (R) 22303431, 22517735 — cbspubs@del3.vsnl.net.in
9810310858, Telefax: 91-11-23276712

C.C.H. (A WOLTERS KLUWER BUSINESS), New Delhi
✆ 46530300, Fax: 91-11-46530399 — vinay.singh@wolterskluwer.com

C.D. ROM, New Delhi
✆ 41040428, Fax: 91-11-28755446 — sales@cdrom.india.com

C.P.I. (M) PUBLICATIONS, New Delhi
✆ 91-11-23711870 — cpim@vsnl.com

C.P.M. DISTRIBUTORS, Mumbai
✆ 23092282, 23094386, Fax: 23098587 — meetac@giasbma.vsnl.net.in

C.P.R.I. BOOK STORE, Shimla
✆ 2624830, Fax: 2624460 — library@cpri.hp.nic.in

C.R. COMPETITION REFRESHER (P) LTD., New Delhi
✆ 23282226/27, Fax: 91-11-23269227 — psbright@ndb.vsnl.net.in

C.R.C. PRESS, Chennai
✆ 24346244, 24346266, Fax: 24346529 — itpsesha@giasmd01.vsnl.net.in

C.S. POCHEE & SONS, Mumbai
✆ 28166135, 28726965 — ranjan@bom5.vsnl.net.in

C.S.I.R. (PUBLICATIONS & INFORMATION DIRECTORATE), New Delhi
✆ 25746024, 25728385, Fax: 91-11-25731353 — paid@sirnetd.ernet.in

CAMBRIDGE BOOK DEPOT, New Delhi
✆ 23363395, 23348805, Fax: 91-11-25546260 — cambridgebooks@hotmail.com

CAMBRIDGE PUBLISHING HOUSE, New Delhi
✆ 24619125, Fax: 91-11-24634935 — ragupta@ndb.vsnl.net.in, galgotia@ndf.vsnl.net.in

CAMBRIDGE UNIVERSITY PRESS INDIA PVT. LTD., New Delhi
✆ 43543500, Fax: 91-11-23288534 — cup@cupind.com, cupdel@cupind.com

CAMPUS BOOKS INTERNATIONAL, New Delhi
✆ 23272541, Fax: 91-11-23257835 — campusbooks@hotmail.com

CAPITAL BOOK DEPOT, Chandigarh
✆ 2702260, 2702594, Fax: 0712-2702594 — ajayacbd@ch.1.vsnl.net.in

CAPITAL PUBLISHING COMPANY PVT. LTD., New Delhi
✆ 23284197, 23288719, Fax: 91-11-41562932 — capitalb@capital-publishing.com

CARE & CURE INTERNATIONAL LTD., New Delhi
✆ 29844012, Fax: 91-11-29847741 — carecure@nde.vsnl.net.in, care@carecure.com

CAREER PLAN, Delhi
✆ 27115656, 31012386 — delhi@careerplanindia.com

CAREER PUBLICATIONS, Nashik
✆ 2311422, Fax: 91-253-2318030 — publications@careerandyou.com

CARTOON PRAKASHANEE, Kolkata
✆ 24155744, 24152822, Fax: 4157443 — saras-cartoon@hotmail.com

CAXTON PRINTERS, Hyderabad
caxton1@hd2.dot.net.in

CENGAGE LEARNING, New Delhi
✆ 30484835, Fax: 91-11-30484834 — alok.srivastava@cengage.com

CENTAX PUBLICATIONS PVT. LTD., New Delhi
✆ 24693001, 24611224, Fax: 91-11-24635243 — centax@del2.vsnl.net.in

CENTRAL BOARD OF IRRIGATION AND POWER, New Delhi
✆ 26875017, 26870117, Fax: 91-11-26116347 — cbip@nda.vsnl.net.in

CENTRAL CHINMAYA MISSION TRUST, Mumbai
✆ 28572367, 28575806, Fax: 28573065 — ccmt@vsnl.com

CENTRAL INSTITUTE OF INDIAN LANGUAGES, Mysore
✆ 2345040, Fax: 81-821-2515032 — chandrashekar@ciil.stpmy.soft.net

CENTRAL NEWS AGENCY PVT. LTD., New Delhi
✆ (O) 23364448, 23364478, 23364508
(R) 26484703, Fax: 91-11-23626036 — info@cna-india.com, nita@cna-india.com

CENTRAL REFERENCE LIBRARY, Kolkata
✆ 24791721-22, Fax: 91-33-24791723 — crlinb@cal.3.vsnl.net.in

CENTRE FOR AMBEDKAR AND DALIT LITERATURE, Delhi
✆ 22270380, Fax: 91-11-22270380 — gautambookcentre@hotmail.com

CENTRE FOR CULTURAL RESOURCES AND TRAINING, New Delhi
✆ 25074252/54/58, 25088630, Fax: 91-11-25088637 — skdgccrt@del3.vsnl.net.in

CENTRE FOR ENTREPRENEURSHIP DEVP., Bhopal
✆ 2766461, 2766437, 2574772, Fax: 2763401 — cedmap@vsnl.com

CENTRE FOR SCIENCE AND ENVIRONMENT, New Delhi
✆ 26981110, 26981124, Fax: 26985879 — cse@cseindia.org

CENTRE FOR STUDIES IN CIVILIZATIONS, New Delhi
✆ 26227831-36, Fax: 91-11-26227836 — csc@del2.vsnl.net.in

CENTRE FOR THE DEVELOPMENT OF ENVIRONMENT AND RESOURCES, New Delhi
✆ 26804269 — suhasini@bol.net.in

CENTURY PUBLICATIONS, New Delhi
✆ 91-11-20281355 — centurypublications@hotmail.com

CHAMPA LAL RANKA & CO., Jaipur
✆ 2654202, 2654155 — iranka@datainfosys.net

CHANAKYA CIVIL SERVICES TODAY, Delhi
✆ 27653240, 27653242, Fax: 91-11-27652337 — ccst@chanakya-iasacademy.com

CHANDNA BOOK HOUSE, Bhopal
✆ 2554269, 3130992, Fax: 0755-2771828 — chandnabookhouse@hotmail.com

CHANNEL PUBLICATIONS, Faridabad
✆ 0129-25272022, Fax: 0129-25272284 — channelpub@hotmail.com

CHAPTER AND VERSE, Pune
✆ 26137870, Fax: 26137870 — candv@pn3.vsnl.net.in

CHAROTAR PUBLISHING HOUSE, Kaira
✆ (O) 02692-256237, 240089 (R) 244422
Fax: 02692-240089 — charotar@icenet.net, charotar@cphbooks.com

CHASVIK TRADES, Delhi
✆ 27132897, 27132902, Fax: 27137735 — chasvik@vsnl.com

CHAUKHAMBA PUBLISHING HOUSE, New Delhi
✆ 32996391, Fax: 91-11-23286537 — chaukhamba@gmail.com

CHAUKHAMBA VIDYA BHAWAN, Varanasi
✆ 2320404 — cvbhawan@satyam.net.in

CHAUKHAMBHA PUBLICATIONS, New Delhi
✆ 23268639, 23259050, Fax: 91-11-23268639 — chaukhambha@mantraonline.com

CHAUKHAMBHA SANSKRIT PRATISTHAN, Delhi
✆ 23856391, Fax: 91-11-41530902 — csp_praveen@rediffmail.com

CHAUKHAMBHA SANSKRIT SERIES OFFICE, Varanasi
✆ 2333458 — cssoffice@satyam.net.in

CHEMTECH BOOKS (P.) LTD., Mumbai
✆ 25912461 — chemtech@bom3.vsnl.net.in

CHETANA PUBLICATIONS PVT. LTD., Mumbai
✆ 23857090, Fax: 91-22-23821910 — cppl@chetanapublications.com

CHETANA PVT. LTD., Mumbai
✆ 22881159, 22824983, Fax: 022-22553412 — karya@chetana.com

CHILDREN BOOK CENTRE, Patna
✆ 2670362 — cbcravi@rediffmail.com

CHILDREN BOOK HOUSE, New Delhi
✆ 24636010/20/30, Fax: 24636011 — neeta@giasdl01.vsnl.net.in

CHILDREN CHOICE PUBLICATION PVT. LTD., Meerut
✆ 2668092, Fax: 91-121-2668093 — children.choice.123@yahoo.com

CHILDREN'S BOOK TRUST, New Delhi
✆ 23316970-74, Fax: 91-11-23721090 — cbtnd@vsnl.com, cbt@vsnl.com

CHILDRENS' BOOKS DISTRIBUTORS, New Delhi
✆ 23276118, 23284898, Fax: 51665736 — rawatrajinder@rediffmail.com

CHINA BOOK CENTRE, New Delhi
✆ 23260022, Fax: 91-11-23911057 — kaushalgoyal@yahoo.com

CHINMAYA JNANPITH, Delhi
✆ 22759139 — sudhirraman@yahoo.com, sudhir20@vsnl.net

CHINMAYA CENTRE OF WORLD UNDERSTANDING, New Delhi
✆ 24697848, 24623301, Fax: 91-11-24643290 — ccwu@vsnl.com, chinmaya@bom2.vsnl.net.in

CHINMAYA MISSION, Kolkata
✆ 24665069, 24647076 — chinmayakolkata@vsnl.net

CHINMAYA MISSION, New Delhi
✆ 24697848, Fax: 91-11-24643290 — ccwu@chinmayamissiondelhi.org

CHINTHANA PRAKASHANA, Bangalore
✆ (O) 080-23354680 (R) 23387121 — anupooja2000@yahoo.com

CHIRAG BOOK DISTRIBUTORS, Baroda
✆ (O) 2410771 (R) 2489003 ▮ 9824080512
Fax: 2449003 — dilchirag@yahoo.com

CHITRA PRAKASHAN, Meerut
✆ (O) 91-121-2662271, 2663271, 2654217, 2644063
(R) 2642116, 2653587 ▮ 9897036095, Fax: 2648704 — rastogimayank@yahoo.com

CHITRANGSU INSTITUTE OF ART & HANDICRAFT, Kolkata
✆ 24663083, Fax: 91-33-24642494 — chitrabhanucomp@vsnl.net

CHOICE INTERNATIONAL, New Delhi
✆ 91-11-64163037 — narkambooks@yahoo.com

CHOWDHARY & CO. (PUBLISHERS) PVT. LTD., Patna
✆ 91-612-2681859 — easternbooks@satyam.net.in

CHOWDHRY EXPORT HOUSE, New Delhi
✆ 25755519, 25720209
Fax: 91-11-25755519 — gphceh@del3.vsnl.net.in, goodwillbooksinternational@gmail.com

CHOWKHAMBA KRISHNADAS ACADEMY, Varanasi
✆ (O) & (R) 2335020 — cssoffice@satyam.net.in

CHRISTIAN LITERATURE SOCIETY (THE), Chennai
✆ (O) 25354296/97 (R) 26414683
▮ 9840442847, Fax: 044-25354297 — jaivanth@yahoo.com

CHRONICLE PUBLICATIONS (P) LTD., New Delhi
✆ 26519761, Fax: 26526443 — chronicl@ndf.vsnl.net.in

CITY BOOK CENTRE, Kashmir
✆ 2470158, 2478288, Fax: 2478266 — citybookcentre@rediff.com

CITY BOOK SHOP, Chandigarh
✆ (O) 0172-2708612 (R) 2662541
▮ 09814017075, Fax: 2714376 — citybookshop123@yahoo.com

CLASSIQUE BOOKS, Kolkata
✆ (O) 2864-0300/2219-0255 (R) 2435-8263
▮ 9830014296, Fax: 22416983 — classiquein@yahoo.com

COLD SPRING HARBOR LAB. PRESS, New Delhi
✆ 26433992, 23243415, Fax: 23243225 — narosadl@nda.vsnl.net.in

COLLEGE BOOK DEPOT, Jaipur
✆ (O) 0141-2320827, 2312156 (R) 2564638
Fax: 0141-2563256 — glp@satyam.net.in

COLLEGE BOOK STORE, Delhi
✆ 23279128, 23269426, Fax: 91-11-23269426 — cbspubs@del3.vsnl.net.in

COMET MEDIA FOUNDATION, Mumbai
✆ 23869052 — comet_media@vsnl.com

COMM. SEARCH (INDIA) PVT. LTD., Chennai
✆ 26286164, Fax: 044-26286165 — hpradeep@giasmd01.vsnl.net.in

COMMONWEALTH HUMAN RIGHTS INITIATIVE, New Delhi
✆ 26859823, 26864678, Fax: 91-11-26864688 — chriall@nda.vsnl.net.in

COMMONWEALTH PUBLISHERS, New Delhi
✆ 23272541, 23257835, Fax: 91-11-23257835 — campusbooks@hotmail.com

COMP-POINT, New Delhi
✆ 25505639, Fax: 91-11-25618305 — comp_point21@yahoo.com

COMP-POINT SYSTEMS (I) PVT. LTD., New Delhi
✆ 25501359, 25512028, Fax: 91-11-25549107 — comppointsystems@gmail.com

COMPETITION SUCCESS REVIEW PVT. LTD., New Delhi
✆ 25761086, 25712898 — info@competitionreview.com

COMPETITION WIZARD, New Delhi
✆ 91-11-27653714 — competitionwizard@gmail.com

COMPETITION WIZARD, New Delhi
✆ 26164551, 26162979, 26106702
Fax: 91-11-26164551 — competition@vsnl.net

COM-POINT PUBLISHERS & DISTRIBUTORS, New Delhi
✆ 25501359, 25512028, Fax: 91-11-25618305 — comp_point21@yahoo.com

COMPUAID ENTERPRISES, New Delhi
✆ 29225821, 29225836, Fax: 91-11-29223621 — vijjip@compuaid-india.com

COMPUTECH PUBLICATIONS LTD., New Delhi
✆ (O) 23280163, 23280164 (R) 55192881, 22154457
Fax: 91-11-23280165 — nap@newasianpub.com

COMPUTER BOOKSHOP (INDIA) (P) LTD., Mumbai
✆ 22070989, Fax: 22623551 — cbs@vsnl.com

COMPUTER DYNAMICS, Indore
✆ (O) 2534676, 2545494 (R) 2494108 ▮ 9826014552 — utidata@sancharnet.in

COMPUTER MART, Kashmir
✆ 91-194-2428758, 2428526 — abhamid@sancharnet.in

COMPUTER ZONE, New Delhi
✆ (O) 26462065, 26227036/37 (R) 27257023
Fax: 91-11-26470740 — computerzonedelhi@hotmail

CONCEPT PUBLISHING COMPANY, New Delhi
✆ 25351460, 25351794, Fax: 91-11-25357103 — publishing@conceptpub.com

CONFLUENCE INTERNATIONAL, New Delhi
✆ 2926832, Fax: 91-11-29217095 — confluence@connectgroup.in

CONSORTIUM FOR EDUCATIONAL COMMUNICATIONS, New Delhi
✆ 26896638, Fax: 91-11-26897416 — cecugc@cec-ugc.org

CONTEMPORARY TARGETT PRAFULL PVT. LTD., New Delhi
▮ 9810120001, Fax: 91-11-24355297 — ctldel@vsnl.com

CONTINENTAL BOOK SUPPLIERS, Mumbai
cbsbooks@indiatimes.com

CORNER BOOKSTORE CO. PVT. LTD., New Delhi
✆ 33163982, Fax: 91-11-26569167 — delhi@thecornerbookstore.com

CORONATION LITHO WORKS (THE), Sivakasi
✆ 222254-57, Fax: 04560-223231 — coronat@vsnl.com

CORPWORTH MARKETING PVT. LTD., New Delhi
✆ 24645132, 24603903, 24604407
Fax: 91-11-24642435 — jaipal@manford.org

COSMO BOOKS, Thrissur
✆ 2335292, 2335570, Fax: 2335642 — cosmoboo@md3vsnl.net.in

COSMO PUBLICATIONS, New Delhi
✆ 23278779, 23280455, Fax: 91-11-23241200 — genesis@ndb.vsnl.net.in

COSMO PUBLISHING HOUSE INDIA, Nasik
✆ 2314870, 2581081, Fax: 2314870 — cosmolog@bomb.vsnl.net.in

COSMOPOLITAN BOOK HOUSE, New Delhi
✆ 23278779, 23280455, Fax: 91-11-23241200 — genesis@ndb.vsnl.net.in

COVER TO COVER BOOKS (P) LTD., Chennai
✆ 24830457, 24672665, Fax: 24881308 — naveens@md3.vsnl.net.in

CRANBURY INTERNATIONAL INDIA, New Delhi
✆ 26535929, 20042143, Fax: 91-11-26969159 — cranburyindia@bol.net.in, techtran@vsnl.com

CRANBURY INTERNATIONAL INDIA/DKG INFO SYSTEMS, New Delhi
✆ 25531842, Fax: 91-11-25541258 — dkinfo@gmail.com

CREATIVE BOOK CENTRE, Chennai
✆ 28272726, 28272749, Fax: 28275039 — dynamic.maa@sm8springtrpg.ems.vsnl.net.in

CREATIVE BOOKS, New Delhi
✆ (O) 25698487, 25699518, 25775737
(R) 25775818 — creativebooks@hotmail.com

CREATIVE BOOKS & PERIODICALS PVT. LTD., Mumbai
✆ 22043342, 22047895, Fax: 22833328 — creat@bom5.vsnl.net.in

CREATIVE EDUCATIONAL AIDS (P) LTD., New Delhi
✆ 23315483, 23720034, Fax: 91-11-23353365 — edutoys@del2.vsnl.net.in

CREATIVE LEARNING, Patna
✆ 2284662, Fax: 2597969 — vijoy_prakash@yahoo.com

CREATIVE PUBLICATION, Delhi
✆ 23279417, 23985175, Fax: 23261030, 23279417 — vikas_aggarwal@vsnl.com

CREATIVE TEACHING PRESS INDIA PVT. LTD., New Delhi
✆ 25381759, 25381813, Fax: 91-11-25381790 — edutoys@del2.vsnl.net.in

CRESCENT PUBLICATIONS, Hyderabad
✆ 55619277, Fax: 55619377 — info@computervignanam.net

CREST PUBLISHING HOUSE, Delhi
✆ 22144204/5/7, Fax: 91-11-22144206 — sethidel@del6.vsnl.net.in

CRITICAL QUEST, New Delhi
✆ 91-11-26502012 — criticalquest@hotmail.com

CROSSWORD, Pune
✆ 0212-6059600/1/2/3/4, Fax: 6059605 — crosswordpune@hotmail.com

CROSSWORD BOOKSHOP, Mumbai
✆ 022-24924882, 24938311, Fax: 24938406 — cwbrd@gdpl.com

CRYSTAL PAGES PUBLICATIONS, New Delhi
✆ 25826880, 25826881, Fax: 91-11-25826882 — sanjay@crystalpages.net

CSDS-SARAI PUBLICATIONS, Delhi
✆ 23942199, Fax: 91-11-23943450 — aftab@sarai.net

C-SOFT CONSULTANTS, New Delhi
✆ 91-11-41550249 — support@csoft.co.in

CULTURE HOUSE ISLAMIC REPUBLIC OF IRAN, New Delhi
✆ 23383232-34, Fax: 91-11-23387547 — ichdelhi@yahoo.co.uk

CULTURE VISTAS MARKETING SERVICES PVT. LTD., Thiruvananthapuram
✆ 2311025, Fax: 91-471-2313170 — info@culturevistas.com

CURRENT BOOKS, Kottayam
✆ (O) 0481-2563114 (R) 2578214, Fax: 0481-2564758 — info@dcbooks.com

CURRENT BOOKS, Thrissur
✆ (O) 2335570, 2335660 (R) 2335593 — cosmobooks@asianetindia.com
Fax: 91-487-2335642

CURRENT SUBSCRIPTION SERVICES, Delhi
✆ 27863662, Fax: 91-11-27556242 — services@del2.vsnl.net.in

CURRENT TECHNICAL BOOK DISTRIBUTORS, Delhi
✆ 27218194, Fax: 91-11-27234817 — lbt@vsnl.net

CURRENT TECHNICAL LITERATURE CO. (P) LTD., Mumbai
✆ 22617616, 22611045, Fax: 22679786 — info@ctlmumbai.com

CYBER MULTIMEDIA (INDIA) LTD., New Delhi
✆ 26491320, 26490019, Fax: 91-11-26496765 — neerajm@cmil.com, cybermm@cmil.com

CYBER MULTIMEDIA (INDIA) LTD., Gurgaon
✆ 2491320, 2490019, Fax: 2496765 — dileshg@cmil.com

CYBER TECH PUBLICATION, New Delhi
✆ (O) 23244078 (R) 25873694, Fax: 91-11-23280028 — cyberpublicationdelhi@yahoo.com

D

D.B. CORP LTD. (MAGAZINE DIVISION), New Delhi
✆ 23[illegible]10452, Fax: 91-11-23355867 — vkgaur@bhaskarnet.com

D.C. BOOKS, Kottayam
✆ 2563114, 2301614, Fax: 2564758 — info@dcbooks.com, ravide@dcbooks.com, dcbooks@sanchar.net.com

D.I. PUBLICATIONS PVT. LTD., Mumbai
✆ 26327007, 26320239 — dipublications@vsnl.com, dip@bom5.vsnl.net.in

D.K. AGENCIES (P) LTD., New Delhi
✆ 25357104-5, Fax: 91-11-25357103 — custserv@dkagencies.com, pubrel@dkagencies.com

D.K. PRINT WORLD (P) LTD., New Delhi
✆ 25453975, 25466019, Fax: 91-11-25465926 — dkprintworld@vsnl.net

D.K. PUBLISHERS DISTRIBUTORS PVT. LTD., New Delhi
✆ 23278368, 23261465, 23279215, 23278584 — dkpd@del3.vsnl.net.in
Fax: 91-11-23264368

D.R. EXPORTS, New Delhi
✆ 24640153, Fax: 91-11-24640153 — ragupta@ndb.vsnl.net.in

D.S. BOOKS INTERNATIONAL, Allahabad
✆ 2560866, Fax: 91-532-2560866 — dsbooksinternational@indiatimes.com

D.S. PUBLISHERS (INDIA), New Delhi
✆ 65253158, 41563757, Fax: 91-11-23244046 — ds_bookmaster@yahoo.co.in

D.V.S. PUBLISHER, Guwahati
✆ 2548965, 2525789, Fax: 2638295
✉ dvs@gw1.dot.net.in, dvsgh@sancharnet.in

DAANISH BOOKS, Delhi
✆ 91-11-22239812 ▮ 9868242343
✉ daanishbooks@gmail.com

DAFFODILS PUBLICATIONS, New Delhi
✆ 47013394, Fax: 91-11-42470122
✉ daffodilspub@yahoo.com

DAFFODILS TECHNOLOGIES, Lucknow
✆ 2208330, 2206852
✉ daffodilstechnologies@rediffmail.com

DAKSHINA, New Delhi
✆ 91-11-25075116
✉ vayttadenvc@rediffmail.com

DALIT BAHUJAN INTELLECTUAL FORUM OF INDIA, Delhi
✆ 22298067 ▮ 9818385185
✉ dbifi777@hotmail.com

DALIT SAHITYA RESEARCH FOUNDATION, Delhi
✆ 22570380, Fax: 91-11-22219239
✉ gautambookcentre@hotmail.com

DANIKA PUBLISHING COMPANY, New Delhi
✆ 91-11-30122482-83
✉ danikabooks@yahoo.com

DAS GUPTA & CO. (P) LTD., Kolkata
✆ 22414609, 22416531, Fax: 22416479
✉ dgboiola@cal.vsnl.net.in

DASTAK PRAKASHAN, Ludhiana
✆ 91-161-2807127 ▮ 989199332
✉ dastak_prakashan@gmail.com

DATANET INDIA PVT. LTD., Mumbai
▮ 9323187101
✉ membership@datanetindia.com

DATTSONS, Nagpur
✆ (O) 2524659 (R) 2532544, Fax: 0712-2537896
✉ dattsons@hotmail.com

DAYA PUBLISHING HOUSE, Delhi
✆ (O) 27383999, 27382765 (R) 23260116
Fax: 91-11-27382329
✉ dayabooks@vsnl.com

DAYITVA BODH, Ghaziabad
▮ 9910462009
✉ dayitvabodh@rediffmail.com

DAYSTAR PUBLICATIONS, New Delhi
✆ 23352438, 22063201, Fax: 91-11-23736679
✉ daystar_publications@yahoo.co.uk

DEEP AND DEEP PUBLICATIONS (P) LTD., New Delhi
✆ (O) 25435369, 25440916, 55479461
(R) 25440855, 32535220, 31075546
Fax: 91-11-25440916
✉ ddpubs@gmail.com, ddpbooks@yahoo.co.in

DEEP BOOK CENTRE, Nasik
✆ (O) 0253-2594498 (R) 0253-2598120
✉ deepbooks2003@yahoo.com

DEEP PUBLICATIONS, New Delhi
✆ (O) 25259514 (R) 25264726
✉ deep_pub@hotmail.com

DEEP PUBLISHING, Agra
✆ 2261220, Fax: 2311012
✉ sumit8@sancharnet.in

DEEPA PRAKASHAN, Ghaziabad
✆ 2900191 ▮ 9811271465, Fax: 91-11-23270889
✉ cbyash@yahoo.com

DEEPAK BOOK STORE, Delhi
▮ 9818564834
✉ pradeepgrewal@redffmail.com

DEEPAK PRAKASHAN, Gwalior
✆ 4040200, Fax: 91-751-2368746
✉ deepakprakashan@hotmail.com

DEEPAK PUBLISHERS & DISTRIBUTORS, Gwalior
✆ 325054, 330209 — anirudh110@sify.com

DEEPSHIKHA BOOKS & INFO SERVICES, Delhi
✆ 35340557, 32361740 — deepshikha_in2000@yahoo.com

DEEPU PRAKASHAN, Delhi
✆ (O) 23258909, 23281911 (R) 27138165 — tarunpub@yahoo.com
Fax: 91-11-23258909

DEHATI PUSTAK BHANDAR, Delhi
✆ 23279417, 23985175, Fax: 91-11-23261030 — hans@ndb.vsnl.net.in

DELHI ARYA PRATINIDHI SABHA, New Delhi
✆ 23360150, 41500589, Fax: 91-11-23365959 — aryasabha@yahoo.com

DELHI BIBLE INSTITUTE, New Delhi
✆ 24611311, Fax: 91-11-24638625 — dbi7bb@gmail.com

DELHI BOOK COMPANY, New Delhi
✆ 23416313, 23417268, Fax: 91-11-23625020 — mybooks@vishvbooks.com

DELHI BOOK STORE, New Delhi
✆ 23283333, 23281202, 23250909 — delhibooks@delnetworks.com,
9811084529, Fax: 91-11-23283781 — vjdelhibook@bol.net.in

DELHI LAW HOUSE, Delhi
✆ (O) 23917627, 23963959 (R) 27241770, 27241716 — sales@delhilawhouse.com,
Fax: 91-11-23941793 — editorial@delhilawhouse.com

DELHI LIBRARY BOOK CENTRE, Delhi
✆ (O) 27557680 (R) 27293793 — delhilibrary@yahoo.com

DELHI PUBLIC COLLEGE OF COMPETITIONS, Delhi
✆ 27187227, 27105555 — vaid@giasd101.vsnl.net.in

DELHI PUSTAK SADAN, Delhi
✆ 22391120, 22912274 — dpsbooks@mantraonline.com

DELHI SARASWAT SANGH, New Delhi
✆ 26302507, Fax: 26524541 — sangram32@yahoo.co.in

DELHI SIKH GURDWARA MANAGEMENT COMMITTEE, New Delhi
✆ 23712580-81, Fax: 91-11-23317511 — dsgmc@rediffmail.com

DELHI WIRELESS INSTITUTE (REGD.) , New Delhi
✆ (O) 25723659, 25723691 (R) 25103758 — arvindm@vsnl.com
Fax: 91-11-25723691

DEPARTMENT OF PUBLICATION, Delhi
✆ 23813764, Fax: 91-11-23817846 — acop.dep@nic.in

DESHI VIDESHI BOOK TRADERS, New Delhi
✆ 26229790, 26221204 — deshivideshi@yahoo.com

DESIGN POINT (THE), Mumbai
honesty@vsnl.com

DESTINATION WORLDWIDE, New Delhi
✆ 25740525 — anju7@vsnl.com

DEV SAMAJ PRAKASHAN, New Delhi
✆ 91-11-26911101 — mnj_1416@yahoo.com

DEVELOPMENT ASSOCIATES, Delhi
✆ 27524081 — da_india@hotmail.com

DHANAM PUBLICATION (P) LTD., Kochi
✆ 2315840, 2316494, Fax: 91-484-2317872 — dhanrubber@vsnl.net

DHANPAT RAI & CO. (P) LTD., Delhi
✆ 23265367, 23250251, Fax: 91-11-27233793 — dhanpatrai@gmail.com

DHANPAT RAI PUBLISHING CO. PVT. LTD., New Delhi
✆ 23257526, 23257511, Fax: 91-11-23257525 — mail@dhanpatrai.in

DHANPAT RAI PUBLICATIONS (P) LTD., New Delhi
✆ (O) 23246573, 23274073, 23246574
(R) 22152148, Fax: 22162852 — ishkapur@vsnl.com

DHANRAJ BOOK HOUSE, Delhi
✆ 27857044, Fax: 91-11-27857044 — dhanraj.books@gmail.com

DHANWANTRA MED. & LAW BOOK HOUSE, Delhi
✆ (O) 23866768, 23865746, 2621653
(R) 26416653, 26224372 ▮ 9810193330 — p.p.khanna@hotmail.com

DHARMYATRA MAHASANGH, New Delhi
✆ 28723934, Fax: 91-11-28724019 — dharm_parvah2007@yahoo.co.in

DHILLON GROUP OF PUBLICATIONS, New Delhi
✆ (O) 26488448 (R) 26239536, 26439536
Fax: 91-11-26488748 — dhillongroup_publication@yahoo.co.in

DHINGRA BOOK HOUSE, Delhi
✆ 22021350, 22059251, 22426053
Telefax: 22059251 — mkdhingra@rediffmail.com

DIAMOND BOOK CENTRE, Pune
✆ (O) 24486093, 4020281 (R) 25464752
Fax: 24486093 — diamond_books@hotmail.com

DIAMOND COMICS (P) LTD., Delhi
✆ (O) 23266232, 23266317, 2401093/94/95
(R) 0124-2354931 ▮ 9810003062
Fax: 91-11-24010393/94/95 — gulshanrai@diamondcomic.com

DIAMOND POCKET BOOKS (P) LTD., New Delhi
✆ 41611861, Fax: 91-11-41611866 — sales@dpb.in

DIANETICS AND SCIENTOLOGY, New Delhi
✆ 41550913/34, Fax: 91-11-41550912 — horstt@airtelbroadband.in

DIKSOOCHI, Bangalore
✆ 23352696, Fax: 23352696 — jeeva@blr.vsnl.net.in

DISCOVERY PUBLISHING HOUSE, New Delhi
✆ (O) 23279245, 23253475 (R) 22414930
Fax: 91-11-23253475 — dphtemp@indiatimes.com

DISHA PUBLICATIONS, New Delhi
✆ 91-11-26691021, 26691713 — aiets@rediffmail.com

DIVINE COMPUTERS PVT. LTD., Faridabad
✆ 2412106, 2410764, 2370806
Fax: 0129-2413493 — mail@divinecd.com, garodia@satyam.net.in

DIVINE SPARK, Delhi
✆ 91-11-22755953 — shenoy_rajaram@hotmail.com

DOABA HOUSE, Delhi
✆ 23274669, 55363037 ▮ 9811137322
Fax: 26968735 — amamikavivek@hotmail.com, doabahouse@hotmail.com

DOCTORS LIBRARY (INDIA) PVT. LTD., Mumbai
✆ 22058916, Fax: 91-22-22088291 — doctors@bom3.vsnl.net.in

DOEACC SOCIETY, New Delhi
✆ 24362824, 24363330-32, Fax: 91-11-24363335 — doeacc@doe.ernet.in

DOLPHIN PRESS, New Delhi
✆ 91-11-41720230 — israelrede@gmail.com

DOLPHIN PUBLICATIONS PVT. LTD., Mumbai
✆ 40763000, Fax: 91-22-40763040 — dolphin3@mtnl.net.in

DOMINANT PUBLISHERS & DISTRIBUTORS, New Delhi
✆ 23281685, Fax: 91-11-23270680 — dominantbooks@post.com

DORLING KINDERSLEY INDIA (P) LTD., New Delhi
✆ 26498851-54, Fax: 91-11-26498885 — saurabh.sri@dk.com

DORLING KINDERSLEY INDIA (P) LTD., Delhi
✆ 43030100, Fax: 91-11-22146071 — mail@pearsoned.co.in

DOVE MULTIMEDIA PVT. LTD., New Delhi
✆ 91-11-32465319 — pebblesdove@gmail.com, dove@vsnl.com

DRAVIDA PUBLICATIONS, Delhi
✆ 22255165, Fax: 91-11-23368376 — keraladir@iname.com

DREAM PALACE BOOK DISTRIBUTORS, New Delhi
✆ 91-11-64163037 — narkambooks@gmail.com

DREAM TEAM NETWORK SOLUTION (P) LTD., Jodhpur
✆ 91-291-2308074, 2308075 — info@lite-rom.com

DREAMLAND PUBLICATIONS, Delhi
✆ 25435657, 25106050, Fax: 91-11-25438283 — dreamland@vsnl.com

DREAMTECH PRESS, New Delhi
✆ 91-11-23284212 — sales@dreamtechbt.com, dreamland@vsnl.com

DRKRUNCH TECHNOLOGIES PVT. LTD., Bangalore
✆ 26681969, Fax: 26680320 — drkrunch@blr.vsnl.net.in

DUGAR BOOKS AND PRINTS, New Delhi
✆ 24621832, Fax: 24627755 — dugarbooks@yahoo.com

DUGGAL PUBLISHERS & DISTRIBUTORS, Kalka
✆ 01733-220360 — duggalpublishers@rediffmail.com

DURGA ENTERPRISES, New Delhi
✆ 91-11-28524316 — durgabooks10@yahoo.com

DYNAMIC PUBLICATIONS (I) LTD., Meerut
✆ (O) & (R) 0121-2644766, 2642946
Fax: 0121-2645855 — sk_kpm@yahoo.com

DYNAMIC SERVICES, Mumbai
✆ 22013123, 22019180, Fax: 22059539 — letterprint@vsnl.net

E

E.D. GALGOTIA & SONS (TECHNICAL SECTION), New Delhi
✆ 23713227-28, 23322876, 23755150 — galgotia@ndf.vsnl.net.in
Fax: 91-11-23327601

E-DIKSHA.COM, New Delhi
✆ 25912191, 25912205, Fax: 91-11-25912205 — vitratra@bol.net.in

EFY INTERPRISES PVT. LTD., New Delhi
✆ 26810601-02/03, Fax: 91-11-26817563, 26812312 — info@efyindia.com

E-FRAME SOLUTIONS PVT. LTD., New Delhi
✆ 41004022, Fax: 91-11-23245011 — info@eframes.in

E-FIRST SOLUTIONS INDIA P. LTD., New Delhi
✆ 26933765, 23289578, Fax: 28611637 — tribhuwan.singh@efirstindia.com

EARLYBIRD BOOKS PVT. LTD., New Delhi
✆ 91-11-23518802, 23610700 — earlybirdbookspvtltd_1999@rediffmail.com

EARTHSCAN INDIA PVT. LTD., New Delhi
✆ 23258325, 23270718, Fax: 91-11-23267224 — viva@mantraonline.com

EARTHWORM BOOKS PVT. LTD., Chennai
✆ 26412314, Fax: 26427484 — ewb.maa@sml.sprintrpg.sprint.com

EAST WEST BOOKS (MADRAS) PVT. LTD., Chennai
✆ 26602003, Fax: 26601974 — ewb@touchtelindia.net

EASTERN BOOK COMPANY, Lucknow
✆ 2223171, 2626517, 2274901 — sales@ebc-india.com, sales@scconline.com, support@ebc-india.com
Fax: 91-522-2624328

EASTERN BOOK HOUSE, Guwahati
✆ (O) 2513876, 2519231 (R) 2636538, Fax: 2519231 — info@easternbookhouse.com

EASTERN BOOK LINKERS, Delhi
✆ 23850287, 32919869 ▮ 9811232913 — ebl@vsnl.net
Fax: 91-11-23970287

EASTERN BOOKS (PUBLISHERS), Delhi
✆ 91-11-22056652 — easternbooks@satyam.net.in

EASTERN EXPORTS, Chennai
✆ 28270975, Fax: 28255724 — eastern@satyem.net.in

EASTERN LAW HOUSE PVT. LTD., Kolkata
✆ 033-27-24989/2301, Fax: 22150491 — elh@cal.vsnl.net.in

EDUCARE PUBLICATIONS, New Delhi
✆ 26602695, Fax: 91-11-26864126 — educare_publication@yahoo.co.in

EDUCATION INTERNATIONAL INDIA, New Delhi
✆ 26897418/19, Fax: 011-26897416 — cec@del2.vsnl.net.in

EDUCATIONAL AIDS & CONSULTANCY SERVICES INDIA, Faridabad
✆/Fax: 2277253 — eacsi@mantraonline.com

EDUCATIONAL BOOK AGENCY, Siliguri
✆ (O) 2424956 (R) 2427499, Fax: 2431100 — ebagency@dte.vsnl.net.in

EDUCATIONAL BOOK AGENCY, Delhi
✆ (O) 23844216, 23842077 (R) 25934928, 55150688 ebaindia2000@yahoo.co.in
Fax: 91-11-23843447

EDUCATIONAL BOOK CENTRE, Mumbai
✆ (O) 25603324, 25685341 (R) 25901148 ebc@vsnl.net
Fax: 25685341

EDUCATIONAL BOOK CENTER, Shimla
✆ 91-177-2650776, Telefax: 2656776 educationalbookcenter@hotmail.com

EDUCATIONAL PUBLISHERS, Delhi
✆ 23216162, 23214465, Fax: 23211540 ephdelhi@yahoo.com, eph@onebox.com

EDUCATIONAL PUBLISHERS & DISTRIBUTORS, Cochin
✆ 2372817, Fax: 2355283 epd-pai@yahoo.com

EDUCATIONAL PUBLISHING HOUSE, Delhi
✆ 23216162, 23214465, Fax: 91-11-23211540 ephindia@gmail.com

EDUCATIONAL SUPPLIES, Bangalore
✆ 26769509, 26761289, Fax: 26769954 jai@blr.vsnl.net.in

EDURITE TECHNOLOGIES PVT. LTD., New Delhi
✆ 46068507, 46068508, Fax: 91-11-46068581 subrotoroy@edurite.com, marketingteam@edurite.com

EFFICIENT BOOK DISTRIBUTORS, New Delhi
✆ 26132262 ▮ 9811380682, Fax: 26132262 effibook@satyam.net.in

EGMONT IMAGINATION (INDIA) LTD., Mumbai
✆ 56924700, Fax: 56924709 ieegmont@bom4.vsnl.net.in

EICHER GOODEARTH LIMITED, New Delhi
✆ 41437600, Fax: 91-11-41437700 maps@eicher.co.in

EKLAVYA, Bhopal
✆ 2463380, 6549033, Fax: 91-755-2461703 pitara@eklavya.in

EKTA BOOK COMPANY, New Delhi
✆ 23388588, 23383875, 23383334, Fax: 23383334 ektalaw@vsnl.com

EKTA BOOK COMPANY (SALES), New Delhi
✆ 30621119, Fax: 91-11-26514798 ektabookcompany_s@yahoo.com

EKTA BOOK DISTRIBUTORS, New Delhi
✆ (O) 56065579 (R) 25640621 ▮ 9811582579 ektabooks@yahoo.com

EKTA LAW HOUSE, New Delhi
✆ 26491875, 26499876 ▮ 9811026696, 9811048086 ektalaw@vsnl.com
Telefax: 26499876

ELIC ENTERPRISES, Nashik
✆ 0253-2580624 elicindia@yahoo.com

ELITE PUBLISHERS & DISTRIBUTORS, New Delhi
✆ (O) 26511961 (R) 26899239 ▮ 9811670046 elitepublishers@vsnl.net
Fax: 91-11-26511961

ELITE PUBLISHING HOUSE PVT. LTD., New Delhi
✆ 26241717, 41004299 ▮ 9810666503 rg_elite@yahoo.com

ELSEVIER (A DIVISION OF REED ELSEVIER INDIA PVT. LTD.), New Delhi
✆ 42890200, Fax: 91-11-42890201 infoindia@elsevier.com

ELSEVIER, New Delhi
✆ 26447160, Fax: 91-11-26447156 esindia@vsnl.net, elservier@giasdol.insl.net.in

ELSEVIER SCIENCE, New Delhi
✆ 26464550, 26280848, Fax: 26475065 — harcourt@vsnl.com

EMBASSY BOOK DISTRIBUTORS, Mumbai
✆ 91-22-22819546 — embassy@vsnl.com

EMERALD PUBLISHERS, Chennai
✆ 28193206, Fax: 28192380 — olivannang@yahoo.co.in

EMKAY PUBLICATIONS, Delhi
✆ 22092191 ▮ 9891156083, Fax: 22046456 — emkay_pub@rediffmail.com

ENCYCLOPAEDIA BRITANNICA INDIA PVT. LTD., Gurgaon
✆ 5012150 ▮ 9810289145, Fax: 5012155 — corporate@ebindia.com, bcd@ebindia.com

ENCYCLOPAEDIA BRITANNICA (INDIA) PVT. LTD., New Delhi
✆ 46536450-53, Fax: 91-11-29245116 — bcd@ebindia.com

ENGINEERING COMPETITION TODAY, Agra
✆ 2156558, 2157671, 2154582, Fax: 2522141 — oswalbooks@vsnl.com, oswalbooks@indiatimes.com

ENGINEERS INDIA RESEARCH INSTITUTE, Delhi
✆ (O) 23918117, 23916431, 23840361
(R) 31082370, Fax: 23916431 — eirisidi@bol.net.in

ENGINEERS TODAY, Jaipur
✆ 2315392, 2201532 — engineerstoday@123india.com

ENGLISH BOOK DEPOT (THE), Dehradun
✆ 22655192, 2710958, Fax: 2658730 — sales@ebdbooks.com, sandeep@ebdbooks.com, ebdbooks@vsnl.com

ENGLISH EDITION, Mumbai
✆ (O) 25243531, 25274464, 55952261/62
(R) 25541853, Fax: 25233158 — english_edition@hotmail.com

ENKAY CORPORATION, Delhi
✆ 27184398, 27180768, 56237493
Fax: 91-11-27180768 ▮ 9810282329 — jdis@del3.vsnl.net.in

ENKAY INTERNATIONAL, Delhi
✆ (O) 22074782 (R) 22076113, Fax: 22076046 — enkayi@eth.net

ESS ESS PUBLICATIONS, New Delhi
✆ 23260807, 23201533, 23274173
Fax: 91-11-23274173 — essess@del3.vsnl.net.in

ESS ESS PUBLICATIONS/REFERENCE PRESS, New Delhi
✆ 23260807, 41563444, Fax: 91-11-41563334 — info@essessreference.com

ESWAR PRESS, Chennai
✆ 52030431, Fax: 24339590 — gempeyes@md3.vsnl.net.in

ET4ALL ENTERPRISES, New Delhi
✆ 91-11-66603600 — ambdded@gmailcom

EURASIA PUBLISHING HOUSE PVT. LTD., New Delhi
✆ 23672080-82 ▮ 9899107446, 9911310888
Fax: 91-11-23677446 — schand@vsnl.com, info@schandgroup.com

EUREKA MARKETING GROUP, Faridabad
✆ (O) & (R) 0129-2512067 ▮ 9818002483,
Fax: 0129-25252222 — pandit@del3.vsnl.net.in

EUROPEAN BUSINESS INFORMATION CENTRE, New Delhi
✆ 24636675, Fax: 24633378 — Ebic@giasbm01.vsnl.net.in

EUROPEAN UNION, New Delhi
✆ 24629237, Fax: 24629206 — eu@delind.cec.eu.int, delegation-india@cec.eu.int

EVEREST PUBLISHING HOUSE, Pune
✆ (O) 2459486, 2364469 (R) 2365790
Fax: 2459486 — everest@adnetindia.com

EVERGREEN PUBLICATIONS (INDIA) LTD., New Delhi
✆ (O) 23283372, 23264528, 23280337
(R) 22151265, Fax: 91-11-23289434, 23262183 — evergreen@del3.vsnl.net.in

EXCEL BOOKS PRIVATE LIMITED, New Delhi
✆ 25795793/94, Fax: 91-11-25791701 — info@excelbooks.com

EXCEL MEDIA, New Delhi
✆ 23251049, Fax: 91-11-23251049 — excelmedia@vsnl.net

EXICOM (INDIA) PVT. LTD., Mumbai
✆ 27634863 /4/5/6, Fax: 27680107 — exipub@bom5.vsnl.net.in

EXPRESS COLOUR SCAN PVT. LTD., New Delhi
✆ 25703345 to 25703348, Fax: 25700111 — castle@giasdl01.vsnl.net.in

EXPOSURE COMMUNICATIONS (P) LTD., Chennai
✆ 28235453, 28215941-42, Fax: 28241799 — exposure@eth.net

F

FABRO DYNAMICS, Hyderabad
✆ 27616512, 27610238, Fax: 27664144 — fabrodynamics@yahoo.com

FACH PRESSE PUBLISHERS PVT. LTD., Mumbai
✆ 24279183, Fax: 22825603 — fach@boms.vsnl.net.in

FALCON BOOKS PVT. LTD., New Delhi
✆ 26432653, 26228514, Fax: 91-11-26448917 — falconbpl@yahoo.co.in

FARID EXPORTS, New Delhi
✆ 23289786, 23256590, Fax: 91-11-23279998 — farid@ndf.vsnl.net.in

FERTILISER DEVELOPMENT AND CONSULTATION ORGANISATION, New Delhi
✆ 26417801, 51633864, Fax: 26862196, 26417801 — fdco@vsnl.net, hls_tandon@mantraonline.com

FILEX SYSTEMS (P) LTD., Delhi
✆ 23925659, 23843404, Fax: 91-11-27781606 — filex@vsnl.com, filexsales@vsnl.net

FILHAAL, Patna
✆ 91-612-2525813 — filhaal_patna@yahoo.com

FIREWALL MEDIA, New Delhi
✆ 23252574, Fax: 23252572 — colaxmi@hotmail.com

FIRMA KLM (P) LTD., Kolkata
✆ 22217294, 22374391, 24813198 — fklm@satyam.net.in
Fax: 91-33-22256742

FIRST CHURCH OF CHRIST SCIENTIST, New Delhi
✆ 91-11-41826022 — juliasappenfield@hotmail.com

FIRST PUBLIC PROTECTION TRUST, Chennai
✆ 24937008, 24950702, Fax: 91-44-24938488 — srinivasan@kmr.net

FLAMINGO BOOKS (EXPORT), New Delhi
✆ 23535454, 23525867, Fax: 91-11-23612870 — sonipub@ndf.vsnl.net.in, sonipub@vsnl.com

FOCUS BOOK SHOP, Bangalore
✆ 3346692, 33445402, Fax: 23424265 — focus@mahiti.org, focusgroup@vsnl.net

FOCUS: THE BOOK SHOP, Pondicherry
✆ 0413-2345513 — m_anony@mailcity.com

FOREIGN LANGUAGE TEACHING AND RESEARCH PRESS, New Delhi
✆ 23263695, Fax: 91-11-23911057 — kaushalgoyal@vsnl.com

FORTUNE BOOKS, New Delhi
✆ 23261597, 23255577, Fax: 23280289 — anmilpublication@vsnl.com

FOUNDATION BOOKS, New Delhi
✆ 23277332, 23285851-2, Fax: 23288534 — cupdel@cupind.com

FOUNDATION MEDIA/FOUNDATION BOOKS, New Delhi
✆ 23277332, 23285851, 23285852, 23274196, 23288533, Fax: 23288534 — cupdel@cupind.com

FOUNTAIN HEAD BOOK SHOP, Chennai
✆ 044-28280867 — fhbooks@satyam.net.in

FOUNTAINHEAD, Bangalore
✆ 2219777 — fhblore@satyam.net.in

FRANK BROTHERS & CO. (PUB.) LTD., New Delhi
✆ 23263393, 23279936 (R) 26107579, Fax: 23269032 — connect@frankbros.com, frankbooks@vsnl.com

FRANK EDUCATIONAL AIDS (P) LTD., Noida
✆ 2537672-73, Fax: 91-120-2536500 — info@frankedu.com, frank@satyam.net.in

FRANKSONS, New Delhi
✆ 23276757, 23265160, 23260796, Fax: 23269032 — connect@frankbros.com

FREE ADS, Secunderabad
✆ 27811025, 27811250, Fax: 27818568 — freeads@hd2.vsnl.net.in

FRENCH BOOK CENTRE PVT. LTD., New Delhi
✆ 24699349, Telex: 31-272143, Fax: 24645917 — fbc@mantraonline.com

FRIENDS PUBLICATIONS (INDIA), Delhi
✆ (O) 27654826 (R) 27659446, Fax: 27654827 — frienpub@ndf.vsnl.net.in

FRONTLINE BOOKS, New Delhi
✆ 23353223, 23320128, Fax: 23721188, 23723366 — fln@del2.vsnl.net.in

FULL CIRCLE PUBLISHING PVT. LTD., New Delhi
✆ 24620063, 55654197, Fax: 24645795 — fullcircle@vsnl.com

FUSION BOOKS, Delhi
✆ 91-11-41611862 — sales@diamondpublication.com

FUTURA BOOKS PONDICHERRY (P) LTD., Pondicherry
✆ 0413-220992 — prpathi@rediffmail.com

FUTURE ARTS, Solan
✆ 91-1795-320762 — info@futurearts.co.in

FUTURE POINT, New Delhi
✆ 26569200-01, 26569800-01, 26850269, 26866000 — mail@futurepointindia.com
Fax: 91-11-26569200-01

■ ■ ■

G

G. RAM BOOKS PVT. LTD., Delhi
✆ 22531066, 22532912, Fax: 91-11-22012811 — info@grambooks.com

G.B.D. BOOKS, New Delhi
✆ 41563695, Fax: 91-11-23911057 — generalbookdepot@yahoo.com

G.D.M.K. PUBLISHERS DISTRIBUTORS, New Delhi
✆ 25415043, 25014181, Fax: 91-11-25635908 — sr_allbooks@vsnl.net

G.K. PUBLISHERS PVT. LTD., Noida
✆ 3250473, 4267181, 4267182 — gkp@gkpublications.com, info@gkpublications.com
Fax: 91-120-4267183

G.R. BATHLA & SONS PUB. & DIST., Meerut
✆ 2660709, 2660802, 4022486 — manojbathla@hotmail.com, grbathla@rediffmail.com
Fax: 91-121-2664539

G.S. SALES CORPORATION, Kolkata
✆ 24639930, 24644139 — gsmacalcal3.vsnl.net.in

GAJANAN PUSTAKALAYA, Surat
✆ 91-261-2424246, 2667419 — info@gajananbooks.com, info@smartinfosys.net

GALGOTIA BOOKSOURCE (P) LTD., New Delhi
✆ 26156455, Fax: 91-11-26156456 — mail@galgotia.com

GALGOTIA PUBLICATIONS (P) LTD., New Delhi
✆ 23263334, 23288132, Fax: 91-11-23281909 — gppl@indiatimes.com

GALGOTIA PUBLISHING COMPANY, New Delhi
✆ (O) 25752918, 25751728 (R) 25751728 — galgotiabooks@rediffmail.com
25788991, Fax: 91-11-23755150

GANASHAKTI, Kolkata
✆ 22458950, Fax: 22448090 — mail@ganashkti.com

GANDHARVA-VED PRAKASHAN (SHRI), Pune
✆ 24493502 — gandharv_ved@hotmail.com

GANDHI LITERATURE CENTRE, New Delhi
✆ 23328310, 23310168, Fax: 91-11-23311793 — gandhimk@nda.vsnl.net.in

GANDHI SMRITI AND DARSHAN SAMITI, New Delhi
✆ 23012843, 23011480, Fax: 91-11-23011480 — mkgandhi@del2.vsnl.net.in

GANGARAMS BOOK BUREAU, Bangalore
✆ 2551618, 25588015 — gangarams@vsnl.com

GARGI PRAKASHAN, Ghaziabad
✆ 9868804857 — gargi_prakashan@yahoo.com

GARGI PRAKASHAN, Saharanpur
✆ 9837315676 — gargi_prakashan@yahoo.com

GAUTAM BOOK CENTRE, Delhi
✆ 22570380 ▮ 9810173667, Fax: 91-11-22119239 — gautambookcentre@hotmail.com

GAUTAMA BROTHERS, Kanpur
✆ (O) 0512-2364601, 2224194 (R) 2544267, 2256026 Fax: 2311314 ▮ 9838009946 — gbrospub@sancharnet.net

GAYATRI PARIVAR, Chandigarh
ajsansthan@awgp.org

GAYATRI PUBLICATIONS, Delhi
✆ 27142802, Fax: 27142802 — mcpur@nda.vsnl.net.in

GEETA GRAPHICS, New Delhi
✆ 25875330, 25871272 — rphbooks@indiatimes.com, gitabooks@rediffmail.com

GEETA INTL. PUBLISHERS & DISTRIBUTORS, Delhi
✆ 22429715 — dvmangla@hotmail.com

GEETA PRIVATE LIMITED (THE), Thrissur
✆ 0487-2334306 — geeta_amrit123@yahoo.com

GEETA PVT. LTD. (THE), Delhi
✆ 22442084 ▮ 9868020790 — geeta_amrit123@yahoo.com

GEETIKA PRAKASHAN, Bijnor
✆ 263232, Fax: 262375 — giriraj3100@rediffmail.com

GEM BOOK DISTRIBUTOR, New Delhi
✆ 26023215 — gbdo15@yahoo.com

GEM BOOK DISTRIBUTOR, New Delhi
✆ 42143438, Fax: 91-11-42143438 — ramlalvani@yahoo.co.in

GENERAL BOOK DEPOT, Delhi
✆ (O) 23263695, 23250635 (R) 23938187, 55351643 Fax: 011-22940861, 23712710 ▮ 9810229648 — contact@goyalbookshop.com

GENERAL PRINTERS & PUBLISHERS, Mumbai
✆ (O) 022-23826854, 23873113 (R) 23642589, 23627547, Fax: 23827197 — thakker@bom3.vsnl.net.in

GENESIS MICRO-LINK PVT. LTD., New Delhi
✆ 25795245, Fax: 25792841 — gmlink@nda.vsnl.net.in

GENUINE PUBLICATIONS & MEDIA (P) LTD., New Delhi
✆ 24352732, Fax: 91-11-24352048 — genuinepublications@yahoo.com

GEOLOGICAL SURVEY OF INDIA, Kolkata
✆ 22861698, Fax: 91-11-22521534 — dydgop4@cal3vsnl.gov.in

GEOLOGISTICS LIMITED, New Delhi
✆ 26130925, Fax: 26130930 — enquiries@geo-logistics.co.in

GERMAN BOOK CENTRE, Chennai
✆ 24346244, 24346266, Fax: 24346529 — germanbk@vsnl.com, itpsesha@giasmd01.vsnl.net.in

GERMAN BOOK SHOP, New Delhi
✆ 23358534, Fax: 91-11-23850961 — goyal@vsnl.com

GHALIB ACADEMY, New Delhi
✆ 24351098, Fax: 91-11-24351098 — ghalibgaacademy05@yahoo.com

GHALIB INSTITUTE, New Delhi
✆ 23232583, Fax: 23236518 — ghalib@vsnl.net

GIRDHARI LAL CHOPRA (AGENTS) P. LTD., Amritsar
✆ 2292295, 2544338, Fax: 0091-0183-2553891 — jp@choprachess.com

GIRI TRADING AGENCY, Chennai
✆ 24940376, 24942530, 24953820
Fax: 91-44-24953821 — giritrading@vsnl.com

GITA ENTERPRISES, New Delhi
✆ (O) 25847377, 25842605 (R) 25726250 — rphbooks@indiatimes.com, gitabooks@rediffmail.com

GITA PRESS, Gorakhpur
✆ 2334721, Fax: 91-551-2336997 — booksales@gitapress.org

GLOBAL BOOK & SUBSCRIPTION SERVICES, New Delhi
✆ (O) 25709439, 25709440, 25709420
(R) 25723241, 25756029, Fax: 011-25756029 — rchandr-gegbss@axcess.net.in, globale@ndf.vsnl.net.in, globalex@bol.net.in

GLOBAL BOOKS, Srinagar
✆ 2410251 — globalbooks-sgr@yahoo.com

GLOBAL CHILDREN CARE & CURE FOUNDATION, New Delhi
✆ 26832036, 26925286, Fax: 26827137 — carecure@nde.vsnl.net.in

GLOBAL INFORMATION SYSTEMS TECHNOLOGY PVT. LTD., Gurgaon
✆ 4001410-13, Fax: 91-124-4052913 — gistdel@gist.com, gistdel@gist.in

GLOBAL MEDIA PUBLICATIONS, New Delhi
✆ 26323985 ▮ 9818327757, Fax: 26323985 — gmpublication@rediffmail.com

GLOBAL VISION PUBLISHING HOUSE, New Delhi
✆ 91-11-23261581, 23276291, 64694271
43575199 ▮ 9810644769 — nsingh_2004@vsnl.net, globalvision.pub@gmail.com, gv.ph@hotmail.com

GLOBAL VOLUNTEERS, Secunderabad
✆ 25550193 ▮ 9861045164 — krajeshg@indiatimes.com

GLOBE BOOK DEPOT (THE), New Delhi
✆ (O) 23329377 (R) 26464826, 26465678 — dsbpa@indiatimes.com

GLOBE PUBLICATIONS PVT. LTD., New Delhi
✆ 45055555, 25770411, 25778875, 25770212
▮ 9810413740, Fax: 91-11-25778876 — info@globepub.com

GOAL PUBLICATION, New Delhi
▮ 9868403166, Fax: 91-11-24621538 — scholarbooks@vsnl.com

GOBIND BALLABH PANT KRISHI EVAM PRADYOGIK VISHWAVIDYALAYA, Udham Singh Nagar
✆ 233579, Fax: 233473 — vc@gbpuat.ernet.in

GOBIND SADAN, New Delhi
✆ 91-11-64517341 — ralph@gobindsadan.org

GOEL BOOK AGENCY, Pune
✆ 020-24453267 — compuhut@pn2.vsnl.net.in

GOEL PUBLISHING HOUSE, Meerut
✆ 01210-2644766, Fax: 2645855 — sk_kpm@yahoo.com

GOLD BOOKS (INDIA), Delhi
✆ 23918311, 22213772 — gold_pub@lycos.com

GOOD COMPANIONS, Vadodara
✆ 2425433 — girish@barodaview.com

GOOD LUCK PUBLISHERS LTD., Delhi
✆ (O) 22015110 (R) 22760953, Fax: 22727104 — deepak3@nde.vsnl.net.in

GOODPRINT, Mumbai
goodprint@vsnl.com

GOODWILL PUBLISHING HOUSE, New Delhi
✆ (O) 25750801, 25755519, 25820556
(R) 25851608, Fax: 91-11-25763428 — goodwillpub@vsnl.net

GOODWORD BOOKS, New Delhi
✆ 24355454, 24356666, Fax: 24357333 — info@goodwordbooks.com

GOPSONS PAPERS LTD., Noida
gopsons@del3.vsnl.net.in

GOSPEL LITERATURE SERVICE, Mumbai
✆ 022-24930116, 56627243, Fax: 24935532 — gls@bom2.vsnl.net.in, glsindia@vsnl.com

GOVINDA BOOK HOUSE, New Delhi
✆ (O) 26851413 (R) 26527481, Fax: 26527481 — govindaberry@hotmail.com, govinda@ndf.vsnl.net.in

GOVINDRAM HASANAND, Delhi
✆ 23977216, 65360255, Fax: 91-11-23977216 — ajayarya@vsnl.com, orders@vedicbooks.com

GOWARSONS PUBLISHERS (P) LTD., New Delhi
✆ (O) 25403312/3 (R) 26961172/3787
Fax: 25403551 — delaae07@giasdl01.vsnl.net.in

GOYAL BROTHERS PRAKASHAN/GOYAL BOOKS OVERSEAS PVT. LTD., New Delhi
✆ 26537772-3, Fax: 26963418 — goyalgbp99@hotmail.com

GOYAL OVERSEAS, New Delhi
✆ 26160476, 26103710, Fax: 91-11-26183237 — goyaloverseas@hotmail.com

GOYAL PUBLISHERS & DISTRIBUTORS PVT. LTD., Delhi
✆ 23912186, 23918362, Fax: 23940861 — goyal@vsnl.com

GOYAL PUBLISHING HOUSE, New Delhi
✆ (O) 23274375, 23274151, 23275092
(R) 23911583, 23964963, Fax: 23274151 — gph2004@yahoo.co.in

GRAIL MESSAGE CENTRE, Hyderabad
✆ 91-40-23608484 — grailindia@gmail.com

GRAIL MESSAGE PUBLICATION CO., New Delhi
✆ 26372301-03 — am.stahl@arcor.de

GRAIL MESSAGE PUBLISHING COMPANY, Hyderabad
✆ 23608484 — grailind@hd2.dot.net.in

GRANADA LEARNING, Bangalore
✆ 56975950 — naveens@vsnl.com

GRANTH ACADEMI, New Delhi
✆ 23264676, Fax: 91-11-23253233 — info@prabhatbooks.com

GRANTHAGAR, Ahmedabad
✆ 26408213 — granthagar@yahoo.com

GRAPHIC PUBLICATIONS (P) LTD., New Delhi
✆ 91-11-23243520 — graphicpublication@yahoo.com

GREENWOOD PUBLISHING, Gurgaon
✆ 91-124-2576796 — overleaf@vsnl.net

GREHLAXMI, New Delhi
✆ 51611861-65, Fax: 51611866 — sulex@diamondpocketbooks.com

GROLIER INTERNATIONAL PVT. LTD., New Delhi
✆ 26281356, 26229088, Fax: 91-11-26281345 — agupta@in.grolier.aspac.com

GROLIER INTERNATIONAL PVT. LTD., New Delhi
✆ 29239088, Fax: 91-11-29231345 — enquiry@grolier.co.in

GUIDE PUBLICATIONS, New Delhi
✆ (O) 25101947 (R) 25101304, Fax: 25122524 — guidepub@del2.vsnl.net.in

GUJARAT SAHITYA PRAKASH, Gujarat
✆ 240161, Fax: 240178 — gsp@satyam.net.in

GULSHAN BOOKS, Srinagar
✆ 2477287, Fax: 91-194-2477287 — gulshanpub@rediffmail.com

GUNA INTERNATIONAL COMPANY, Madurai
dolphin@md5.vsnl.net.in

GUPTA BROTHERS, Ajmer
✆ (O) 2460919 (R) 2627870 — guptabrothersajmer@hotmail.com

GUPTA BROTHERS BOOKS, Visakhapatnam
✆ 2754454, 2748412, 2700899, Fax: 2747580 — guptabrothersbooks@hotmail.com

GUPTA PRAKASHAN, New Delhi
✆ 24616351, 24619125, Fax: 24634935 — ragupta@del2.vsnl.net.in

GURJAR DESH CHARITABLE TRUST, Jammu
✆ 462049, Fax: 463190 — gurjarct@jla.vsnl.net.in

GURJAR GRANTH RATNA KARYALAYA, Ahmedabad
✆ (O) 22144663, 22149660 (R) 26446413 26621539, Fax: 22149660 — allbooks@sity.com

GURUKUL KANGRI VISHVAVIDYALAYA, Haridwar
✆ 243037, Fax: 91-1334-246811 — queries@gkvharidwar.org, mayank@gkvharidwar.org

GYAN BOOKS PVT. LTD., New Delhi
✆ (O) 23282060, 23261060 (R) 27215974, 27459472 Fax: 011-23285914 — books@gyanbooks.com

GYAN DEEP, New Delhi
✆ 23842930 ▮ 9810154549 — gyandeep@mantraonline.com

GYAN GANGA, Delhi
✆ 23257555, Fax: 23253233 — shubham@id.eth.net

GYAN SAGAR PUBLICATIONS, Delhi
✆ 23275594, 22528110 ▮ 9811625372 Fax: 23253832 — gyan@vsnl.net

GYAN VIGYAN RESEARCH INSTITUTE, Jabalpur
✆ 2314697, Fax: 2516771 — divinesx@bom6.vsnl.net.in

GYAN YAGYA PRAKASHAN, Delhi
✆ 27112592, 27242994, Fax: 91-11-27425700 — ipcoldstorage@yahoo.com

H

H.F.Y. ENTERPRISES, Noida
✆ 95120-2583702 — hfy@homoeopathyforall.com

H.J. BOOK AGENCY, Delhi
✆ 30919830, Fax: 91-11-23918777 — hjbookag@yahoo.com

H.M. DAMODAR, Ulhasnagar
✆ 2567401 — damodar_mansharamani@hotmail.com

H.M. PUBLISHERS HOLDING LTD./PALGRAVE MACMILLAN, New Delhi
✆ 23272010, Fax: 91-11-23272010 — palgrave@vsnl.com

H.P.C. PUBLISHERS DISTRIBUTORS PVT. LTD., New Delhi
✆ (O) 23254401, 23254402 (R) 26193544
Fax: 91-1i-26193511, 23274405 — hpc@vsnl.com

HABITAT COMMUNICATIONS PVT. LTD., Ahmedabad
✆ 079-26467919, Fax: 26467919 — habcom@yahoo.com

HAMDAM BOOK DISTRIBUTORS, New Delhi
✆ 26986019 — uzair_quddusi@rediffmail.com

HAMMERARTAG.COM, Delhi
▮ 9213310716 — gayatry_070@yahoo.co.in

HANS PRAKASHAN, Allahabad
✆ 22623077 — ar@nde.vsnl.net.in

HAPPY BOOK DEPOT, Rohtak
✆ 211615, Fax: 91-1262-210614 — hbdrohtak@yahoo.com

HAR ANAND PUBLICATIONS PVT. LTD., New Delhi
✆ 416303490/91/92, Fax: 91-11-41708607 — haranand@rediffmail.com

HARCOURT EDUCATION, UK, New Delhi
✆ 26169147 — overleaf@vsnl.net

HARLEQUIN MILLS AND BOON INDIA (P) LTD., Mumbai
✆ 91-22-4050926 — manish.singh@hmbindia.com

HARE KRISHAN TRUST, Chandigarh
✆ 2567009, 2702378 — hktvibhu@yahoo.com, hktindia@sancharnet.in

HARKRISHNAN BOOK COMPANY, Delhi
✆ 27884306 ▮ 9811373613 — harkrishanbook@rediffmail.com

HARMAN PUBLISHING HOUSE, New Delhi
✆ 25708193 — harmanpublishing@yahoo.com

HARNAM DASS & BROTHERS AGENCIES, Jammu
✆ (O) 2542175, 2574428 (R) 2470210, 2470209
▮ 9419180999 — rahul_nph@rediffmail.com

HARNANDI PUBLISHERS & DISTRIBUTORS (INDIA), New Delhi
✆ (O) 25718135 (R) 25813432-3, Fax: 25764347 — goelvkg@vsnl.com, geelvkg@vsnl.com

HARPER COLLINS PUBLISHERS INDIA, New Delhi
✆ 23352233, 23351736/38, Fax: 23712998 — harper@ndf.vsnl.net.in

HARSH BOOKS CORNER, Delhi
✆ 56218070 — bhanu262@rediffmail.com

HARVARD BUSINESS SCHOOL PRESS, New Delhi
✆ 25819304-7, 25732841, 25732918
Fax: 25819302, 25819303 — marketing_india@mcgraw-hill.com, xlderl/tmh/roystan@tmh.satyam.net.in

HARYANA POLICE ACADEMY, Haryana
✆ 2350101, Fax: 91-184-2350101 — dirhpambam@yahoo.co.in

HARYANA SCIENTIFIC CORPORATION, Hissar
✆ 235849, 235860, 236880, Fax: 236880 — sursavi2001@yahoo.com

HATHWAY INVESTMENTS PVT. LTD., New Delhi
✆ 26191421-24, Fax: 26191420 — outlook@outlookindia.com

HAY HOUSE PUBLISHERS, New Delhi
✆ 41761620, Fax: 91-11-41761630 — contact@hayhouse.co.in

HEALING BOOKS, Gurgaon
✆ 2322779, 2322005, Fax: 91-2324782 — ind-doc-ser@satyam.net.in

HEALTH & WEALTH CARE CENTRE, New Delhi
✆ 25121880 ▮ 9811482650 — rk_suneja@rediffmail.com

HEALTH TIMES, Jodhpur
✆ 2759042, Fax: 91-291-2759042 — info@acupressure.com

HELLO FRIEND BOOKS, Noida
✆ 2423846/47/48, Fax: 91-120-2420324 — info@hellofriendbooks.com

HEMDIP AGENCIES, Vadodra
✆ (O) 22422603, 22337503 (R) 22645502
Telefax: 0265-22422603 — hemdip@lawbooksagency.com

HEMKUNT PUBLISHERS PVT. LTD., New Delhi
✆ 25790032, 25792083, 25795079
Fax: 91-11-6113705 — hemkunt@ndf.vsnl.net.in

HERITAGE PUBLISHERS, New Delhi
✆ 23264444, 23266633, Fax: 91-11-23263050 — info@heritagepublishers.in, heritage@nda.vsnl.in, info@meditechbooks.com

HI-TECH BOOK SERVICES, New Delhi
▮ (O) & (R) 9811140844, Fax: 011-26362326 — htbooks@yahoo.com

HIGGINBOTHAMS LIMITED, Chennai
✆ 28520640, 28521841-43, Fax: 28528101 — higginbothams@vsnl.com

HIGH COMMISSION OF CANADA, New Delhi
✆ 41782312, Fax: 91-11-41782021 — malti.bhandari@international.gc.ca

HILAL PUBLICATIONS, Delhi
✆ 23288523, Fax: 91-11-23288234 — reyazul@giasdla.vsnl.net.in

HIMACHAL ACADEMY OF ARTS, CULTURE AND LANGUAGES, Shimla
✆ 2624330, Fax: 2623149 — hpstateacademy@gmail.com

HIMALA PUBLISHERS, New Delhi
✆ 26109397, 26107969 — himpub@nda.vsnl.net.in

HIMALAYA PUBLISHING HOUSE PVT. LTD., New Delhi
✆ 23270392, Fax: 91-11-23256286 — himpub@vsnl.com

HIMALAYAN INSTITUTE HOSPITAL TRUST, Dehradun
✆ 2412068, Fax: 91-135-2412008 — hintsee@sancharnet.in

HIMALAYAN INSTITUTE PUBLICATIONS, New Delhi
✆ 26405422, 26445422, 26446368, Fax: 26476432 — arun@himalayaninstitute.org, hidelhi@himalayaninstitute.org, hip34@hotmail.com

HIMANSHU BOOK COMPANY, Ahmedabad
✆ 079-26579685, 6583782 — hbc@icenet.net

HIMANSU BOOK DEPOT, Vizianagram
✆ 25422, Fax: 22134 — himansu@siffy.com

HIND BOOK HOUSE, New Delhi
✆ (O) 26831827, 26843576 (R) 26843576
Fax: 26831827, 23725881 — hindbookhouse@vsnl.com, hindbookhouse@rediffmail.com

HIND PUSTAK BHANDAR, New Delhi
✆ 23276539, 23272783-84, Fax: 23260518 — info@pustakmahal.com

HIND-YUGM, Faridabad
98117416106 — hindyugm@gmail.com

HINDI ACADEMY, Delhi
✆ 23693118, 23694562, Fax: 91-11-23696897 — hindiacademy_delhi@vsnl.net

HINDI BOOK CENTRE, New Delhi
✆ 23286757, 23258993, 23261696, 23268651
Fax: 91-11-23273335, 26481565 — info@hindibook.com, starpub@satyam.net.in

HINDI SAHITYA NIKETAN, Bijnor
✆ (O) 01342-262375 (R) 263232 — giriraj3100@rediffmail.com

HINDI SAHITYA SADAN, New Delhi
✆ 51545969, Fax: 23553624 — indiabooks@rediffmail.com

HINDUSTAN BOOK AGENCY (INDIA), New Delhi
✆ 26163294-96, Telefax: 011-26193297 — hba@vsnl.com

HINDUSTAN LAW BOOK COMPANY, Kolkata
✆ 24405837, Fax: 24407669 — Jagadish@cal-vsnl.net.in, hlbc@cal2.vsnl.net.in

HINDUSTAN PUBLISHING CORPORATION, New Delhi
✆ (O) 23254401, 23254402 (R) 26193544
Fax: 91-11-26193511, 23274405 — hpc@vsnl.com, hpcpd@hpc.cc

HINDUSTAN SUBSCRIPTION SERVICE, Chennai
✆ 24342219, Fax: 24342219 — hindsub@vsnl.com

HODDER ARNOLD INDIA, New Delhi
✆ 23270718, Fax: 23267224 — arnoldindia@vivagroupindia.net

HOLYFAITH INTERNATIONAL, New Delhi
✆ 22518122, Fax: 91-11-22546557 — holyfaith1@vsnl.net

HOPE INDIA PUBLICATIONS, Gurgaon
✆ 2367308, Fax: 91-11-26211396, 9911402692 — info@hopeindiapublications.com

HORIZON: THE BOOK SHOP, Mumbai
✆ 26186278, 26188475 — horizonbookshop@vsnl.com

HORIZON PUBLISHERS, Allahabad
✆ 2461159, 2642780 — horizonpub@hotmail.com

HOUSE PRIDE BOOKS, Goa
✆ 2515030, 2513429, Fax: 2513020 — manda_nana@hotmail.com

HUMANA PRESS INC., Chennai
✆ 24346244, 24346266, Fax: 24346529 — itpsesha@giasmd01.vsnl.net.in

I

I.A.B. PUBLISHERS AND DISTRIBUTORS PVT. LTD., Delhi
✆ 22161701, 22161702, 23266480, 23266681
Fax: 011-22167103, Telefax: 031-79002 GITI-IN — amit_iabpd@hotmail.com

I.B. PUBLICATIONS & DISTRIBUTORS, Delhi
✆ 55298293 ▮ 9891190178, Fax: 22823839 — sanjeev-seth_in@yahoo.com

I.B.A. PUBLICATIONS, Ambala
✆ 2630125, 2640126, Fax: 91-11-2601862 — ibapublications@rediffmail.com

I.B.D. PUBLISHER AND DISTRIBUTORS, New Delhi
✆ 23251094, 23259102 ▮ 9811225032
Fax: 23259102 — piyush_gahlot@rediffmail.com

I.B.I. DOTCOM PVT. LTD., New Delhi
✆ 25875330, 25871272, Fax: 25786769 — ibicom@bol.net.in, ibicom@rediffmail.com

I.B.M. BOOK CENTRE, Mumbai
✆ (O) 24150178 (R) 24149880, 24168220
Fax: 4162561 — ibm@bom3.vsnl.net.in

ICFAI UNIVERSITY PRESS, New Delhi
✆ 66601854, Fax: 91-11-41617429 — srikar@icfaipress.org

I.D.G. BOOKS INDIAN PVT. LTD., New Delhi
✆ 23260877, 23270877, Fax: 23275895 — idgbooks@vsnl.com, idgbooks@bol.net.in

I.I.M.S. PUBLICATIONS, New Delhi
✆ 24329106, 24316915, 24311946
Fax: 91-11-24313503 — iimspub@nde.vsnl.net.in

I.J.C.P. GROUP OF PUBLICATIONS, New Delhi
✆ 26239415, 26239416, Fax: 26239411 — kkhcfl@giasd01.vsnl.net.in

I.K. INTERNATIONAL PVT. LTD., New Delhi
✆ 41755552-4, 26532251 ▮ 9810489922
Fax: 91-11-26532252 — ik_in@vsnl.net

I.K.S. PUBLISHERS & DISTRIBUTORS, Srinagar
ikssgr@del1.vsnl.net.in

I.Q. TECH MEDIA PVT. LTD., Mumbai
✆ 55969222, Fax: 91-22-55969739 — janardhan@iqtechmedia.com, info@developeriq.com, raulojanardhan@hotmail.com

ISPCK (INDIAN SOCIETY FOR PROMOTING CHRISTIAN KNOWLEDGE), Delhi
✆ 23866323, Fax: 91-11-23865490 — ashish@ispck.org.in

ICON PUBLICATIONS PVT. LTD., New Delhi
✆ (O) 23290091 (R) 22374923 ▮ 9818261853
Fax: 23290067 — iconpub@eth.net

IDARA EXPORTS, New Delhi
✆ 26956832-33, Fax: 91-11-26942787 — sales@idara.com

IDEAL PUBLISHING HOUSE PVT. LTD., Chennai
✆ 91-44-42154259, 42154359 — idealpublishinghouse@yahoo.co.in

IMPEX STATISTICS SERVICES, Mumbai
✆ 22080518, 22088151, Fax: 22055444 — booksell@vsnl.net

IMRAN BOOK DEPOT, Delhi
✆ 22507486, 23287486, Fax: 22428786 — imranbookdepot@vsnl.net

INDEPENDENT PUBLISHERS GROUP, New Delhi
✆ 26491448, 27666067 ▮ 9811692261 — ipg.delhi@gmail.com

INDEX INTERNATIONAL, New Delhi
✆ 22714005, 22713475, Fax: 22714005 — dorai@del3.vsnl.net.in

INDIA BOOK CENTRE, Patna
✆ 2670681 (R) 2648345 ▮ 9835022986 — ibcpatna@yahoo.com

INDIA BOOKS COMPANY, New Delhi
✆ 91-11-25331361, 64527190 — indiabookscompany@yahoo.co.in

INDIA BOOK DISTRIBUTORS (BOMBAY) LTD., Mumbai
✆ 40769200-01/15-16, 22825220, 22824646, 22872528, 22872532, 22824691, Fax: 91-22-22872531 — ibdho@ibd.co.in, websales@ibd.co.in

INDIA BOOK FAIR, Delhi
✆ 27403422, 27213267, Fax: 27462079 — sales@indiabookfair.com

INDIA BOOK HOUSE, New Delhi
✆ 23313014, 23313015, Fax: 23351974 — magazines-delhi@ibhworld.com

INDIA BOOK HOUSE LTD., Mumbai
✆ 22840165, 22840626, Fax: 22835099 — info@ibhworld.com, indiabookhouse@vsnl.com

INDIA BOOK HOUSE (P) LTD., Mumbai
✆ 66529500, Fax: 91-22-66529570 — info@ibhworld.com

INDIA CLUB INC. (THE), New Delhi
✆ 26851864 — bkbk@nda.vsnl.net.in

INDIA RESEARCH PRESS, New Delhi
✆ 24694610, 24694855, Fax: 24618637 — contact@indiaresearchpress.com

INDIA RESEARCH PRESS/TARA PRESS, New Delhi
✆ 24694610, 24694855
Fax: 91-11-24618637, 41757113 — contact@indiaresearchpress.com, editor@indiaresearchpress.com

INDIA TODAY BOOK CLUB, New Delhi
bahrisons@vsnl.com

INDIALOG PUBLICATION PVT. LTD., New Delhi
✆ (O) 26320504, 26839936, 26935221
(R) 26913990, Fax: 26935221 — publishing@silicondocs.com, gagan@silicondocs.com, basant@oxdocs.net.au

INDIAN BIBLOGRAPHIC CENTRE, Varanasi
✆ 221337, Fax: 222337 — sullas80@hotmail.com

INDIAN BOOK DEPOT (MAP HOUSE), Delhi
✆ 23673927, 23523635, Fax: 91-11-23552096 — ibdmaps@ndb.vsnl.net.in

INDIAN BOOKS & PERIODICAL SYNDICATE, New Delhi
✆ 2572444 Fax: 25766699 — ibps@del3.vsnl.net.in

INDIAN BOOKS & PERIODICALS, New Delhi
✆ 55354142 ▮ 9811393986 — ibp@ndf.vsnl.net.in

INDIAN BOOKS CENTRE, Delhi
✆ (O) 27434930, 27126497 (R) 27130893
Fax: 27227336 — ibcindia@ibcindia.com, ibcindia@vsnl.com

INDIAN COMMITTEE FOR CULTURAL FREEDOM, Mumbai
✆ 22843416 — freedom@vsnl.com

INDIAN COUNCIL OF AGRICULTURAL RESEARCH, New Delhi
✆ 25843657, Fax: 91-11-25843567 — bnicar@kab.delhi.nic.in

INDIAN COUNCIL FOR CULTURAL RELATIONS, New Delhi
✆ 23370229, 23379158, Fax: 233784441, 23378639 — iccr@vsnl.com

INDIAN COUNCIL OF HISTORICAL RESEARCH, New Delhi
✆ 23382321, 23386973, Fax: 91-11-23383421 — support@ichrindia.org

INDIAN COUNCIL OF MEDICAL RESEARCH, New Delhi
✆ 26588895, 26588980, 26589794
Fax: 91-11-26588662, 26588713 — headquarters@icmr.org.in, icmrhqds@sansad.nic.in

INDIAN COUNCIL OF PHILOSOPHICAL RESEARCH, New Delhi
✆ 26094405, 26094403, Fax: 26092129 — icpr@del2.vsnl.net.in

INDIAN COUNCIL OF SOCIAL SCIENCE RESEARCH, New Delhi
✆ 26192059, 23073438, 23383091
Fax: 23381571, 26179834 — rupa_chatterjee@hotmail.com, chna14@hotmail.com

INDIAN DOCUMENTATION SERVICE, Gurgaon
✆ (O) 2324782, 3093753 (R) 2322779
Fax: 2324782 — indoc@indiatimes.com

INDIAN EXPRESS NEWSPAPERS (B) P. LTD., Mumbai
✆ 26411453, Fax: 26411455 — ieegmont@bom4.vsnl.net.in

INDIAN HYPNOSIS ACADEMY, Delhi
✆ 91-11-27524081 — info@indianhypnosisacademy.com

INDIAN INSTITUTE OF ADVANCED STUDY, Shimla
✆2831390, Fax: 91-177-2831390 — iiasaro@iias.org, proiias@iias.org

INDIAN INSTITUTE OF PUBLIC ADMINISTRATION, New Delhi
✆ 22372400/366, Fax: 23072440 — iipaitc@nda.vsnl.net.in

INDIAN INSTITUTE OF SINDHOLOGY, Kutch
✆ 261569, 263851, Fax: 91-2836-260336 — contact@sindhology.org

INDIAN JOURNAL OF APPLIED ECONOMICS, Bangalore
✆ 23303198, 23350484, Fax: 080-23303239 — ijae.kps@axcess.net.in

INDIAN MAP SERVICE, Jodhpur
✆ 2740874, 2740574, Fax: 5102248 — indianmap@satyam.net.in

INDIAN MUSEUM, Kolkata
✆ 22861679, 22861702, Fax: 91-33-22861696 — imbot@cal2.vsnl.net.in

INDIAN NATIONAL SCIENCE ACADEMY, New Delhi
✆ 23221931-50, Fax: 23235648 — insa@giasd101.vsnl.net.in

INDIAN PETROLEUM PUBLISHERS, Dehradun
✆ 0135-2654074 — ipp@garhwalhimalayas.com

INDIAN PUBLISHERS DISTRIBUTORS, New Delhi
✆ 55354581 ▮ 9312400620
Fax: 91-11-23846233
✉ info@indianpublishersdistributors.com, sales@indianpublishersdistributors.com

INDIAN SOCIAL INSTITUTE, New Delhi
✆ 24611745, 24635096, 24694602
Fax: 91-11-24690660
✉ isi@isidelhi.org.in

INDIAN SOCIETY FOR PROMOTING CHRISTIAN KNOWLEDGE (THE), Delhi
✆ 22966323, 22966322, Fax: 011-22965490
✉ ispck@nde.vsnl.net.in

INDIAN SOCIETY FOR TRAINING & DEVELOPMENT, New Delhi
✆ 26867710, 26857157, Fax: 26867607
✉ istd@ren02.nic.in

INDIAN THOUGHT PUBLICATION, Chennai
✆ 24344529, Fax: 44-24342009
✉ ksm@md2.vsnl.net.in

INDIAN WRITING, Chennai
✆ 42009601, Fax: 91-44-43009701
✉ support@nhm.in

INDIANA, New Delhi
✆ 24622827, Fax: 91-11-24623923
✉ indiana@nda.vsnl.net.in

INDIANE-BOOKS.COM, Delhi
✆ 27452453, 27401672
✉ lpp@nde.vsnl.net.in

INDICA BOOKS, Varanasi
✆ 3294999, Fax: 91-542-2450818
✉ indicabooks@satyam.net.in, indicabs@nde.vsnl.net.in

INDICA PUBLISHERS & DISTRIBUTORS PVT. LTD., New Delhi
✆ (O) 23243027, 23243028 (R) 27435512
Fax: 23243006
✉ ipdplbooks@yahoo.co.in

INDICUS ANALYTICS PVT. LTD., New Delhi
✆ 29222638, 29226711
✉ indic@indicus.net

INDIRA GANDHI NATIONAL CENTRE FOR THE ARTS, New Delhi
✆ 23381303, Fax: 23388280
✉ kauladvait@rediffmail.com

INDIRA GANDHI NATIONAL OPEN UNIVERSITY—ELECTRONIC MEDIA PRODUCTION CENTRE, New Delhi
✆ 26962450, Fax: 26855083
✉ ignoumkt@ignou.ac.in

INDIRA PRINTERS, New Delhi
✆ 26829337, 26316876, 26830401
Fax: 91-11-26830493, 26852280
✉ krishan@ned.vsnl.net.in

INDIRA PUBLISHING HOUSE, Bhopal
✆ 0755-2465238
✉ landmark_no1@satyam.net.in

INDO-AMERICAN BOOKS, Delhi
✆ 27138609, 27412409
Fax: 91-11-27122052
✉ vijay.sharma@iabooks.com, iab@iabooks.com

INDO-US BOOKS CORPORATION, New Delhi
✆ 23265523, 23260783, Fax: 23272766
✉ manaspublication@vsnl.com

INDOLOGICAL BOOK HOUSE, Delhi
✆ 30901148, Fax: 23922137
✉ ioph@rediffmail.com

INDRAPRASTHA PRAKASHAN, Delhi
✆ 22099764, Fax: 91-11-22002274
✉ indraprastha04@yahoo.com

INDUS INTERNATIONAL, New Delhi
✆ 25151333, 25935289
Fax: 91-11-25115667
✉ indus@indus-intl.com

INDUS PUBLISHING COMPANY, New Delhi
✆ 42133022, 42133622, 25151333
Fax: 91-11-42133985
✉ indus@indus-publishing.com

INFINITEBOOKS.COM PVT. LTD., Chennai
✆ 91-44-24423744, 24423722, Fax: 24917441
✉ books@beslcc.com, gopi@besl.cc.com

INFINITY BOOKS, New Delhi
✆ 25264771, 25264782, Fax: 011-25255492
✉ rsethi@vsnl.net

INFO BOOK DISTRIBUTORS, Bangalore
✆ 2206175, 5484300, Fax: 2206175
✉ infob@vsnl.net

INFORMATIC BOOKS, Delhi
✆ 55298293
✉ ibd@rediffmail.com

INFORMATICS (INDIA) LTD., Bangalore
✆ 23367867, 23365940, Fax: 23344598
✉ info@informindia.co.in

INFOTECH STANDARDS INDIA (P) LTD., New Delhi
✆ (O) 56020164, 56020178, 55659120
(R) 26645636, 25509439 ▮ 9811224190
Fax: 011-51642947
✉ standards@bol.net.in

INNOSERV SYSTEMS PVT. LTD., New Delhi
✆ 28619112, 28619113, 26855341, 26226680
Fax: 91-11-26286640, 26966911
✉ rakesh@cdindia.com, sales@cdindia.com

INNOVATIVE BOOKS, Faridabad
▮ 9999035066
✉ innovativebooks4u@yahoo.co.in

INNOVATIVE PUBLISHERS, New Delhi
✆ 23353951, Fax: 23713275
✉ rajuprim@vsnl.com, oxford@vsnl.com

INSAT BOOKS & PERIODICALS, New Delhi
✆ 23264151, 41562759, Fax: 91-11-23276109
✉ insatbp@airtelbroadband.in

INSTITUTE OF PROFESSIONAL PSYCHOLOGY, Cochin
✆ 6517050, Fax: 91-984-6110021
✉ kaliaden@gmail.com

INSTITUTE OF SELF RELIANCE, Bhubaneswar
✆ 2354662, Fax: 91-674-2354662
✉ isrindia@sify.com

INSTITUTO CERVANTES, New Delhi
✆ 41293013, Fax: 91-11-41293020
✉ dirndel@cervantes.es

INTEGRAL BOOKS, Payyanur
✉ booksintegral@yahoo.com

INTEL BOOK DISTRIBUTORS PRIVATE LIMITED, Bangalore
✆ 26611448, 2601963, Fax: 26611448
✉ ibd@satyam.net.in

INTER UNIVERSITY PRESS (P) LTD., Delhi
✆ 27134725, 27455876, Fax: 27431133
✉ iup@iuppublisher.com

INTERCONTINENTAL BOOK AGENCY, New Delhi
✆ 23271108, 23254330, Fax: 91-11-23271108
✉ iba@vsnl.net

INTERLUDE TECHNOLOGIES, New Delhi
✆ 91-11-25524087, 25506100, 25506200, 39583441
✉ info@interludetech.com, sales@interludetech.com

INTERNATIONAL AGRICULTURAL RESEARCH CENTRES, Patancheru
✆ 23296161, Fax: 2241239
✉ icrisat@cgiar.org

INTERNATIONAL BIBLE SOCIETY INDIA, Hyderabad
✆ 23559322, Fax: 23559322
✉ ibssasia@hdl.vsnl.net.in

INTERNATIONAL BOOK BUREAU, Mumbai
✆ 24149995, 24147631, Fax: 24147631 — arjunibb@bom5.vsnl.net.in

INTERNATIONAL BOOK DISTRIBUTING CO., Lucknow
✆ 22450004, 22450007, 22459058, Fax: 22458629 — ibdco@sancharnet.in, sushil@1w1.vsnl.net.in

INTERNATIONAL BOOK DISTRIBUTING CO., Lucknow
✆ 2209542-45, Fax: 91-522-4045308 — ibdco@airtelbroadband.in

INTERNATIONAL BOOK DISTRIBUTORS, Dehradun
✆ (O) 0135-2657497, 2656526 (R) 2650949
Fax: 2656554 — ibdbooks@sancharnet.in, rpsinghgahlot@yahoo.co.in

INTERNATIONAL BOOK DISTRIBUTORS, New Delhi
✆ (O) 23271052 (R) 25888239, Fax: 23252951 — ibdnewdelhi@airtelbroadband.in

INTERNATIONAL BOOK HOUSE PVT. LTD., Mumbai
✆ 22021634, 22044859, 22021795-0765
Fax: 22851109 — ibh@vsnl.com, ibh@vsnl.in

INTERNATIONAL BOOK TRADERS, Delhi
✆ (O) 27143827, 27218194, 27234159
(R) 27233896, Fax: 91-11-27234817 — ibt@vsnl.net

INTERNATIONAL BOOKS, Trichy
✆ (O) 2703743, 2711599 (R) 2780447 — try_intbook@sancharnet.in

INTERNATIONAL BOOKS & PERIODICALS SUPPLY SERVICES, Delhi
✆ 27107078, 27182217, Fax: 27020538 — hkjain1975@yahoo.com

INTERNATIONAL BOOKS UPDATE, Delhi
✆ 27130049, Fax: 91-11-27435724 — buntyw@hotmail.com

INTERNATIONAL GAUDIYA VEDANT TRUST, New Delhi
✆ 91-11-25533568 — krsnakauta@gmail.com

INTERNATIONAL LAW BOOK COMPANY, Delhi
✆ 23867810, 23864769 — ilbco@vsnl.com

INTERNATIONAL OBSERVER, Delhi
9810602915 — internationalobserver@rediffmail.com

INTERNATIONAL PERIODICALS SUPPLIERS, Delhi
✆ (O) 27018098, 7018097 (R) 27021469 — ips268@hotmail.com

INTERNATIONAL PUBLICATIONS, Delhi
✆ 23557888, 23677888, 23357888
Fax: 91-11-23557888 — mappeople@liveindia.com, maskpd@sify.com, mail@mappeople.com

INTERNATIONAL PUBLISHING HOUSE, Meerut
✆ 4006365, Fax: 91-121-2664890 — info@iph-india.com

INTERNATIONAL RANKA AND CO., Jaipur
✆ 91-141-2654155, 2654202 — iranka@datainfosys.net

INTERNATIONAL SCIENTFIC PUBLISHING ACADEMY, New Delhi
✆ 23250398, Fax: 91-11-25351521 — ispabooks@gmail.com

INTERNATIONAL SOCIETY FOR KRISHNA CONSCIOUSNESS, New Delhi
✆ 26280060, Fax: 91-11-26215421 — delhi@pamho.net

INTERNATIONAL SUBSCRIPTION AGENCY, Lucknow
✆ 22789506, 2789103, 3110103 — intl@sancharnet.in

INTERNATIONAL THOMSON PUBLISHING ASIAN, Chennai
✆ 24346529 — itpsesha@giasmd01.vsnl.net.in

INTERNATIONAL YOGA SOCIETY, Ghaziabad
✆ 0120-2600237, 2166237 — @ iys@vsnl.com, iys@ndf.vsnl.net.in

INTERPRINT, New Delhi
✆ 25704450/51/52, 25704234, 25707474 — @ mopl@del3.vsnl.net.in
Fax: 91-11-2570644

INTIME BOOKS SERVICES, New Delhi
✆ 26220958, 26426566, 35905898, 32035429 — @ itbookservices@yahoo.co.in
Fax: 26212122, 26288018

INVIS MULTIMEDIA, Thiruvananthapuram
✆ 2311832, 2319892, Fax: 0471-2313170 — @ infor@invismultimedia.com

IOS PRESS BV, New Delhi
✆ 45055540, Fax: 91-11-25778876 — @ p.sing@iospress.in

IPD ALTERNATIVES, New Delhi
✆ 91-11-26492040 — @ ipd.alternatives@gmail.com

IRRAWADDY PUBLICATIONS, New Delhi
✆ 25504169, 25613636, Fax: 25614759 — @ mawthiri@hotmail.com

ISKCON, Kolkata
✆ 2476075, 2473757, Fax: 2478515 — @ iskcon.calcutta@pamho.net

ISLAMIC BOOK SERVICE, New Delhi
✆ (O) 23253514, 23265380, 23286551, 23272292 — @ ibsdelhi@del2.vsnl.net.in, islamic@eth.net
(R) 26941065, Fax: 011-23277913

ISLAMIC FOUNDATION TRUST, Chennai
✆ 26424401, 26426181, 26624401 — @ iftchennai12@email.com
Telefax: 044-24835120, Fax: 91-44-25365086

ISLAMIC PUBLISHING HOUSE, Calicut
✆ 91-495-2720072, 2724618 — @ iphcalicut@dataone.in

ITALIAN EMBASSY CULTURAL CENTRE, New Delhi
✆ 26871901, 26871903, Fax: 26871902 — @ italcult@del3.vsnl.net.in

J

J.B.A. PUBLISHERS, New Delhi
✆ 28726165, 91-11-41513850 — @ sales@jba.in

J.B.C. PUBLISHERS AND DISTRIBUTORS, New Delhi
✆ 41564445, Fax: 91-11-41564440 — @ jbcpd@airtelbroadband.in

J.B.D. BOOK DISTRIBUTOR, New Delhi
✆ (O) 36821450, 23629902 (R) 27420558 — @ jbdbook@yahoo.com

J.K. LAW HOUSE, Jammu
✆ 2570061, Fax: 2573652 — @ jklaw@sancharnet.in

J.M. JAINA & BROTHERS, Delhi
✆ (O) 23966603, 23915064, 23950936 — @ akalank@vsnl.com
(R) 23964707, 23976292, Fax: 23986793

J.P. PRINT SYSTEMS (P) LTD., Hyderabad
✆ 23732972, 23734117, Fax: 23750647 — info@jpeamcet.com

J.P. PUBLICATIONS, Vijayawada
✆ 2627484 — srinivasjp99@hotmail.com

JAGDAMBA BOOK CENTRE, New Delhi
✆ 23250048, 23258536 ▮ 9810576314 — jadgambabc@yahoo.com

JAGDAMBA PUBLISHING COMPANY, New Delhi
✆ 23250048, 23258536 ▮ 9810576314 — jagdambhabc@yahoo.com

JAGMANDER BOOK AGENCY, New Delhi
✆ (O) 28713985, 28715483 (R) 28711147
28711149, Fax: 91-11-28711147, 28714987 — jba@ndf.vsnl.net.in

JAGRAN PRAKASHAN LTD., Noida
✆ 2425961-62, Fax: 91-120-2425203 — delhi@nda.jagran.com

JAGRAN RESEARCH CENTRE, Kanpur
✆ 2216161-64, Fax: 2216972, 2298040 — jrc@jagran.com

JAMA'AT AHMEDIYYA INTERNATIONAL, New Delhi
✆ 26059094, Fax: 91-11-29958055 — dawood.ahmad@tcs.com

JANBAAT DISTRIBUTORS, Delhi
▮ 9868078123 — janbatt@yahoo.com

JANCHETNA, Lucknow
✆ 91-551-2241922 — janchetna@rediffmail.com

JAI PRAKASH NATH PUBLICATIONS, Meerut
✆ 2762403, 2762414, Fax: 2600013 — jpnpmrrt@rediffmail.com

JAICO PUBLISHING HOUSE, Mumbai
✆ 22676702, 22676802, 22672969
Fax: 91-22-22656412 — jaicobom@bom5.vsnl.com, jaicowbd@vsnl.com, jaicopub@vsnl.com

JAIN BOOK AGENCY, New Delhi
✆ (O) 23321663, 23320806, 23326728
23416390-94, 51513851 (R) 25738897
Fax: 91-11-23731117 — govtbooks@del3.vsnl.net.in, sales@jainbookagency.com

JAIN BOOK DEPOT, Delhi
✆ 31027550 — jainbookdepo@hotmail.com

JAIN BOOKS & PERIODICALS, Delhi
✆ 27383728, Fax: 91-11-27182715 — jainbooks@vsnl.net, ibptn@hotmail.com

JAIN BROTHERS, New Delhi
✆ 23618426, 23619023, 27518426
Fax: 91-11-23638444 — jain_bros@hotmail.com

JAINSON BOOK SHOP & STATIONERS, Indore
✆ 2538787 — kitab2000@rediffmail.com

JALALI ACADEMY, New Delhi
✆ 23265480, Fax: 91-11-23257189 — aakif@del3.vsnl.net.in

JAMBAWAN BOOK AGENCY, Thanjavur
✆ 04362-288840 — rajchristy@hotmail.com, jambawanbooks@hotmail.com

JANAM MARKETING, Mumbai
✆ 022-27691318, Fax: 022-27697788 — janamark@vsnl.net.in

JANE'S INFORMATION GROUP, New Delhi
✆ 26516105, Fax: 26516105 — janesindia@sify.com

JANTA BOOK DEPOT, New Delhi
✆ (O) 24692352, 24621791 (R) 26416656
Fax: 24604413 — mukkug@yahoo.com, milli@bol.net.in

JAY BOOK HOUSE, Thane
jaybookhouseindia@rediffmail.com

JAY CEE PUBLICATIONS, New Delhi
✆ 23552591, 25382500
Fax: 91-11-25382100 — info@jaypeepublications.com

JAY KAY BOOK HOUSE, Jammu Tawi
✆ 2573560, 2470195 — jkbh@rediffmail.com

JAY KAY BOOK SHOP (REGD.), Kashmir
✆ (O) 0194-2421135 (R) 2425937
Fax: 0194-2476686, 2426811 — jkbookshop@yahoo.com

JAYPEE BROTHERS MEDICAL PUBLISHERS (P) LTD., New Delhi
✆ 23272143, 23282021, 23272703
Fax: 23276490, 23281761 — jaypee@jaypeebrothers.com

JEEVAN SOFTECH LIMITED, Hyderabad
✆ 23205739 — jeevan@hd2.vsnl.net.in

JEEVANSONS PUBLICATIONS, Delhi
✆ 23911358 — jpubin@yahoo.com.in

JEEVANVIDYA MISSION, Mumbai
✆ 28879015-16, Fax: 91-22-28845480 — wamanrao@jeevanvidya.org

JEFFSON PRINT MEDIA HOUSE, Delhi
✆ (O) 20059037, 30931801 ▮ 9868286356
(R) 27226906, Fax: 27138119 — jeffry@ndf.vsnl.net.in

JINDAL BOOK SERVICES, New Delhi
✆ (O) 23255012 (R) 23845862, Fax: 23282127 — sshjbs@yahoo.com

JINGLE ZONE ANIMATIONS (P) LTD., New Delhi
✆ 26224301, Fax: 91-11-26237785 — jinglezone@epaathshala.com

JIWAN BOOKS INTERNATIONAL (P) LTD., New Delhi
✆ 43541944, Fax: 91-11-43541900 — info@jiwanbooks.co

JIWAN PUBLISHING HOUSE (P) LTD. INDIA, New Delhi
✆ 25462358, 25932219, 25937039
Fax: 25449314, 25453365 — info@jphbooks.com, jphpltd@nde.vsnl.net.in

JNANADA PRAKASHAN, New Delhi
✆ 91-11-23272047 — jnanadabooksdelhi@yahoo.com

JNANADA PUBLISHERS, Patna
✆ 2689059 — jnanada@rediffmail.com

JNANPITH PRATISHTHAN, New Delhi
✆ 24656201, Fax: 91-11-24654197 — jnanpith@satyam.net.in

JNANPITH PUSTAK KENDRA/JNANPITH VIKRAI KENDRA, New Delhi
✆ 24626467, 24698417
Fax: 91-11-24654197 — jnanpith@satyam.net.in

JODO GYAN EDUCATIONAL SERVICES, Delhi
✆ 27102820 ▮ 9811949635
Fax: 91-11-27102820 — jodogyandel@yahoo.com

JOHN WILEY & SONS, New Delhi
✆ 26518365, 26858760, 26969502 — aindia@wiley.com.sg
Fax: 91-11-26858760

JOURNALS SUBSCRIPTION SERVICE, New Delhi
✆ 25447609, 25447684 — jssindia@hotmail.com

JYOTI ASHRAM, Pune
✆ 91-20-26832632 — jyotiashram@gmail.com

JYOTI BOOK DEPOT, Visakhapatnam
✆ (O) 0891-2746020, 2541201, 5566062-63 — jbdvizag@yahoo.com, jbdindia@yahoo.com
▮ 9849121001, Fax: 2541203

JYOTI BOOK DEPOT, New Delhi
✆ 23268121, Fax: 23268122 — jbdindia@rediffmail.com

JYOTI ENTERPRISES, Delhi
✆ 91-11-23858405 — jyoti_enterprises_1979@indiatimes.com

JYOTI PUBLISHERS, New Delhi
✆ 25786163, 25737566, Fax: 25782601 — jyotipub@yahoo.co.in

JYOTI PUBLISHERS AND DISTRIBUTORS, Dehradun
jyotiannfor@hotmail.com

JYOTI STORES, Nashik
✆ 2504026, 2597026, Fax: 2573630 — joytistore@sify.com

JYOTSNA PRAKASHAN, Mumbai
✆ 022-23877019, 23824071 — jyotsnaprakashan@vsnl.com, vlp@vsnl.net

K

K. KRISHNAMURTHY, Chennai
✆ 24344519, Fax: 24342009 — service@kkbooks.com, kkbooks@eth.net

K.K. PUBLICATIONS, New Delhi
✆ 27637048, 27636984, 27636835 ▮ 9818020120 — kkpdevinder@vsnl.net
Fax: 91-11-30125577

K.L. MALIK & SONS PVT. LTD., New Delhi
✆ 23274161, Fax: 91-11-23254407 — klmalik_23@yahoo.com

K.M. VARGHESE COMPANY, Mumbai
✆ 24149074, 24144601, Fax: 24146904 — km@varghese.net

K.P. BAGCHI & COMPANY, Kolkata
✆ (O) 22367474 (R) 2236-9496 — kpbagchi@hotmail.com
Fax: 033-22369496

K.P.B. BOOKS PVT. LTD., Kolkata
kpbbooks@hotmail.com

K.S.K. BOOK DISTRIBUTORS, Delhi
✆ (O) 22593323 (R) 26188253 ▮ 9810881414 — kskbooks@hotmail.com

K.S.V. BOOK SUPPLIERS, Ghaziabad
✆ 95120-2771651 — ksvbooksuppliers@yahoo.co.in

KAANTHALAKAM, Chennai
✆ 2834505, Fax: 2834728 — sachi@Giasmd01.vsnl.net.in

KABIR, Delhi
✆ 22485139, Fax: 91-11-22485139 — neeraj.com@gmail.com

KABIR PATH PRAKASHAN, New Delhi
✆ 25894637 — kabirpath@yahoo.co.in

KADAMBARI PRAKASHAN, Delhi
✆ 91-11-65352060 — kadambari_prakashan@yahoo.com

KAGZI HAND MADE PAPER IND., Jaipur
✆ 730019, 730076, Fax: 732065 — kagzi@jpl.dot.net.in

KAILASH ASHRAM, New Delhi
✆ 23201505, 23256437 — swbikash@hotmail.com, kailashmansarovar@usa.net

KAILASO BOOKS, New Delhi
✆ 30910969, 23445103, Fax: 2345103 — kilaso@mantraonline.com

KALACHUVADU PATHIPPAGM, Nagercoil
✆ 2278525, Fax: 2231160 — kalachuvadu@sancharnet.in

KALI FOR WOMEN, New Delhi
✆ 26964947, 26524129, Fax: 26496597 — womenunltd@vsnl.net

KALPNA BOOK DISTRIBUTORS, New Delhi
✆ 27637048, Fax: 91-11-30125577 — kkpdevinder@vsnl.net

KALPAZ PUBLICATIONS, Delhi
▮ 9212729499 — kalpaz@hotmail.com

KALRA PUBLICATIONS (P) LTD., New Delhi
✆ 23256606, 23275451, Fax: 27654141 — kpplbooks@hotmail.com

KAMAL BOOKS INTERNATIONAL, New Delhi
✆ 26101076, 26103896, 23270654 ▮ 9810228919
Fax: 011-26185044, 26103896 — kamalbooks@yahoo.com

KAMAL LAW HOUSE, Kolkata
✆ 22101558, 22209841, Fax: 22202822 — lawpointcal@rediffmail.com

KAMLA-RAJ ENTERPRISES, Delhi
✆ 23284126, Fax: 91-124-4361193
▮ 9873186386, 9899513686 — kre@vsnl.com, kre@airtelmail.in

KANISHKA BOOK CENTRE, Delhi
✆ 20038210, 20036278 ▮ 9810927808
Fax: 23214634 — kanishka_book@yahoo.com

KANISHKA PUBLISHERS AND DISTRIBUTORS, New Delhi
✆ 23270497, 23288285, Fax: 91-11-23288285 — kanisha_publishing@yahoo.co.in

KANNADHASAN PATHIPPAGAM, Chennai
✆ 044-24332682, 24332681, Fax: 24338712 — kannadasan@vsnl.com, kanna@md2.vsnl.net.in

KANOON PRAKASHAK, Jodhpur
✆ 2628979 — ncj@kanoonprakashak.com

KANOON PRAKASHAN, New Delhi
✆ 24692616 — dk@kanoonprakashak.com

KAPIL PUSTAK SADAN, Gwalior
✆ 0751-3540717 — kapilsahni@mantrafreenet.com

KARNATAKA PUBLISHERS ASSOCIATION, Bangalore
✆ 26617755, 91-80-26617100 — ankitapustaka@rediffmail.com

KASHMIR BOOK DEPOT, Kashmir
✆ 2457968, Fax: 2457968 — k_bookdepot@indiatimes.com

KASHMIR LAW HOUSE, Srinagar
✆ 2428758, Fax: 2428526 — telehamid1@rediffmail.com

KAT INDUSTRIAL CONSULTANTS PVT. LTD., New Delhi
✆ 23411360, 51528137, 23849959 ▮ 9868182357
Fax: 23413183, 23842632 — katcon@del2.vsnl.net.in

KATHA, New Delhi
✆ 26524350, 26524511, Fax: 91-11-26514373 — katha@katha.org, katha@vsnl.com, marketing@katha.org

KAVERI BOOK SERVICES, New Delhi
✆ 23288140, 23245799 — kaveri@del3.vsnl.net.in, kaveribooks@vsnl.com

KENDRIYA HINDI SANSTHAN, Agra
✆ 2530684, 2530159, Fax: 91-11-2530684 — registrarkhs@yahoo.co.in

KERALA BOOK MARKETING SOCIETY/BOOKMARK, Trivandrum
✆ 91-0471-2473921 — keralabookmark@yahoo.com

KERALA EXPORTERS & TRADERS, Mumbai
✆ 28345112, 28214403, Fax: 28221497 — kerextra@vsnl.com

KHAAS KITAB FOUNDATION, New Delhi
✆ 26859641, Fax: 91-11-26859641 — vjafa@bol.net.in

KHANDELWAL BOOK DEPOT, Rampur
✆ (O) 2324636, 2327963 (R) 2340906 — khandelwal123@vsnl.com

KHANNA BANDHU, Dehradun
✆ 2621485, 2621689, Fax: 2621689, 2760240 — khannabandhu@vsnl.com, khannabandhu@sanchanet.in

KHANNA BOOK PUBLISHING CO. PVT. LTD., Delhi
✆ 23283211, 23256658, Fax: 91-11-23256658 — contact@khannaedu.com

KHEL SAHITYA KENDRA/KSK PUBLISHERS AND DISTRIBUTORS, New Delhi
✆ 65190343 ▮ 9811088729, Fax: 91-11-42564726 — khelsahitya1@rediffmail.com

KHEMRAJ SHRIKRISHNADASS, Mumbai
✆/Fax: 23857456 — khemraj@vsnl.com

KHUDA BAKHSH ORIENTAL PUBLIC LIBRARY, Patna
✆ 2301507, Fax: 91-612-2300315 — pat_kbopl@dataone.in

KHURANA PUBLISHING HOUSE, Delhi
✆ 91-11-22386293, 22391292 — khuranapublishing@gmail.com

KHURMI BOOKS, New Delhi
✆ 26314690, 26323759, Fax: 26921585 — khurmieducation@yahoo.com

KILASO BOOKS, New Delhi
✆ 41562653, 41563798, Fax: 91-11-41562653 — kilasobooks@airtelbroadband.in

KINDERSTON PUBLICATIONS, New Delhi
✆ 23272402 — inquiry@kp-ed.com

KINSEY BROTHERS, New Delhi
✆ 23324446, Fax: 23328731 — kinse@del2.vsnl.net.in

KISALAYA PUBLICATIONS PVT. LTD., New Delhi
✆ 26804169, 26800956 — suhasini@bol.net.in

KITAB BHAVAN, New Delhi
✆ 23277392, 23277393, 23274686
Fax: 91-11-23263383 — nasri@vsnl.com, nasri@nda.vsnl.net.in

KITAB GHAR, New Delhi
✆ 23271844, 23281844, Fax: 91-11-23281244 — kitabghar@hotmail.com

KITAB MAHAL, Cuttack
✆ (O) 2648333 (R) 2613666, 2613999
Fax: 0674-2613301 — info@kitabmahal.net

KITAB MAHAL, Allahabad
✆ 2423466, Fax: 23289285 — kitab_mahal@hotmail.com

KITAB MAHAL DISTRIBUTORS, New Delhi
✆ 23273230, 23289285, Fax: 23289935 — kitab_mahal@hotmail.com, kmahal@del3.vsnl.net.in

KITAB MAHAL (REGD.), Srinagar
✆ 2421135 — kitabmahalpublishers@rediffmail.com

KITAB PUBLISHING HOUSE, New Delhi
✆ 2520124, 23543786 ▮ 9810049590
Fax: 27538699 — snchalta@giasdla.vsnl.net.in, kitab@vsnl.com

KITABGHAR PRAKASHAN, New Delhi
✆ 91-11-23271844, 23266207 — kitabghar_prd@yahoo.com

KITABI DUNIYA, Delhi
✆ 23288452, 35972589 — kitabiduniya@rediffmail.com

KITS & CONCEPTS (INDIA) PVT. LTD., Chennai
✆ 24895335-36, Fax: 91-44-25910549 — kits_con@yahoo.com

KIZHKKU PATHIPPAGAM, Chennai
✆ 42009601, Fax: 91-44-43009701 — support@nhm.in

KLUWER ACADEMIC PUBLISHERS, Faridabad
✆ 0129-2373639, Fax: 091-2273641 — kluwer@nde.vsnl.net.in

KNOWLEDGE BOOKS INC., Noida
✆ 0120-2572246, 2574810, 2575981 ▮ 9810191394 — komal@ndb.vsnl.net.in

KNOWLEDGE CITY BOOKS, Thane
✆ 2384718 — knowledgecity@rediffmail.com

KNOWLEDGE STORE (THE), New Delhi
✆ 26531279-80, Fax: 26532252 — ik_in@vsnl.net

KNOWLEDGE WORLD, New Delhi
✆ 23263488 ▮ 9810483435, Fax: 23263498 — kwi@mantraonline.com

KOHINOOR BOOK CENTRE, Hyderabad
✆ 23320602, Fax: 23309038 — kohinoorbookcentre1@rediffmail.com

KOMAL PUBLICATIONS, Nagaland
✆ 25344, Fax: 02764-24504 — bharatp200in@yahoo.com

KONARK PUBLISHERS PVT. LTD., Delhi
✆ 22455731, 22504101, 22507103, 55244972
Fax: 22507103 — kpp123@eth.net, kprn@bol.net.in

KOSHAL BOOK DEPOT, Delhi
✆ 91-11-65860877 — koshal.bookdepot@gmail.com

KOTAK BROS, Mumbai
✆ 28769572, Fax: 91-22-28769726 — kketan@bom5.vsnl.net.in

KRANTZ PUBLICATIONS, New Delhi
✆ 26252146, Fax: 91-11-26252146 — anilkrantz@vsnl.com

KRISHNA BOOK DISTRIBUTORS, Delhi
✆ 22116098 ▮ 9810834859, Fax: 22131719 — krishnabooks@yahoo.com

KRISHNA PRAKASHAN MEDIA (P) LTD., Meerut
✆ 0121-2644766, 2642946, Fax: 2645855 — sk_kpm@yahoo.com

KRISHNA TRADERS, Mumbai
✆ 22011357, 22012103, Fax: 22083184 — k_tee@vsnl.com

KRISHNAMURTI FOUNDATION INDIA, Pune
✆ 91-20-27284463 — kbooks2000@yahoo.com

KRISHNAMURTI FOUNDATION INDIA, Varanasi
✆ 2331289, 2332536, Fax: 0542-2330218 — publications@kfionline.org

KRISHNAMURTI FOUNDATION INDIA, Chennai
✆ 24937803, 2332536 — publications@kfionline.org

KUMAR BOOK DEPOT, New Delhi
✆ 32411029, Fax: 91-11-27321743 — kumar_bookdepot@yahoo.co.in

KUMAR PUBLICATIONS, New Delhi
✆ 25720718, 25760718, Fax: 25841718 — kumarpublications@rediffmail.com

KUMARAN PATHIPPAGAM, Chennai
✆ 28264046, 28241865, Fax: 91-44-28264046 — thambi@md2.vsnl.net.in

KUMUD BOOK MARKETING SERVICES, Sahibabad
✆ 95120-2639303 ▮ 9891371403 — come2_kbms@indiatimes.com

KUNAL SUBSCRIPTION AGENCY, Ahmedabad
✆ 7641553, 6563075 — pravinpnchal@jinpalonline.com

KURUKSHETHRA PRAKASHAN (P) LTD., Kerala
✆ 2338324, Fax: 91-484-2338324 — kurukshethraprakasan@yahoo.co.in

KUSUM PUBLISHING SERVICES P. LTD., New Delhi
✆ 26892495, 26892498, Fax: 26130069 — surit@vsnl.com

KUTUB KHANA ANJUMAN E-TARAQQI-E-URDU, Delhi
✆ 23282740, 23274339, Fax: 23263567 — sgagan@nde.vsnl.net.in

KUTUB KHANA ISHYAT-UL-ISLAM (REGD.), New Delhi
✆ 26412015, 26291371, 51623889, Fax: 51623890 — sgagan@del5.vsnl.net.in

KUWAIT EMBASSY INFORMATION OFFICE, New Delhi
✆ 26884946, 24100791, Fax: 26881115 — kuinfo@kuwait-info.com

KW PUBLISHERS PVT. LTD., New Delhi
✆ 23263498, 43528107 — knowledgeworld@vsnl.net

L

L.B. ASSOCIATES, Noida
✆ 4506666 — hawkolba@satyam.net.in

L.B. PUBLISHERS & DISTRIBUTORS PVT. LTD., Bangalore
✆ 25587621, 25587302, Fax: 25586463 — lbpdshp@bgl.vsnl.net.in

L.B. PUBLISHERS & DISTRIBUTORS PVT. LTD., New Delhi
✆ 26486816, 26217240, Fax: 91-11-26428684 — delhi@timelifeindia.com

L.B.S. PUBLICATIONS, New Delhi
bdbauruah@lbsbooks.com

L.C.A. SOFT PVT. LTD., New Delhi
✆ 66605878 — lca4cd@yahoo.com

L.C.A. SOFTWARE, New Delhi
9212735340 — mk5165620@yahoo.com

L.M. FURTADO & CO., Mumbai
✆ 22013105, 2756/3656, Fax: 22058750 — furtados@vsnl.com

L.R. BOOK DISTRIBUTORS, New Delhi
✆ 23718081, 23725154, Fax: 23356444 — lovdevandsons@w3c.com

LABDHI PRAKASHAN, Ahmedabad
labdhiprakashan@hotmail.com

LAHORE BOOK HOUSE (THE), Indore
✆ 2704435, Fax: 2554542 — lahorebook@yahoo.com

LALIT KALA AKADEMI, New Delhi
✆ 23387241, Fax: 91-11-23782485 — lka@lalithala.gov.in

LANCER PUBLISHERS & DISTRIBUTORS, New Delhi
✆ 26854691, Fax: 91-11-26960404 — lancer@lancerpublishers.com

LANDMARK, Chennai
✆ 28279637, 28259067, 28220147, Fax: 28259047 — landmark@md2.vsnl.net.in, landmark@vsnl.com

LANDMARK, Bhopal
✆ 2465238, Fax: 2411907 — landmark_no1@satyam.net.in

LAW JOURNAL PUBLICATIONS, Gwalior
✆ (O) 0751-2322-340, 2570591 (R) 2540118, 2369638 — lawjournal@mantramail.com

LAW PUBLISHERS, Allahabad
✆ 2660758, Fax: 91-532-2260781 — lawpub@sancharnet.in

LAWMAN (INDIA) PVT. LTD., New Delhi
✆ 41724129-30, Fax: 91-11-41724167 — abooks@vsnl.com

LAWZ MEDIA PVT. LTD., New Delhi
✆ 23073522, Fax: 91-11-23073522 — lawzmagazine@gmail.com, lawz@lawmagazine.com

LAXMI PUBLICATIONS PVT. LTD., New Delhi
✆ 43532500, 43532501
Fax: 91-11-23252572, 43532528 — info@laxmipublications.com, order@laxmipublications.com

LAZWAL PUBLISHERS & DISTRIBUTORS, Aligarh
✆ 0571-2405493, Fax: 0571-2401209 — maas@ndb.vsnl.net.in

LEADERSHIP KNOWLEDGE CONSULTING, Gurgaon
✆ 4103460-62, Fax: 91-124-4301464 — response@franklincoveyshouthasia.com

LEELA PRAKASHAN, Delhi
✆ 22118411, 22584998 — trimurtibooks@hotmail.com, trimurtibooks@yahoo.com

LEFTWORD BOOKS, New Delhi
✆ 23359456, 23356966, Fax: 23356966 — leftword@vsnl.com

LEXICON BOOK DISTRIBUTOR, New Delhi
✆ 91-11-65937423 — lexicon.books@yahoo.co.in

LIBCO BOOK DISTRIBUTORS, Delhi
✆ (O) & (R) 22371125 ▮ 9810274860 — libcobooks@email.com

LIBERTY INSTITUTE, New Delhi
✆ 25079214, Fax: 91-11-25079101 — info@libertyindia.org, liberty@nda.vsnl.net.in

LIBRARY BOOK CENTRE, Delhi
✆ 23262043 — sudhir20@vsnl.net

LIBRARY SERVICES UNLIMITED, Delhi
✆ (R) 27216750, 27476150 — tsut@rediffmail.com

LIMCA BOOK OF RECORDS, Gurgaon
✆ 2366907, Fax: 91-2366020 — vghose@abix.vsnl.net.in

LINGUAPHONE, New Delhi
✆ 26239663 — sami2982002@yahoo.com

LINGUAPHONE HIGHLIGHTS, New Delhi
✆ 22371212 ▮ 9811346542 — deepikamago@hotmail.com

LITRICO, Delhi
✆ 22320635, Fax: 91-11-22320761 — litrico@vsnl.com

LITTLE DARLING EDUCATIONAL RHYTHMS, New Delhi
✆ (O) & (R) 25599327 — abishekpublications@hotmail.com

LITTLE GENIUS, New Delhi
✆ 25980771, Fax: 91-11-28114164 ▮ 9868108195 — littlegeniusrk@yahoo.com

LITTLE FLOWER CO. (THE), Chennai
✆ 24341538, 24336467, Fax: 24310659 — varadan@lifcobooks.com

LIVING LITERATURE CRUSADE, New Delhi
✆ 24618818, 26670744, Fax: 24615121, 26420005 — loyall@ndf.vsnl.net.in

LIVING MEDIA INDIA LTD., New Delhi
✆ 23325453, 23736970, Fax: 91-11-23327322 — ramarao@intoday.com

LOGOS PRESS, New Delhi
✆ 23272187, Fax: 91-11-26351794 — mail@logospressindia.com

LOKAVANI-HALL MARK PRESS PVT. LTD., Chennai
lokavani@md2.vsnl.net.in

LOKBHARATI PRAKASHAN, Allahabad
✆ 91-532-2623314 — info@lokbhartiprakashan.com

LOTUS EDUCATION NETWORK PVT. LTD., New Delhi
✆ 26418944, 26963509, Fax: 26474646 — mystique_india@hotmail.com

LOTUS GROUP OF COMPANIES, Delhi
✆ 25692831, 25699044 — usharma16@hotmail.com

LOTUS LEARNING PVT. LTD., Mumbai
✆ 26400199, 26435052, 26441641, Fax: 2690458 — lotusmk@vsnl.com

LOTUS PRESS (PUBLISHERS & DISTRIBUTORS), New Delhi
✆ 91-11-32903912, 23280047 — lotus_press@sify.com

LOV DEV & SONS, New Delhi
✆ 23311844, 31010029, Fax: 23356444 — lovdevandsons@w3c.com

LOW COST TEACHING AIDS, Delhi
✆ 27130661, 27216115, Fax: 27435724 — lctas@oscarindia.com

LOW PRICE PUBLICATIONS, Delhi
✆ 91-11-27452453, 27401672 — lpp@nde.vsnl.net.in

LUCKY BOOK SELLERS, Jalgaon
✆ 226750, Fax: 223399 — luckybooksellers@rediffmail.com

M

M.B.D. ALCHEMIE PVT. LTD., New Delhi
✆ 41509995, Fax: 91-11-41509996 — info@mbdalchemie.com

M.C. BHANDARI FOUNDATION (MYSTIC INDIA MAGAZINE), New Delhi
✆ 23931393, 26521888, Fax: 23986100 — mysticindiamag@rediffmail.com

M.C.C. PUBLICATIONS, Bangalore
✆ 26549560, 26549561, Fax: 26656242 — mccpublications@vsnl.com

M.D. PUBLICATIONS (P) LTD., New Delhi
✆ 41562846, Fax: 91-11-23275542 — contact@mdppl.com

M.J.P. PUBLISHERS, Chennai
✆ 28441043, Fax: 91-44-28443347 — mjptnbh@rediffmail.com

M.K. BOOK DISTRIBUTORS, Ahmedabad
✆ (O) 6306545 (R) 6305322,
Fax: (079) 6304097, 6421344 — mkbooks@egujarat.net

M.M. BOOK PLAZA, Bangalore
✆ 5486200 ▮ 9886029882 — mmbplaza@hotmail.com

M.M.C. DIGIPRESS PVT. LTD., New Delhi
✆ 91-11-25927467, 25432580, 64530632
▮ 9212314134 — sales@mmcdigipress.com

M.P.P. HOUSE, Bangalore
✆ 22265901, 22260706, Fax: 22265901 — mphouse@vsnl.com

M.R. BOOK CENTRE, Hyderabad
✆ 23205684 — mrbookstall@usa.net

M.R. BOOKS, Guwahati
✆ 0361-2470746 — mrbooks2002@hotmail.com

M.R. PUBLICATIONS, New Delhi
▮ 9810784549 — abdus26@hotmail.com

M.S. BHALLAS & CO. (P) LTD., New Delhi
✆ 23257725, 23245609, Fax: 23256883 — info@msb.in

M.Y. PUBLICATIONS, New Delhi
✆ 91-11-65860770, 65728240 — manjuli_prakashan@rediffmail.com

MAANSI BOOK DISTRIBUTORS, Delhi
✆ 23206479, 23276669 — mansibookdist@hotmail.com, sonutraders@yahoo.com

MACMILLAN GLOBAL ACAMEDIC PUBLISHING, New Delhi
✆ 23271010 — jagat@del2.vsnl.net.in

MACMILLAN INDIA LTD., Bangalore
✆ 080-25586563, 25587878, Fax: 25588713 — rberi@bgl.vsnl.net.in

MACMILLAN PRESS LTD., New Delhi
✆ 23272010, 23257714, Fax: 23272010 — jagat@del2.vsnl.net.in

MADHAV VIDYA BHAVAN, Delhi
✆ 27249680 ▮ 9810563659, Fax: 27249680 — premacharyaji@yahoo.co.in

MADHUBAN EDUCATIONAL BOOKS, Noida
✆ 4078900, Fax: 91-120-4078999 — info@madhubanbooks.com

MADHUBAN EDUCATIONAL BOOKS, New Delhi
✆ 24314605, 24315313, Fax: 24310879 — helpline@vikaspublishing.com

MADHUR SANDESH SANGAM, New Delhi
✆ 26753327, Fax: 91-11-23276741 — madhursandeshsangam@yahoo.co.in

MADHYAM BOOKS, Delhi
✆ 22521081, 22432054, Fax: 22524233 — kaval@nde.vsnl.net.in

MADHYAMIK SHIKSHA NIDESHALAYA, Bikaner
✆ 2528875, Fax: 201861 — diredu@raj.nic.in

MADRAS BOOK AGENCY, Chennai
✆ 26260385, 25340962, 26289269 — mbamani@md3.vsnl.net.in

MAGIC TECH INDIAN PVT. LTD., New Delhi
✆ 26423988, 26422149, Fax: 26482338 — bdewan@mtipl.com

MAGNETIC POWER PUBLICATIONS, Hyderabad
✆ 23221057, 56641057 — alpspprinter@uyahoo.com

MAGNUM BOOKS (P) LTD., New Delhi
✆ 26090280, 31027384, Fax: 26090280 — arvindpassi@now-india.net.in

MAGNUM ENTERPRISES (REGD.), New Delhi
✆ (O) & (R) 26990280, 26995986, Fax: 26995986 — magbooks@mantraonline.com

MAGUS MEDIA PVT. LTD., New Delhi
✆ 26327595/6/7, 26315108, 51616562
Fax: 91-11-26311243, 51616561 — india@lifepositive.com

MAHAVEER & SONS, New Delhi
✆ 91-11-23287638 — mahaveersonspub@rediffmail.com

MAHALAXMI ENTERPRISES, Bangalore
✆ 23357433, 26742950, Fax: 23201967 — hrr@vsnl.com, hrr@bgl.vsnl.net.in

MAHAMAYA PUBLISHING HOUSE, New Delhi
✆ 91-11-23275538 — mahamayaph@rediffmail.com

MAHATMA GANDHI ANTARRASHTRIYA HINDI VISHWAVIDYALAYA, New Delhi
✆ 26254830, 26259308, Fax: 91-11-26263779 — hindiunv@nda.vsnl.net.in

MAKKIA BOOKS PLC, New Delhi
✆ 26841617, Fax: 91-11-26841618 — info@makkiabooks.com
▮ 9899228866

MAKTABA-AL-HASANT, New Delhi
✆ 91-11-41563256 | 📧 m_alhasanat@rediffmail.com, faisalfaheem@rediffmail.com

MALAYALA MANORAMA CO. LTD., Kottayam
✆ 2563646, Fax: 2562479 | 📧 mmdelhi@mmkerala.com

MALHOTRA BOOK DEPOT, New Delhi
✆ 23317931, 23317787, 23318301
Fax: 011-23319471 | 📧 mgulab@del.2vsnl.net.in

MALHOTRA PUBLISHING HOUSE, New Delhi
✆ (O) 25157006 (R) 25558788, 25610139
Fax: 91-11-25934597 | 📧 mph@vsnl.com

MALIK & COMPANY, Jaipur
✆ (O) 2575258, 2564858 (R) 2721417, 2721418
Fax: 0141-2396758 | 📧 sales@nationalpublishinghouse.com

MALIK BOOK DEPOT, Delhi
📱 9899711762 | 📧 aadilaseer@hotmail.com

MALLIGAI BOOK CENTRE, Madurai
✆ 2540534, 2341739 | 📧 malligaibc@eth.net

MALLIKA BOOKS, Delhi
✆ (O) 27612927 (R) 27615096, Fax: 27617546 | 📧 mallikabooks@vsnl.net, mallika@now-india.net.in

MANAK PUBLICATIONS PVT. LTD., Delhi
✆ 22453894, 22042529, Fax: 22418599 | 📧 manak_publications@hotmail.com

MANAS PUBLICATIONS, New Delhi
✆ (O) 23260783, 23265523 (R) 27131660, 27143052
Fax: 91-11-23272766 | 📧 manaspublications@vsnl.com

MANGAL DEEP PUBLISHERS & DISTRIBUTORS, Jaipur
✆ 0141-5102022, 2365086, Fax: 5102022 | 📧 mdpbk@sancharnet.in

MANIPAL PRINTERS & PUBLISHERS LTD., Manipal
✆ 270845, Fax: 08252-270563 | 📧 info@manipalpress.com

MANJUL PUBLISHING PVT. LTD., Bhopal
✆ 4240340, 2545952, 2543624
Fax: 91-755-2736919 | 📧 manjul@manjulindia.com

MANJULI PRAKASHAN, New Delhi
✆ 91-11-65728240, 65860770 | 📧 manjuli_prakashan@rediffmail.com

MANNEYS BOOK SELLERS, Pune
✆ 2651683, 2623214, Fax: 2634867 | 📧 manneys@vsnl.com

MANOHAR PUBLISHERS & DISTRIBUTORS, New Delhi
✆ 23289100, 23262796, 23284848, 23260774
Fax: 91-11-23265162 | 📧 sales@manoharbooks.com

MANOHARA GRANTHA MALA, Dharwad
✆ 91-836-2441822 | 📧 ramakantjoshi@rediffmail.com

MANOJ PUBLICATIONS, Delhi
✆ 27611116, 27611349, 27611118, Fax: 27611546 | 📧 swan_gupta@mantraonline.com, manojpublication@mantraonline.com

MANORAMA BOOK STALL, Punalur
✆ (O) 0475-2223391 (R) 2222491 | 📧 josea@md5.vsnl.net.in

MANSEE BOOKS (P) LTD., New Delhi
✆ (O) 23283115 (R) 28126407, Fax: 23286610 | 📧 mansibooks@vsnl.net

MANUPATRA INFORMATION SOLUTIONS PVT. LTD., Noida
✆ 4014444, 4014515, Fax: 91-120-2443723 — support@manupatra.com, contact@manupatra.com

MANUSHAM PUBLICATIONS, Kottayam
✆ 0481-2426550 — manusham@md3.vsnl.net.in, vattamattam@vsnl.com

MAP AND AGENCIES, Chennai
✆ 22431941 — mapsandagencies@mantraonline.com

MAP EDUCATIONAL SERVICES PVT. LTD., Gurgaon
✆ 26321669, 26325207, Fax: 26321865 — mapintledu@sify.com

MAPIN PUBLISHING (P) LTD., Ahmedabad
✆ 27545390-91, Fax: 91-79-27545592 — mapin@mapinpub.com

MARG PUBLICATIONS, Mumbai
✆ 022-22842520, 22821151, Fax: 22047102 — margpub@tata.com

MARIGOLD BOOKS, Chennai
✆ 24492307, 24491195, 24928209
Fax: 24491195, 24928209 — marigoldbks@satyam.net.in

MARKAZI MAKTABA ISLAMI PUBLISHERS, New Delhi
✆ 26971652, 26954341, Fax: 91-11-26947858 — mmipub@nda.vsnl.net.in

MARY ANN LIEBERT INC, New Delhi
✆ 45055555, Fax: 91-11-25778876 — varora@globe.pub.com

MARY MARTIN BOOKSELLERS, Coimbatore
✆ (O) 0422-2499030 (R) 2495780, Fax: 2495781 — mmbooks@vsnl.com

MASS EDUCATIONAL TECHNICAL TRAINING INSTITUTE, West Bengal
✆ 24771447, 24772010, Fax: 24772010 — mass@cal.vsnl.net.in

MASTERMIND PUBLICATIONS (INDIA) PVT. LTD., Meerut
✆ 4020511, 4020519, Fax: 91-121-2760824 — rastoginischal@rediffmail.com

MATHRUBHUMI PRINTING AND PUBLISHING CO. LTD., New Delhi
✆ 23733122, Fax: 91-11-23733124 — mbidelhi@gmail.com

MATRUSHRI, Hyderabad
✆ 27619469, 27669606 — matrushri@nettlinx.com

MAXLATIVE TRADING CORPORATION, Bangalore
✆ 41124411, 91-80-41124411 — md@maxlative.com

MAYA PUBLISHERS PVT. LTD., New Delhi
✆ 26892495, 26892498, Fax: 26130069 — surit@vsnl.com

MAYUR PAPERBACKS, Noida
✆ 4338365, Fax: 91-11-23254407 — sales@nationalpublishinghouse.com

MCGRAW-HILL BOOK CO., New Delhi
✆ 25882743-46, 25882918, Fax: 25885154 — marketing_india@mcgraw-hill.com

MCGRAW-HILL EDUCATION (INDIA) PVT. LTD., Noida
✆ 4383400, Fax: 91-120-4383401-03 — michael_cruz@mcgraw-hill.com, prakash_tiwari@mcgraw-hill.com

MECRON PUBLISHERS (P) LTD., Sivakasi
✆ 04562-27423738, 221108, Fax: 04562-272089
226655 — mecron@md3.vsnl.net.in

MEDHA BOOKS, Delhi
✆ 22323672, Fax: 91-11-22321818 — medhabooks@gmail.com

MEDIA 2000, New Delhi
✆ 26445191/2/3, Fax: 91-11-26217027 — info@media2k.com

MEDIA HOUSE, Delhi
✆ (O) 22750667 (R) 22751317 ▮ 9810301010
Fax: 22757040
[@] books@indiancurrents.com, mediabooks@hotmail.com

MEDIA STAR PVT. LTD., Mumbai
✆ 22815538, Fax: 91-22-22839619
[@] ravi@mediastar.co.in

MEDIA-CENTER/RUPOSHI BANGLA, Kolkata
✆ 31069767, 23372549, Fax: 23336567
[@] hapipaul@rediffmail.com

MEDIA-CENTER/UJJAL BOOKS, Kolkata
✆ 91-33-23607869
[@] hapipaul@rediffmail.com

MEDIAMATICS, New Delhi
✆ 43031100, Fax: 91-11-43031144
[@] mediam@dataone.in

MEDIAWARE SYSTEMS INDIA PVT. LTD., Chennai
[@] mediazmarket@yahoo.com

MEDICAL HOUSE, Delhi
✆ 65398987, 65675891, Fax: 91-11-23559348
[@] medicalhouse@airtelbroadband.in, medicalhouse@hotmail.com, medicalhouse@gmail.com

MEDICO REFRESHER PUBLICATIONS, New Delhi
✆ 32019798, Fax: 91-562-2811145
[@] sumit8@sancharnet.in

MEDITECH BOOK DISTRIBUTORS, Bangalore
[@] medibook@rediffmail.com

MEGH PRAKASHAN, Delhi
✆ 91-11-23278761, 65278761
[@] megh_prakashan@rediffmail.com

MEGHA BOOK DEPOT, Delhi
✆ 27455172
[@] mehta7455172@rediffmail.com, mehta7455172yahoo.com

MEHARCHAND LACHHMANDAS PUBLICATIONS, New Delhi
✆ (O) 23271568, 23281568 (R) 0124-5051104
Fax: 23271568
[@] atulnaahar@vsnl.com

MEHRAS, New Delhi
✆ 91-11-23273838
[@] mehras_delhi@vsnl.net

MEHTA BOOK SELLERS, Kolhapur
✆ (O) 0231-2542304, 2541881 (R) 2543260
Fax: 0231-2541881
[@] mehtabooks@eth.net

MEHTA PUBLISHERS, New Delhi
✆ 25704450, 25707667, Fax: 25704234
[@] mopl@vsnl.com

MEHUL BOOK SALES, Mumbai
✆ (O) 22654657, 22694145, 22674944
(R) 24141216, 24184679, Fax: 22654657
[@] mehulbks@vsnl.com

MEMORY RETENTION WORKSHOP, Delhi
✆ 22542805, 22548006, Fax: 22248006
[@] gunjan-kapadia@rediffmail.com

MENTA BOOK DISTRIBUTORS PVT. LTD., Bangalore
✆ 26769509, 26761289, Fax: 26769954
[@] jai@blr.vsnl.net.in

MERIDIAN INTERNATIONAL, Tuticorn
✆ 328116, Fax: 327116
[@] sageer@vsnl.com

METRO BOOKS PVT. LTD., New Delhi
91-11-43541022
[@] metrobooks@rediffmail.com

METROPOLITAN BOOK CO. PVT. LTD., New Delhi
✆ 23271661, 23255914, Fax: 23272497
[@] metrobks@ndf.vsnl.net.in

MICRO E-COMMERCE LTD., Noida
✆ 2421544, 2421545, Fax: 95-120-2420330 — vipul@microecommerce.net, mecom@microecommerce.net

MIDLAND BOOK SHOP, New Delhi
✆ (O) 26867121 (R) 25266048, Fax: 26962718 — midbook@bol.net.in

MILIND PRAKASHAN, Hyderabad
✆ (O) 24753737, 31052988 (R) 27562595 — milindprakshan@rediffmail.com

MILLAT BOOK CENTRE, New Delhi
✆ 23274339, 23282740, Fax: 23263567 — sgagan@vsnl.com

MILLENNIUM BOOKS, Patna
✆ 220647, Fax: 229079 — uks@vsnl.com

MILLENNIUM PUBLISHERS, New Delhi
✆ 24621791, 24692352, Fax: 24604413 — milli@bol.net.in

MILTON BOOK COMPANY, Dehradun
✆ 0135-2658692, 2659601 — milton@ndb.vsnl.net.in

MIND & BODY RESEARCH CENTRE, New Delhi
✆ (O) 26412432, 26430337 (R) 516430337 — dayanandverma@yahoo.com

MINDSTORM COMPUTER INFORMATION PVT. LTD., Chennai
✆ 26427633, 26427454, Fax: 25321076 — info@compuserve.com

MINERVA BOOK HOUSE, Shimla
✆ 2203078, 2250523, Fax: 2254802 — minerva@nde.vsnl.net.in, minerva_shimla@yahoo.com

MINERVA BOOK STALL, Thrissur
✆ (O) 2335478, 2335578 (R) 2383878, 2383879
Fax: 0487-2383878 — minerva@md5.vsnl.net.in

MINERVA PUBLICATIONS, Chennai
✆ 28445674, Fax: 28445674 — minerva@hathway.com

MIRA ADITI CENTRE, Mysore
✆ 0821-2330380 — miraditi@hclinfinet.com, miraditi@hotmail.com

MITTAL BOOK DISTRIBUTORS, Delhi
✆ 23263913, 23257587, Fax: 23940285 — dkm@ndb.vsnl.net.in

MITTAL PUBLICATIONS, New Delhi
✆ 25648725, 23250398, 25351493, Fax: 25351521 — mittalp@ndf.net.in, info@mittalbooks.com

MOBEL BOOK DISTRIBUTORS, Ahmedabad
✆ 26756476, Fax: 079-6767618 — mobelabad@yahoo.co.in

MODERN BOOK CENTRE, Trivandrum
✆ 2331816, 2331826, 2333987, Fax: 2333186 — modern@techpark.net

MODERN BOOK DEPOT, New Delhi
✆ 23241471, 56022599, Fax: 91-11-27241674 — vinmedia@bol.net.in, modbook@caltigen.com

MODERN BOOK DEPOT, Bhubaneswar
✆ 0675-534374 — modbooks@cal2.vsnl.net.in

MODERN BOOK DEPOT (THE), Kolkata
✆ 22493102, 22490933, Fax: 22497455 — modcal@vsnl.com

MODERN BOOK DEPOT (THE), Guwahati
✆ 2517059, 2546244, Fax: 2544791 — unipub@gw1.dot.net.in, modbook@caltigen.com

MODERN BOOK HOUSE, Jodhpur
✆ (O) 0291-2624850 (R) 0291-2548326 — vikpankj@sancharnet.in

MODERN INTERNATIONAL PVT. LTD., Delhi
mpml@ndf.vsnl.net.in

MODERN LAW PUBLISHERS, Allahabad
modernip@sancharnet.in

MODERN PUBLISHERS, New Delhi
✆ 22518122, Fax: 91-11-22546557 — holyfaith1@vsnl.net

MODERN SUBSCRIPTION AGENCY, Delhi
✆ 27123293 — modern_in@yahoo.com

MOHIT PRAKASHAN, New Delhi
✆ (O) 27224337 (R) 27253552, Fax: 27486529 — mohitpra@ndf.vsnl.net.in

MONA ASSOCIATES, Bangalore
✆ 25285476 — monassociates@yahoo.com, ojaeyk@yahoo.com

MONIKA BOOK DISTRIBUTORS, New Delhi
✆ 23243979 ▮ 9810562673, Fax: 23251437 — monika_books@hotmail.com

MONITOR INFORMATION SERVICES, Hyderabad
✆ 55787065, Fax: 27552390 — emonitor@hd2.dot.net.in

MORNING STAR (EDUCATIONAL PUBLISHERS), New Delhi
✆ 23244660, 23246113, Fax: 91-11-23244660 — pinto_anl@vsnl.com, latikap@ndy.vsnl.net.in

MOSAIC BOOKS, New Delhi
✆ 51720230, Fax: 29813869 — israel4@vsnl.com

MOTILAL BANARSIDASS PUBLISHERS PVT. LTD., Delhi
✆ 23858335, 23851985, 23852747, 23854826
Fax: 91-11-23850689 — mlbd@vsnl.com

MOTIVE BOOKS, New Delhi
✆ 65860009, 32436524, Fax: 91-11-65860009
▮ 9810338636, 9310338636 — info@motivebooks.com, sales@motivebooks.com, editor@motivebooks.com, chairman@motivebooks.com

MOUJI RAM SMRITI NYAS, New Delhi
✆ 24636010/30, Fax: 91-11-24636011 — neetabooks@vsnl.com

MUDIT PRAKASHAN, New Delhi
✆ 45521005, Fax: 91-11-45521005 — umesh1955@gmail.com

MUDRA PRAKASHAN, New Delhi
✆ (O) 23277230, 23280711, 26564461, 2356743
(R) 22927668, 22911185, Fax: 23277230, 26963361 — selina@vsnl.com, mudrit@hotmail.com

MULBERRY PUBLICATIONS, Kozhikode
✆ 740746, 403603, Fax: 765531 — shalvyd@com

MULTI MEDIA HRD (P) LTD., Mumbai
✆ 22042281, 22826312, Fax: 22836478 — info@multimediahrd.com

MUNSHIRAM MANOHARLAL PUBLISHERS PVT. LTD., New Delhi
✆ 23671668, 23673650, 23636097
Fax: 91-11-23612745 — mrml@mrmlbooks.com

MUSIC BOOKS, Delhi
✆ 91-11-27013346 — music@musicbooks.in

MURUGAN MAGAZINE DISTRIBUTOR, Mumbai
✆ 28310574, 28262118, Fax: 28381201
bombay@muruganmagazine.com, info@muruganmagazne.com

MYTEC PROCESS (P) LTD., Bangalore
✆ 22233328/3279, Fax: 080-2233262
mytec@blr.vsnl.net.in

■ ■ ■

N

N.A.V. SUBRAMANIAN BOOK AGENCY, Chennai
✆ 24724018, Fax: 24724018
navsba@md3.vsnl.net.in

N.B. MODERN AGENCIES, Siliguri
✆ 2521297, 2432349, Fax: 2432349
anand_prakash68@hotmail.com, sig_nbmodern@sancharnet.in

N.C. KANSIL & SONS, New Delhi
✆ 23550178, 23670178, Fax: 91-11-23550340
nckmaps@gmail.com, mail@nckmaps.com

N.G.C. NETWORK (INDIA) PVT. LTD., Bangalore
✆ 66947827, 91-80-66947902
farhan@in.startv.com

N.G.P.A. PUBLICATIONS, New Delhi
✆ 91-11-27043600
ngpa@ngpacollege.com

N.P.T. OFFSET PVT. LTD., Chennai
nptoffset@vsnl.com

N.R. BOOK DISTRIBUTORS, Delhi
✆ (O) 27383169 (R) 27187496 📱 9810047770
nrbd@mantraonline.com, nrbd@vsnl.com

N.R. BOOK SYNDICATE, Delhi
✆ (O) 27011652, 27196269 (R) 27018098
27187496, Fax: 91-11-27276256,
Telefax: 31-79055
nrbooks@email.com

N.R. BROTHERS, Indore
✆ (O) 2701337, 2701640 (R) 2461821, 2462786
Fax: 0731-2701337
nrbros@sancharnet.in, nrbros@bom4.vsnl.net.in

N.S. PRINTERS AND PUBLISHERS, Delhi
✆ 23285932
swanitee@hotmail.com

NABA MUDRAN PVT. LTD., Kolkata
✆ 25555094, 25556558, Fax: 22511876
santk@cal.vsnl.net.in

NABHI PUBLICATIONS, New Delhi
✆ 23354823, 43640045, Fax: 91-11-23416103
23731117
sales@nabhipublications.com

NAG PUBLISHERS, Delhi
✆ 91-11-23857975, 23855883
nagpublishers@rediffmail.com

NAGARAJ & CO. (P) LTD., Chennai
✆ 24413133, 24911725, Fax: 28256982
amranagaraj@cyberwaveindia.com

NAGEEN PRAKASHAN PVT. LTD., Meerut
✆ (O) 2660099, 2663154, 2643154 (R) 2660098 2663153, Fax: 2643153
✉ nageenprakashan@yahoo.com, nageen@rediffmail.com

NAISADAK COMPANY, Delhi
✉ deepak2107@rediffmail.com

NAI SADI PRAKASHAN PVT. LTD., Delhi
✆ 27658461-2, Fax: 27652700
✉ naisadi@vsnl.com

NALANDA BOOK STORE, Bangalore
✆ 25510307
✉ ikon_maya@hotmail.com, ikonmaya@bgl.vsnl.net.in

NAMDHARI DARBAR, New Delhi
✆ 25191122, 25156625, Fax: 25446060
✉ info@namdhari-world.com

NANDA BOOK SERVICE, Delhi
✆ 22530838, Fax: 22459177
✉ nandabook@hotmail.com

NARAYAN KUTTI SANYAS ASHRAM, Dewas
✆ 91-11-23381403
✉ urmil95@yahoo.co.in

NARENDRA BOOK AGENCY & PUBLISHING HOUSE, Delhi
✆ 23268470, 23259412, Fax: 23259412
✉ info@ebooksvision.com, info@nph-india.com

NARESH PUBLISHERS, New Delhi
✆ 25723235, 25754442, 25746485, Fax: 25746485
✉ narpubs@nda.vsnl.net.in

NARNE PUBLICATIONS PVT. LTD., Secunderabad
✆ 27800728, Fax: 27840246
✉ deepa@narne.com

NAROSA BOOK DISTRIBUTORS PVT. LTD., New Delhi
✆ 23258579, 23259263, Fax: 91-11-23258934
✉ info@narosa.com

NATIONAL ATLAS AND THEMATIC MAPPING ORGANISATION, Kolkata
✆ 033-23346460, Fax: 23346460
✉ natmo@giascl01.vsnl.net.in

NATIONAL BOOK AGENCY, Madurai
✆ 0452-2341304
✉ nba_mduss@rediffmail.com

NATIONAL BOOK CENTRE, Nashik
✆ 2314821
✉ nationalbooks@rediffmail.com

NATIONAL BOOK DEPOT, Gorakhpur
✆ 2339533, 2340342
✉ national_book_depot@hotmail.com

NATIONAL BOOK DEPOT (THE), Mumbai
✆ 24131362, 24165274, Fax: 24130877
✉ prachint@bom7.vsnl.net.in

NATIONAL BOOK ENTERPRISES, Hyderabad
✆ 27561890, 27564442, Fax: 27560146
✉ nbe77@rediffmail.com

NATIONAL BOOK SHOP, Delhi
✆ 23278392, 23264342
✉ nbs_books@sify.com

NATIONAL BOOK STALL, Hubli
✆ (O) 0836-2367902 (R) 2353209
✉ nationalbook1@rediffmail.com

NATIONAL BOOK TRUST, INDIA, New Delhi
✆ 26569962, 26568052, 26561684, 26564020 Fax: 26851795
✉ nbtindia@ndb.vsnl.net.in

NATIONAL COUNCIL FOR PROMOTION OF URDU LANGUAGE, New Delhi
✆ 26103381, 26103938, 26179657 Fax: 91-11-26108159
✉ urducouncil@gmail.com, alijaved40@hotmail.com

NATIONAL COUNCIL OF EDUCATIONAL RESEARCH AND TRAINING, New Delhi
✆ 26560620, 26864811, Fax: 91-11-26868419 — proncert@yahoo.co.in

NATIONAL GANDHI MUSEUM, New Delhi
✆ 23328310, 23310168, Fax: 23311793 — gandhimk@nda.vsnl.net.in

NATIONAL INSTITUTE OF CONSTRUCTION MANAGEMENT & RESEARCH, Mumbai
✆ 24952453, 24927847, Fax: 24961183 — nicmarmb@giasbm01.vsnl.net.in, giasbm01.vsnl.net.in

NATIONAL INSTITUTE OF DESIGN, Ahmedabad
✆ 26639692-3-4, Fax: 26605242, 26621167
Telex: 1216322 — publication@nid.edu

NATIONAL INSTITUTE OF EDUCATIONAL PLANNING & ADMINISTRATION, New Delhi
✆ 26962120, 26962126, 2696780
Fax: 26853041, 26865180 — niepa@vsnl.com

NATIONAL INSTITUTE OF INDUSTRIAL RESEARCH, Delhi
✆ 23823955, 23835654, 23845886, Fax: 23841561 — niir@vsnl.com

NATIONAL INSTITUTE OF OPEN SCHOOLING (NIOS), New Delhi
✆ 26452331, Fax: 26481569 — bhdhyani@hotmail.com

NATIONAL INSTITUTE OF SCIENCE COMMUNICATION, New Delhi
✆ 25843359, 25786301, Fax: 25843359 — niscom@sirnetd.ernet.in, sales@niscom.res.in

NATIONAL PUBLISHING HOUSE, New Delhi
✆ 23274161, 23275267, Fax: 23254407 — sales@nationalpublishinghouse.com

NATIONAL SCHOOL OF BANKING, Hyderabad
✆ 23387715, Fax: 23387846 — csvepa@yahoo.com

NATIONAL SCHOOL OF DRAMA, New Delhi
✆ 23389402, 23387137, 23382821, Fax: 23384288 — nsdr@rediffmail.com, info@nsd.gov.in

NATRAJ BOOK CENTRE, Ahmedabad
✆ 26587930, 26588750, Fax: 079-26440767 — natrajbooks@yahoo.com

NATRAJ PUBLISHERS, Dehradun
✆ 2653382, 2654584, Fax: 2749914, 2651108 — natrajbooks@vsnl.com

NATURE PUBLISHING GROUP, Gurgaon
✆ 2881053-54, Fax: 91-124-2881052 — j.srinivasan@nature.com

NATURE PUBLISHING GROUP, New Delhi
✆ 23244186, Fax: 23272010 — harpal@nature.com

NAV BHARAT PUBLICATIONS CO., Chennai
✆ (O) 044-28114560 (R) 28111751, Fax: 28111554 — navbharat@kmronline.com

NAVAKARNATAKA PUBLICATIONS (P) LTD., Bangalore
✆ 22203580-81-82, Fax: 22203582 — nkp@bgl.vsnl.net.in

NAVAYUGA BOOK HOUSE, Hyderabad
✆ 24754688 — navayuga79@hotmail.com

NAVDEEP PUBLICATIONS, New Delhi
✆ 24697006, 24697009, Fax: 91-11-24618474 — info@navdeepublications.com

NAVEEN PRAKASHAN (REGD.), Ghaziabad
✆ (O) 24790157, 24794554 (R) 0575-27523535
2734698, Fax: 24790868 — navpr@ndf.vsnl.net.in

NAVJYOTHI BOOK HOUSE, Bhopal
✆ 0755-2754487 ▮ 9826088242 — pvanraj@yahoo.co.in, vanrajpaul@rediffmail.com

NAVNEET EDUTAINMENT LIMITED, Mumbai
✆ 24989898, Fax: 24934343 — support@connectschool.com

NAVNEET PUBLICATIONS (INDIA) LTD., Mumbai
✆ 66626565, Fax: 91-22-66626470 — npil@navneet.com

NAVODAYA PUBLISHERS, Vijayawada
✆ 0866-2573500, 2574500 — booklik@md4.vsnl.net.in

NAVRANG BOOKSELLERS & PUBLISHERS, New Delhi
✆ 25835914, 25833803, Fax: 25833803 — navrang@navrangbooks.com

NAVYUG BOOKS (INDIA), Delhi
▮ 9910910967 — navyugbookindia@yahoo.com

NAYA GYANODAYA, New Delhi
✆ 24626467, 24654196, 24698417, 24656201
Fax: 91-11-24654197 — sales@jnanpith.net, jnanpith@satyam.net.in

NAYA PROKASH, Kolkata
✆ (O) 033-23542130, 24110987 (R) 25387794
Fax: 25382897 — npsales@cal2.vsnl.net.in

NAYA UDYOG, Kolkata
✆ 22414709, 22413540, 22190799 — navudyog@vsnl.net

NAZ PUBLISHING HOUSE, Delhi
✆ 23246409, Fax: 91-11-23279392 — nazp@del2.vsnl.net.in

NEELKAMAL PUBLICATIONS PVT. LTD., Hyderabad
✆ 24757140, 24757944, 24757197
Fax: 91-40-24757951 — suresh@neelkamalpub.com

NEERAJ BOOK CENTRE, Delhi
▮ 9312869947 — neerajmittal_2002@rediffmail.com

NEERAJ PUBLICATIONS, Delhi
✆ 23260329, 65817881, Fax: 91-11-23285501 — info@neerajbooks.com

NEETA PRAKASHAN, New Delhi
✆ 24636010, 24636030, 24653600, Fax: 24636011 — neetabooks@vsnl.com

NELSON THORNES, Gurgaon
✆ 91-124-2576796 — overleaf@vsnl.net

NEOVISION PUBLISHERS (P) LTD., New Delhi
✆ 26241848, Fax: 26241559 — neovisionpublishers@mail.com

NETTIKADAN BOOKS (P) LTD., Cochin
✆ 2366067, 2369784, Fax: 0484-2354695 — mail@nettikadan.com

NETWORK (INDIA) BOOK DISTRIBUTORS, New Delhi
✆ (R) 24631478 ▮ 9810398699
Fax: 011-24635783 — kishor_megha@vsnl.net

NETWORKS 18 PUBLICATIONS PVT. LTD., Mumbai
✆ 40019477, Fax: 91-22-66618985 — kannaniyer@network18online.com

NEW ACADEMIC PUBLISHERS, Delhi
✆ 22413394, 22420827 — alsindia@sigmaonline.net

NEW AGE BOOKS, New Delhi
✆ 25895218-19, 23922151, Fax: 25797221 — info@newagebooksindia.com, nab@vsnl.net.in

NEW AGE INTERNATIONAL, New Delhi
✆ 23252574, Fax: 23252572 — colaxmi@hotmail.com

NEW AGE INTERNATIONAL (P) LTD., New Delhi
✆ 23276802, 23258865, Fax: 91-11-23267437 — orders@newagepublishers.com, info@newagepublishers.com, sales@newagepublishers.com

NEW ASIAN PUBLISHERS, New Delhi
✆ 23280163-65, Fax: 23280165 — mehta_anil@mailcity.com

NEW BHARATIYA BOOK CORPORATION, Delhi
✆ 91-11-23851294, 65195809 — newbbc@indiatimes.com

NEW BHARATIYA BOOK CORPORATION, Delhi
✆ 23981294, Fax: 23956241 — deepak_nbbc@hotmail.com

NEW BOOK CORNER (THE), Kolkata
✆ 23374872/0059, Fax: 24930043 — nbccal72@vsnl.net, anuttam@vsnl.net

NEW BOOK CENTRE, New Delhi
✆ 91-11-23356663 — newbookcentre@rediffmail.com

NEW BOOK DEPOT, New Delhi
✆ (O) 23320020, 23755124, 23318045
(R) 24697423, Fax: 91-11-23354027 — rakeshchandra@mantraonline.com

NEW BOOK DEPOT (THE), Guwahati
✆ 2517059, Fax: 2544719 — modbook@caltigen.com

NEW BOOK HOUSE, Allahabad
✆ (O) & (R) 0532-2622879, 3150898 — sprakash@nde.vsnl.net.in

NEW CENTRAL BOOK AGENCY (P) LTD., Kolkata
✆ 22418411, 22418537, 22419094
Fax: 91-33-22413852, 22418537 — central@cal2.vsnl.net.in, ncba@cal2.vsnl.net.in, ncbapvtltd@eth.net

NEW CENTURY BOOK HOUSE (P) LTD., Chennai
✆ 26258410, Fax: 91-44-26858410 — ncbhbook@yahoo.co.in

NEW CENTURY PUBLICATIONS, Delhi
✆ 27247805, 27138192, Fax: 91-11-27464774 — indiatax@del2.vsnl.net.in

NEW CENTURY PUBLICATIONS, New Delhi
✆ 23247798, 65396605, Fax: 91-11-41017798
Mobile: 9811266355 — indiatax@vsnl.com, info@newcenturypublications.com

NEW CONCEPTS, New Delhi
✆ 56223494 Mobile: 9868026219, Fax: 25587139 — newkconcepts@yahoo.com

NEW ERA BOOK AGENCY, Chandigarh
✆ 2702318, 2702189 — nebaaph@sancharnet.in, nebaaph@hotmail.com

NEW ERA BOOKS, Bangalore
✆ 080-26603244, 26420049, Fax: 26750079 — newera-rbs@hotmail.com, newrabooks@vsnl.net

NEW ERA PUBLICATIONS PVT. LTD., New Delhi
✆ 26601548 — tgoeldenite@gmx.net

NEW INDIA PUBLISHING AGENCY, New Delhi
✆ 27341717, 27343030, Fax: 91-11-27341616 — newindiapublishingagency@gmail.com

NEW JACK PRINTING WORKS PVT. LTD., Mumbai
✆ 24925481/82, 24925473 — newjack@vsnl.com

NEW LIGHT PUBLISHERS, New Delhi
✆ (O) 25737448, 25721761, 25712649
(R) 25764425, 25764479, 25711116
Fax: 25812385
✉ newlight@vsnl.net, readwell@sify.com

NEW OSCAR PUBLICATIONS PVT. LTD., New Delhi
✆ 23682766, 23520716, Fax: 011-23520716
✉ newoscarpub@yahoo.com

NEW ROYAL BOOK COMPANY, Lucknow
✆ (O) 0522-2285607 (R) 2240644, 2248003
Fax: 2231569
✉ nrbc@rediffmail.com

NEW STUDENTS BOOK CENTRE, Guntur
✆ (O) 2233332 (R) 2233335
✉ nsbc74@yahoo.com

NEW STUDENTS BOOK CENTRE, Vijayawada
✆ 2572222, 2572211, Fax: 0866-2578333
✉ babjee48@rediffmail.com, babjee48@yahoo.com

NEWS & LITERATURE HOUSE, Kota
✆ (O) 0744-2451339, 2364155, 2330779
(R) 0744-2422752, Fax: 0744-2330779, 2360275
✉ nlh@kappa.net.in

NEWSJOY PUBLICATIONS PVT. LTD., New Delhi
✆ 26480505, 26448682, Fax: 26474646
✉ newsjoy@satyam.net.in, editor@newsjoy.com

NEXT DIMENSION MULTIMEDIA, New Delhi
✆ 26237787, 51617787, Fax: 26237787
✉ nextd@vsnl.net

NEXUS INFORMATION SERVICES CO. (P) LTD., Delhi
✆ 27001517, 22254625, Fax: 26859444
✉ nisc@vsnl.com, aiiebip@nisc.co.in

NIDHI PUBLISHERS (INDIA), Bikaner
✆ 0151-543261
✉ nidhipub@rediffmail.com

NIIR PROJECT CONSULTANCY SERVICES, New Delhi
✆ 23843955, 23845654, 23845886
Fax: 91-11-23841561 ▮ 9811043595
✉ niir.india@gmail.com

NINSACH TECHNOLOGIES, Hissar
✉ nitinrgoel@rediffmail.com

NIRALA PUBLICATIONS, New Delhi
✆ 22453992
✉ nirala32@hotmail.com

NIRALI PRAKASHAN, Pune
✆ 24450842, 24451512, Fax: 91-20-24495422
✉ pragatibooks@vsnl.net

NIRMAL BOOK AGENCY, Kolkata
✆ 2415728, 2414003, Fax: 2419238
✉ pradip-saha@hotmail.com

NIROG SUKH, Jaipur
✆ 2302995, 2233273, Fax: 2303558
✉ nirogsuk@datainfosys.net.in

NISHKAAM PEETH PRAKASHAN, New Delhi
✆ 26512504, 26512523
✉ editor@jyotirved.com

NITA MEHTA CULINARY ACADEMY PVT. LTD., New Delhi
✆ 65976202, Fax: 91-11-29225218
✉ nitamehta@email.com

NITA MEHTA PUBLICATION, New Delhi
✆ (O) 29218574, 29218727, 23252948
(R) 29218727 ▮ 9810053070, 9810632282
Fax: 29225218, 23252948
✉ nitamehta@email.com

NITHYANANDA DHYANAPEETAM, Bangalore
✆ 91-80-65591844, 27202084
✉ mail@nithyananda.org

NIYOGI OFFSET PRIVATE LIMITED, New Delhi
© 26826301, 26813350-52 ▮ 9810645410
Fax: 91-11-26813830, 26810483
@ bikash12@nda.vsnl.net.in

NOBEL FOUNDATION, New Delhi
© 26845477, 26845542, Fax: 26831814
@ webmaster@nobletfoundation.org

NORTHERN BOOK CENTRE, New Delhi
© 23271626, 23280295, 23264519, 23280195
23271626, Fax: 23252651
@ scs@del2.vsnl.net.in,
nbcnd@ndb.vsnl.net.in

NOVA PUBLICATIONS, New Delhi
© 23283372, Fax: 23262183
@ evergreen@del3.vsnl.net.in

NOVATECH SCIENTIFICS & INFORMATICS, Moradabad
© 0591-2310723 ▮ 09412139878, Fax: 2440070
@ sanjeev_seth_in@yahoo.com

NOVELTY & COMPANY, Patna
© (O) 2672775, 2687561 (R) 2650873, 2657183
Fax: 2687641
@ noveltyandco.@yahoo.com,
noveltyandcompany@yahoo.com

NOVELTY BOOK DISTRIBUTORS, New Delhi
© (O) 23242323 (R) 25798942
▮ 9811211264, Fax: 25422776
@ novelty@ndb.vsnl.net.in,
noveltybook@vsnl.com

■ ■ ■

O

O.B.I. EXPORTS, New Delhi
© 23263363, 23265303, Fax: 91-11-23278091
@ obi@del2.vsnl.net.in

OASIS EDUCATIONAL SERVICES PVT. LTD., New Delhi
© 26124025-7, Fax: 26124028
@ oescare@vsnl.net

OBEROI BOOK SERVICE, Jammu
© 2471723, 2580017, Fax: 2472906
@ obs@rediffmail.com

OCEAN BOOKS PVT. LTD., New Delhi
© 23289555, 23289666, 23289777
Fax: 91-11-23253233
@ info@oceanbooks.in,
prabhat1@vsnl.com

OCTOPUS INDIA, New Delhi
© 23284894, Fax: 23281819
@ aparmar@vsnl.com

OFFICE OF THE REGISTRAR GENERAL, INDIA, New Delhi
© 23020629, Fax: 91-11-23383145
@ rgoffice.rgi@nic.in

OJASAVI PUBLICATIONS, New Delhi
© 22155169, 91-11-22144806
@ ojasvipublication@yahoo.com

OLD & NEW BOOKS, New Delhi
© 28538200
@ coinbooks@rediffmail.com

OM BOOK SERVICE, Delhi
© 23279323, 23274303, Fax: 23278091
@ obl@del2.vsnl.net.in

OM BOOK SHOP, New Delhi
© 24653792, 24653793, Fax: 24653794
@ sales@ombooks.com,
leoamitvig@yahoo.com

OM BOOKS, Secunderabad
✆ 2861282, Fax: 863956 — ombooks@omb.ind.com.org

OM BOOKS INTERNATIONAL, New Delhi
✆ 23265303, 23278091 — sales@ombooks.com

OM PUBLICATIONS, Faridabad
✆ 2272892, 3535574 — ipb@ndf.vsnl.net.in

OM SAI PUBLISHERS & DISTRIBUTORS, New Delhi
✆ (O) 26232172 (R) 31061215 — bkumar_y&k@yahoo.com

OM SAKTHI BOOK HOUSE, Chennai
✆ 23811923, Fax: 23811923 — omsbh@rediffmail.com

OMEGA SCIENTIFIC PUBLISHERS, New Delhi
✆ 26846071, 26918517, Fax: 26823869 — israel4@vsnl.com

OMSONS PUBLICATIONS, New Delhi
✆ 25412452, Fax: 23289353 — omsons@hotmail.com, omsons@satyam.net.in

ONKAR BOOK AGENCY, New Delhi
✆ 26172096, 65691896, Fax: 91-11-41030456 — onkarbooks@hotmail.com

OORJA MUSIC, Pune
✆ 2630815, 2633880, Fax: 2622512 — sahil@pn2.vsnl.net.in

OPTOMETRY TODAY, New Delhi
✆ (O) 25599839 (R) 25612301 — kumars@vsnl.com

ORIENT EDUCATIONAL STORES, New Delhi
✆ 23264156, Fax: 91-11-23271065 — orientda@airtelbroadband.in

ORIENT LAW HOUSE, New Delhi
✆ 26415150, 26483300 — orientlaw@now-india.net.in

ORIENT BLACKSWAN PVT. LTD., Hyderabad
✆ 27662849/2850/5446/5447, Fax: 040-27645046 — info@orientblackswan.com

ORIENT PAPERBACKS, New Delhi
✆ 23278877, Fax: 91-11-23278879 — orientpbk@vsnl.com, sales@orientpaperbacks.com

ORIENT PUBLICATIONS, Delhi
✆ (O) 22370737 (R) 22374753 ▮ 9810693391 — orient_pub@rediffmail.com

ORIENTAL ENTERPRISES, Dehradun
✆ 0135-2654218, Fax: 2652111 — oriental@samcharet.in

ORIENTAL WATCHMAN PUBLISHING HOUSE, Pune
✆ 020-4261441, 4273017, Fax: 020-4261638 — owph@pn2.vsnl.net.in

ORIGINALS, Delhi
✆ 27452453, 27401672 — lpp@nde.vsnl.net.in

ORION BOOKS, Delhi
✆ 22298067 — orionbooks74@hotmail.com

OSA BOOKS & PERIODICALS PVT. LTD., New Delhi
✆ 23259171, 26460705, Fax: 23259161 — osabooks@hotmail.com

OSCAR PUBLICATIONS, Delhi
✆ 27130449, 27435724, Fax: 27435724 — info@oscarindia.com, oscar@del2.vsnl.net.in

OSHO LOVE AFFAIR, Delhi
✆ 23967450, 23981989, Fax: 23935532 — osholoveaffair@vsnl.com

OSHO MEVLANA MEDITATION CENTER, Hyderabad
✆ 55629311 — mahacon@hd1.vsnl.net.in

OSHO PUBLICATIONS, Pune
✆ 4019999, Fax: 4019900 — distrib@osho.net

OSHO WORLD FOUNDATION, New Delhi
✆ 65694869, Fax: 91-11-26691074 — contact@oshoworld.com

OSWAAL BOOKS, Agra
✆ 2856558, 2857671, Fax: 91-562-2854582 — contact@oswaalbooks.com

OSWAL COMPETITION BOOKS, Agra
✆ 0562-215655-8, Fax: 2522141 — oswalbooks@indiatimes.com

OTHER INDIA BOOK STORE (THE), Goa
✆ 263305, 263306, Fax: 263305 — aibs@bom2.vsnl.net.in, oib@goatelecom.com

OUTLOOK PUBLISHING (INDIA) PVT. LTD., New Delhi
✆ 26191421-24, Fax: 91-11-26191420 — yourhelpline@outlookindia.com

OVERLEAF, Gurgaon
✆ 95-124-2576796 — overleaf@vsnl.net

OVERSEAS BOOKS, New Delhi
✆ 25463308, 55394449, Fax: 91-11-25114297 — overseas_bks@yahoo.co.in

OVERSEAS PRESS (INDIA) PVT. LTD., New Delhi
✆ 23269503, Fax: 91-11-23250262 — info@overseaspub.com

OXFORD & IBH PUBLISHING CO. PVT. LTD., New Delhi
✆ (O) 23415896, 23416951, 23324578, 23320518
(R) 26862327, 26967714, Fax: 51517559 — oxford@vsnl.com

OXFORD BOOK & STATIONERY CO., New Delhi
✆ (O) 23315896, 23315308 (R) 24623066
Fax: 91-11-23713275 — oxford.pubs.@axcess.net.in

OXFORD BOOK COMPANY, Jaipur
✆ 2762072, 2594705, Fax: 0141-2593892 — abdpublishers@rediffmail.com

OXFORD BOOK STORE GALLERY, Kolkata
✆ 2298509, 2297662, Fax: 22499250 — oxfordbooksstore@hotmail.com, a-jairam@hotmail.com

OXFORD EXPORT HOUSE, New Delhi
✆ 23324578, 23320518, Fax: 23710090 — oxford@vsnl.com

OXFORD UNIVERSITY PRESS, New Delhi
✆ 43600300, Fax: 91-11-23360897 — admin.in@oup.com

P

P.A.V. AUDIO VISUAL, Delhi
✆ 22112976, 22286071, Fax: 22112976 — pavaudiovisual@yahoomail.com

P.B. INTERNATIONAL, Kolkata
✆ 033-23541386 ▮ 9831143468
Fax: 033-25520278 — pbinternational@rediffmail.com

P.B.D. PUBLISHERS & DISTRIBUTORS (REGD.), Delhi
✆ 23285501, 23260329, Fax: 23285501 — info@neerajbooks.com

P.C. JAIN & COMPANY, Imphal
✆ 0385-221756, 225004 — newsagency1@rediffmail.com

P.C.M. BOOK SHOP, Chennai
✆ 044-24337329 — mdspcm@yahoo.com

P.G.T. BOOKS INTERNATIONAL, New Delhi
✆ (O) 26167998 (R) 25500143, Fax: 011-26196409 — pgtbooks@indiatimes.com

P.K. ENTERPRISES, Hyderabad
✆ 23308329 — rahulchoudhary18@hotmail.com

P.S. MULTIMEDIA, New Delhi
✆ 23278368, 23261465, Fax: 91-11-23264368 — psm@dkpd.com, dkpd@del3.vsnl.net.in

PACIFIC PRESS, Delhi
✆ 27108207, 32324154 — pacificpress@red.com

PAI & COMPANY; Cochin
✆ 0484-2382068, 2381515, Fax: 2353163 — paico@paicoindia.com

PAI & SONS, Coimbatore
✆ 2393024, 5586050 — paisons@md3.vsnl.net.in

PAL BOOK DISTRIBUTORS, Ludhiana
✆ (O) 0161-2446858 (R) 2459923 — book-pal@yahoo.com

PALANI PARAMOUNT PUBLICATIONS, Palani
✆ 04545-242332, 243212, Fax: 244316 — spalani1@md4.vsnl.net.in

PALANIAPPA BROTHERS, Chennai
✆ (O) 044-28132863 (R) 28275685, Fax: 28133350 — sales@palbrothers.com

PALGRAVE MACMILLAN, New Delhi
✆ 23272010, 23259643, Fax: 23272010 — jagat@del2.vsnl.net.in

PALJOR PUBLICATION, New Delhi
✆ (O) 24325643, 24325644, 25312952
(R) 24312416, Fax: 011-24325643 — palpub@vsnl.com, palpub@tibet.net

PANCHSHEEL PRAKASHAN, Jaipur
✆ 2315072, Fax: 2326554 — panchsheel_j@sify.com

PANIMA BOOK DISTRIBUTORS, New Delhi
✆ 23264039, 23282623, Fax: 23264039 — panimabooks@satyam.net.in

PANIMA EDUCATIONAL BOOK AGENCY/ PANIMA PUBLISHING CORPORATION, New Delhi
✆ 23264039, 23282623, 26866488
Fax: 26863145 — panimabooks@satyam.net.in

PANKAJ PUBLICATION, New Delhi
© 30955771, 23363395, 23348805, Fax: 23363395 — vikas@pankajbooks.com, book@vsnl.com

PANKAJ PUBLICATIONS INTERNATIONAL, Delhi
© 33100770 — support@pankajpublicationint.com, pankaj_arora@sandesh.com

PANTHER PUBLISHERS PVT. LTD., Bangalore
© 5505836, 5505837, 5537145, Fax: 5505981 — panther_publishers@vsnl.com

PARAGON ENTERPRISE, Kolkata
© 2808924, 2808925, Fax: 2801620 — southest@cal2.vsnl.net.in

PARAMVIR ENTERPRISES, Jalandhar
© 236248, 241248, Fax: 241248 — parament@jla.vsnl.net.in

PARAS AGENCIES, Delhi
© 22391636 — paras_agencies@rediffmail.com

PARAS MEDICAL BOOKS PVT. LTD., Hyderabad
© 66821071, 91-40-24731903 — parasmedicalbooks@gmail.com

PARAS MEDICAL PUBLISHERS, Hyderabad
© 24742239, Fax: 91-40-66366642 — parasmedpub@hotmail.com, parasmedicalbooks@indiainfo.com

PARAVIDYA RESEARCH FOUNDATION, New Delhi
© 22202142, 22210663, 22424057, Fax: 22424057 — healing@bol.net.in

PARIDRISHYA PRAKASHAN, Mumbai
© 22019268, 38918055, Fax: 22019268 — hindikitaben@rediffmail.com

PARIJAT PRAKASHAN, Patna
9910170711 — parijat.publication@gmail.com

PARIKALPANA PRAKASHAN, Lucknow
© 91-522-2786782, 3096414 — parikalpana@gmail.com

PARIMAL PUBLICATION, Delhi
© 91-11-23845456, 47015168, 65441516 — parimal@ndf.vsnl.net.in

PARIVARTAN PUBLICATION, Delhi
9873383398 — parivartanpublication@yahoo.co.in

PARRAGON PUBLISHING INDIA PVT. LTD., New Delhi
© 42828750, Fax: 91-11-42828756 — sales@parragonpublishing.co.in

PARROT READS PUBLISHERS, New Delhi
© 26492710-11, Fax: 91-11-26742382 — rajivjha@parrotreads.com

PASCHIMBANGA PRAKASHAK SABHA, Kolkata
© 23506720, Fax: 2413852 — asen.central@axcess.net.in

PATRIKA BOOKING CENTRE, New Delhi
© 25761619, 30932031, Fax: 25720390 — patrika@vsnl.com

PATRIKA SYNDICATE PVT. LTD., New Delhi
© 23274443, 23259353, 23255118, Fax: 23261290 — bidel@ndb.vsnl.net.in

PAULINE BOOK & MEDIA CENTRE, New Delhi
© 25851260, 25785465 — paulinedel@mantraonline

PAULSON PRESS PVT. LTD., New Delhi
© 23547532, 55379214, Fax: 91-11-23545182 — paulson@nde.vsnl.net.in, paulson_press_ltd@vsnl.net.in

PAVAI PUBLICATIONS, Chennai
© 28482441, Fax: 91-11-28482973 — pavai123@yahoo.com

PEACOCK BOOKS, New Delhi
✆ (O) 23273880, 23285873 (R) 25413460 Fax: 23285873 — info@atlanticbooks.com

PEARL BOOKS, New Delhi
✆ 23258245, 23258254, Fax: 91-11-23280028 — pearlbooks.delhi@gmail.com

PEARL (INDIA) PUBLISHING HOUSE PVT. LTD., New Delhi
✆ 25812253, 25815254, Fax: 25754739 — info@sumanprakashan.com, info@pearl-india.com

PEARSON EDUCATION (SINGAPORE) PVT. LTD., Delhi
✆ 22146067-70, Fax: 22146071 — mail@personed.co.in

PEEPEE PUBLISHERS AND DISTRIBUTORS (P) LTD., Delhi
✆ 91-11-55195868 Mobile: 9811156083 — pawan_vij@peepeepub.com, anupam_vij@peepeepub.com, peepee160@yahoo.com, peepee160@rediffmail.com

PEHEL - BFC, New Delhi
✆ 51640571-76 — kirans@pehel-bfc.org

PEN-TIMES PUBLISHERS AND DISTRIBUTORS, Delhi
✆ 33336030 Mobile: 9891460555, Fax: 22561933 — pentimes@yahoo.com

PEN BOOKS PVT. LTD., Cochin
✆ (O) 0484-2621668, 2620377, 2625414 (R) 2620668, Fax: 2620668 — penbooks@md3.vsnl.net.in

PENCRAFT INTERNATIONAL, New Delhi
✆ 27120156, 23277084, Fax: 27443784 — pencraft@nda.vsnl.net.in

PENGUIN BOOKS INDIA PVT. LTD., New Delhi
✆ 26494401, 26494405/02, Fax: 26494403 — penguin@del2.vsnl.net.in

PENMAN PUBLISHERS, Delhi
✆ 27112806, Fax: 2398642 — penman_bks@hotmail.com

PENTA BOOK DISTRIBUTORS, Calicut
✆ 0495-2725746 — pentabooks@yahoo.com

PENTAGON PRESS, New Delhi
✆ (O) 23415198, 23415205 (R) 25137459 Fax: 51517091 — rajanarya@vsnl.com

PENTAGON PRESS, New Delhi
✆ 25490455, 25491263, Fax: 25403549 — rajanarya@vsnl.com

PENTAGON PRESS, New Delhi
✆ 26491568, 64706243, Fax: 91-11-26490600 — rajan@pentagon-press.com, pentagon_press@yahoo.com

PEPPIN THOMAS, Thrissur
✆ 235292, 27033487, 2335593 — cosmobooks@sancharnet.in

PETER LANG PUBLISHING GROUP, New Delhi
✆ 64613894, 91-11-26742382 — info@parrotreads.com

PHARMA BOOK SYNDICATE, Hydrabad
✆ 23445666, Fax: 91-40-23445611 — info@pharmabooksyndicate.com

PHAROS MEDIA & PUBLISHING PVT. LTD., New Delhi
✆ 26927483, 26932825, 26822883 Fax: 26835825, 24697333 — zik.pharos@axcess.net.in

PHILHAL, Patna
✆ 2500476 — filhal@rediffmail.com

PHOENIX PUBLISHING HOUSE PVT. LTD., New Delhi
✆ 23276688, 23276611, 23276625, 23259222 23270743, Fax: 23283141
✉ ouseph@del3.vsnl.net.in

PIE EDUCATION, New Delhi
✆ 26527444, 26568545, Fax: 26962662
✉ info@pieeducation.com

PILGRIMS BOOK HOUSE, Varanasi
✆ 2314060, 2312496, 2312456 ▮ 9811300970
Fax: 91-542-2312456
✉ pilgrimsbooks@sify.com, pilgrims@satyam.net.in

PINKY BOOK DISTRIBUTORS, Delhi
✆ 23246089, 23246362, Fax: 23246535
✉ ouseph@del13.vsnl.net, pinky@ndb.vsnl.net.in

PINNACLES BOOKS PVT. LTD., Patna
✆ (O) 2671356, 2689717 (R) 2674079
Fax: 2670010
✉ bbpdpat@gisclol.vsnl.net.in

PITAMBAR PUBLISHING COMPANY PVT. LTD., New Delhi
✆ (O) 23670067, 23625528, (R) 25883437
Fax: 91-11-25883427 ▮ 9811080291
✉ pitambar@bol.net.in

PITARA-EKLAVYA, Bhopal
✆ 2463380, Fax: 91-755-2461703
✉ pitara@eklavya.in

PIXIE PUBLICATIONS INDIA (P) LIMITED, Karnal
✆ 2242174, 2242175, Fax: 2204619
✉ info@poultrytimesofindia.com

PLANET MULTI MEDIA, New Delhi
✆ 25740588, 25730546
✉ sales@cdrom-india.com

PLANMAN MEDIA PVT. LTD., New Delhi
✆ 41799616, Fax: 91-11-41799555
✉ bhupinn@yahoo.co.in

POINTER PUBLISHERS, Jaipur
✆ 2568159, 2518286, Fax: 2568159, 2562000
✉ pointerpub@hotmail.com

POLYMER RESEARCH CENTRE, Bangalore
✆ 5289359
✉ pcenterbangalore@usa.net

POOJA PRAKASHAN, New Delhi
✆ 23533737 ▮ 9811249405
✉ poojaprakashan@yahoo.com, surendersharmadel@hotmail.com

POONAM BOOK SERVICE CENTRE, New Delhi
✆ (O) 30908197, 23285054 (R) 22777367
Fax: 23285055
✉ pbsco2@yahoo.com, poonam02@rediffmail.com

POORNA PUBLICATIONS, Kozhikode
✆ 0495-2720085-6, Fax: 0495-2721414
✉ tbsbook@vsnl.com

POORVANCHAL PRAKASHAN, Delhi
✆ 22178983
✉ poorvanchalprakashan@yahoo.com

POOVAZHAKI PATHIPAGAM, Chennai
✆ 24800325, 24833180, Fax: 24811755
✉ aruram@md2.vsnl.net.in

POPULAR BOOK HOUSE, Pune
✆ 5671737, 5673315, Fax: 2375600
✉ pop@pn2.vsnl.net.in

POPULAR PRAKASHAN (P) LTD., Mumbai
✆ 23530303, Fax: 91-22-23535294
✉ sales@popularprakashan.com

PRABHAT BOOK CENTRE, Gwalior
✆ 322879, 334108
✉ anirudh110@sify.com

PRABHAT BOOK DISTRIBUTORS, Delhi
✆ 22436362, 22427066
✉ exposofttech@rediffmail.com

PRABHAT PRAKASHAN, New Delhi
✆ (O) 23289555, 23289666, 23289777, 23264676
(R) 22540400, Fax: 23253233
✉ prabhat@indianabooks.com, prabhat@vsnl.com

PRABHU BOOK HOUSE, Kochi
✆ 0484-354012
✉ skrpai@stayam.net.in

PRABHU BOOK SERVICE, Gurgaon
✆ (O) 26320588 (R) 26306778, Fax: 26329805
✉ prabook@del3.vsnl.net.in

PRABHUS BOOKS, Thiruvananthapuram
✆ (O) 0471-2478397, 2473496 (R) 2478393
Fax: 91-471-2473496
✉ books@prabhusbooks.com

PRACHI (INDIA) PVT. LTD., Delhi
✆ 23656678, 23659695, Fax: 23659209
✉ info@prachipublications.com

PRACHI PUBLICATIONS (INDIA) PVT. LTD., Delhi
✆ 23653191, Fax: 91-11-23659209
✉ info@prachipublications.com

PRAGATI BOOKS PVT. LTD., Pune
✆ (O) 020-24450842, 24451512, 4022708
(R) 25430133, Fax: 24495422
✉ pragatibooks@vsnl.net

PRAGATI PERIODICALS SUBSCRIPTION AGENCY, Delhi
✆ 27521237 ▮ 9810202312, Fax: 27521237
✉ ppsa@vsnl.net, ppsa@mantraonline.com

PRAGATI PRAKASHAN, Meerut
✆ (O) 2661657, 2640642, 2651907
(R) 2663838, 2654661, Fax: 2663838
✉ pragatiprakashan@yahoo.com

PRAGATI PUBLICATIONS, New Delhi
✆ 23280585
✉ pragati1@ndf.vsnl.net.in

PRAJASAKTI BOOK HOUSE, Hyderabad
✆ 23660013, 27635136, Fax: 27639921
✉ pbhhyd@yahoo.co.in

PRAKASH AND COMPANY, Meerut
✆ 2771049
✉ jaiprakash_co@rediffmail.com

PRAKASH BOOK DEPOT, New Delhi
✆ 23416566, 23416897, Fax: 23246975
✉ accounts@prakashbooks.com

PRAKASH BOOK DISTRIBUTORS, Delhi
✆ 22118400, 22138251, 22181230, Fax: 22118400
✉ prakashbooksd@rediffmail.com

PRAKASH BOOKS INDIA PVT. LTD., New Delhi
✆ 23247062-65, Fax: 91-11-23246975
✉ sales@prakashbooks.com, info@prakashbooks.com

PRAKASH PUBLICATIONS, Muzaffarnagar
✆ (O) 0131-2403263, 2433530
(R) 2406562, 2403354, Fax: 2430676
✉ manojbathla@hotmail.com

PRAMCO (INDIA) PVT. LTD., New Delhi
✆ 26922072, 26934735, Fax: 26934734
✉ pramcolearning@vsnl.net, pramco@usa.net

PRANIC HEALING FOUNDATION OF DELHI, New Delhi
✆ 28660565/66/67, Fax: 91-11-28660567
✉ phfd@vsnl.com

PRANJAL ART PUBLISHERS, Lucknow
▮ 9935799066
✉ pranjal_art@gmail.com

PRASANNA TRUST, Bangalore
✆ 41535832, Fax: 91-80-23444112
✉ prasannatrust@vsnl.com

PRASAR BOOKSELLERS, Bhavnagar
✆ 0278-568452 — prasaradl@sancharnet.in

PRASHANT BOOK AGENCY, New Delhi
✆ 65398961, Fax: 91-11-23251390 — prashantbooks@hotmail.com

PRASHANT BOOK HOUSE & PUBLICATIONS, Jalgaon
✆ (O) 0257-2227231 (R) 0257-2252374 — prashantbook@yahoo.com

PRASHANT PUBLICATIONS, Delhi
✆ (O) 27480144, 27482403 (R) 27481259
Fax: 27480144, 27482403 — prashantbooks@indiatimes.com, prashantbooks@yahoo.co.in

PRATAP HOMOEO PHARMACY & CLINIC, New Delhi
✆ 24623859, 24645728, 24623856, Fax: 24647774 — kpsdhama@bol.net.in

PRATHAM BOOKS, New Delhi
✆ 65684113, Fax: 91-11-26716083 — info@prathambooks.org

PRATIBHA PRAKASHAN, Delhi
✆ 91-11-23848485, 23840390
Mobile: 9350884227, 9350906327 — info@pratibhabooks.com

PRATIBHA PRATISHTHAN, New Delhi
✆ 23257555, Fax: 23253233 — prabhat@indianabooks.com

PRATIYOGITA DARPAN, Agra
✆ 2531101, 2602653, Fax: 2531940 — upkarl@sancharnet.in

PRATIYOGITA SAHITYA SERIES, Agra
✆ 351665, 353400, Fax: 351568 — kanhaiya@ndb.vsnl.net.in

PRAVEEN PRAKASHAN, Delhi
Mobile: 9312492269 — praveenbooksdist@rediffmail.com

PRAVEEN PRAKASHAN, New Delhi
✆ 91-11-65651098 — info@praveenbooks.com

PRAYAS PUBLISHERS & BOOKSELLERS, Kolkata
✆ 2241-0176, Fax: 25124630 — prayasbook2@hotmail.com

PRECISE COMPUTER TOOLING CO., New Delhi
✆ 26836173, Fax: 26813896 — elcon@del2.vsnl.net.in

PREFACE BOOKS, Mumbai
✆ 24988054, Fax: 24988048 — preface@vsnl.com

PREMA PIRASURAM, Chennai
✆ 24800325, 24833180, Fax: 044-24811755 — aruramdmd2.vsnl.net.in

PREMIER PUBLISHING PVT. LTD., Chennai
premierbooks@hotmail.com, manahabi2002@hotmail.com

PRENTICE-HALL OF INDIA PRIVATE LIMITED, New Delhi
✆ 23411779, 23418078, 23415326
Fax: 91-11-23417179 — phi@phindia.com

PRESCHOOL LEARNERS.COM, New Delhi
✆ 24311060 — sireeshbhatnagar@hotmail.com

PRESENTATION BOOKS, Srinagar
presentbooks@yahoo.com

PRESTIGE TUTORIAL SAMITHI, Uttar Pradesh
✆ 91-5568-222005, 248180 — prestigetutorial@mail.com

PRIME BOOK SHOP, Nagpur
✆ (O) 2524659 (R) 2532544, Fax: 0712-2537896 — primebookshop@hotmail.com

PRIME MAG. SUBSCRIPTION SERVICES PVT. LTD., Delhi
✆ 27441746, Fax: 27210420 — primemag@mantraonline.com

PRIME PUBLISHING HOUSE, Ghaziabad
✆ 95120-2900076 ▮ 9818478547 — primehouse@rediffmail.com

PRIME TIME PUBLICATIONS (P) LTD., New Delhi
✆ 25713032, 25820554, Fax: 25741149 — hitads@ndb.vsnl.net.in

PRINT & BLOCK CONCERN, Kolkata
✆ 22339207, 22392696, Fax: 22392696 — kishorebinani@vsnl.net

PRINT INN (HOUSE OF BOOKS), Pune
print.inn@netkracker.com

PRINT LINE BOOKS, Delhi
✆ 22163582, 43023727, Fax: 91-11-22143023 — tinytotpub@hotmail.com

PRINT PUBLISHING, New Delhi
✆ 26405715, Fax: 26405716 — khuranas@del2.vsnl.net.in

PRINTS INDIA, New Delhi
✆ 23268645, 23271378, 23257864
Fax: 23275542, 6475450 — printsin@nde.vsnl.net.in

PRISM BOOK PVT. LTD., Bangalore
✆ 26713991, 26714108, 26714060
Fax: 26713979 — pranesh@prismbooks.com, prism@vsnl.com

PRITHVI BOOK AGENCY, Bangalore
✆ 6703939, 6701060 — prithvibooks@hotmail.com

PRITIMAN PRAKASHAN PVT. LTD., Bhopal
✆ 550291, 555442, Fax: 555449 — rajonas@vsnl.com

PRIYA BOOK DISTRIBUTORS, Delhi
✆ (R) 35902598 ▮ 9811167944 — priyabook_prompt@yahoo.com.sg

PRIYAM BOOK DEPOT, New Delhi
✆ 91-11-25639146 — priyambookdepot@rediffmail.com

PRODUCTIVITY PRESS (I) (P) LTD., Chennai
✆ 24344519, Fax: 044-24342009 — k.k.cheenu@ppl.sprintrgp.ems.vsnl.net.in, ksm@md2.vsnl.net.ins

PROFESSIONAL BOOK HOUSE, Mumbai
✆ 28728072 ▮ 9821226410 — professionalbkhouse.com.india

PROFESSIONAL BOOK SERVICE, Hyderabad
✆ 27664180, 55595618 — huk2bux_pbs@yaboo.com.in, pbs_prob@tatanova.com

PROFESSIONAL BOOKS TRADER, Chennai
✆ 044-24723998 — pbtvijay@eth.net

PROGRESS PUBLISHERS, Delhi
✆ (O) 22243463 (R) 22212513, Fax: 22211791 — progress.india@vsnl.com

PROGRESSIVE CURRICULUM MANAGEMENT PVT. LTD., Kochi
✆ 2354047, 2352778, 2333604, Fax: 2339823 — ekmpcm@sancharnet.in

PROMILLA & CO., PUBLISHERS, New Delhi
✆ 26864124, 33335186 — ashok@ashokbutani.com, abutani@biblioasia.com

PROMINENT PUBLISHERS DISTRIBUTORS, Delhi
✆ 22158906, 22150526, Fax: 011-22140454 — vipinm48@hotmail.com, prominent_publishers@hotmail.com

PROMOD BATRA VIJAY BATRA & ASSOCIATES, New Delhi
✆ 24359898, 24356038, Fax: 91-11-24357980 — thinkinc@vsnl.com, thinkinc@successcorners.com

PSC & SCHMIDT PERIODICALS, Lucknow
✆ 2789506, 91-522-4012302 — sanjay@periodicals.com

PUBLICATION BUREAU, Delhi
✆ 23676503, 23656950 ▮ 9811647980
Fax: 23656950 — pubbureau@now-india.net.in, sales@publicationbureau.com

PUBLICATION SCHEME, Jaipur
✆ 5104038, 2601801, 2320680, Fax: 2376922 — parampsj@datainfosys.net

PUBLICATIONS DIVISION, New Delhi
✆ 24365610, 24367260, Fax: 91-11-24365609 — dpd@sb.nic.in

PUBLISHERS & BOOKSELLERS GUILD, Kolkata
✆ 23604588, 23544417, 23577717, Fax: 23604566 — guild@cal2.vsnl.net.in

PUNASCHA, Kolkata
✆ 22413572, Fax: 91-33-23732427 — pnbooks@sify.com

PUNEET BOOKS, Jaipur
▮ 9414035174 — vikal_goyal@yahoo.com

PUNJAB BOOK CENTRE, Chandigarh
✆ 232052, 2701952, Fax: 2601304 — punjabbookcentre@usa.net

PUNJABI ACADEMY, New Delhi
✆ 23616265, 23615979, 23616243
Fax: 23615979 — punjabiacademydelhi@rediffmail.com

PURVODAYA PRAKASHAN, New Delhi
✆ 23274956, Fax: 91-11-43541934 — purvodaya1950@yahoo.com

PUSHPAK SALES AGENCY, New Delhi
✆ 23257939, 23258184, Fax: 23258184 — pushpakbooks@yahoo.com

PUSTAK BAZAR COM, New Delhi
✆ 26410316, 26951188, Fax: 25816394 — corpris@vsnl.com

PUSTAK BHAWAN, Kanpur
✆ 2365223 — pustakbhawan@yahoo.com

PUSTAK MAHAL, New Delhi
✆ 23272783-84, 23276539, Fax: 91-11-23260518 — pustakmahal@vsnl.net.in, info@pustakmahal.com

PUSTAK PETH VITRAN, Aurangabad
✆ 347271 — pustakpeth@yahoo.com

PUSTAKALATO SNEHAM, Secunderabad
✆ 27015295 — sureshkosaraju@yahoo.co.in

PUSTAKYAN, New Delhi
✆ 23274513, 23278858 — subodhbooks@vsnl.net

Q

QAZI PUBLISHERS & DISTRIBUTORS, New Delhi
✆ 24352732, 23259526, Fax: 24352048 — qazipublishers@yahoo.com

QUALITY SALES & SERVICES, Thiruvananthapuram
✆ 2326789, 2332158, Fax: 2491491 — qssbooks@rediffmail.com

QUARTETTE BOOKS DISTRIBUTORS P. LTD., Mumbai
✆ 24965864, 24965865, Fax: 24965866 — qartett@bom3.vsnl.net.in

QUEST BOOKS COMPANY, New Delhi
✆ 56020164, 56020178, 26264946, 26264947 — qbc@bol.net.in
9811224190, Fax: 51642947

QUIXOT MULTIMEDIA PVT. LTD., New Delhi
✆ 28313048, Fax: 91-11-28313048 — sales@quixotmultimedia.com

R

R. CHAND & COMPANY, New Delhi
✆ 23273566, 23257796, Fax: 23268760 — rchand-co@rediffmail.com

R.A. BOOK AGENCY, Delhi
✆ (O) & (R) 22430805, 22513962 9810158917 — raba1@sify.com, raba@del2vsnl.net.in
Fax: 91-11-22430805

R.B.S.A. PUBLISHERS, Jaipur
✆ 2575826, Fax: 91-141-2575826 — info@rbsapublishers.com

R.K. BOOKS, New Delhi
✆ (O) 23278337, 23261774 (R) 22048678 — rkbooks@vsnl.net
9312654192, Fax: 91-11-51562798

R.K. BOOKS AGENCIES, Nanded
✆ 02462-33655, Fax: 51955 — ek_patil2001@yahoo.com

R.K. TECHNO SCIENCE AGENCY, New Delhi
✆ (O) 26524341 (R) 26969531 — rktsa@ndf.vsnl.net.in
Fax: 011-26524769

R.K. PUBLISHERS & DISTRIBUTORS, New Delhi
✆ 23272868 9810828952 — rkpddelhi@yahoo

R.K.V. MEDIA PVT. LTD., New Delhi
✆ 41651841-2, Fax: 91-11-41651843 — wecare@eternall.org.in

R.N.B. MERCHANTILE PVT. LTD./ R.N.B. OVERSEAS PVT. LTD., New Delhi
✆ 25166761, Fax: 25447253 — info@rambajaj.com

R.R. SHETH & CO., Ahmedabad ✆ (O) 25356573 (R) 26589508, Fax: 25321732	sales@rrsheth.com
R.S. BOOK & PRINTS, New Delhi ✆ 26257095, Fax: 26253011	rsbooks@spectranet.com
R.S. PUBLISHERS & DISTRIBUTORS, Navi Mumbai ✆ 27579974/75	rspdbooks@hotmail.com
R.V. PUBLISHERS, Faridabad ✆ 3315310, Fax: 3710090	rajuprim@vsnl.com
RACHNA BOOKS & PERIODICALS, Gangtok ✆ 03592-24336	rachna_books@yahoo.co.in
RACHNA PRAKASHAN PVT. LTD., Ghaziabad ✆ 32980, Fax: 32982	rachnaprakashan@mantraonline.com
RACHNA SAGAR (P) LTD., New Delhi ✆ (O) 23285568-69, 23246027, 23201691 (R) 27459316, 27418469, Fax: 23243519	rachnasagar@hotmail.com
RADHA KRISHNA ANAND & CO., Jammu ✆ (O) 2546691 (R) 248357, Fax: 2578357	radhakrishananand2000@rediffmail.com
RADHA PUBLICATIONS, New Delhi ✆ 91-11-23254306	radhapublications@yahoo.com
RADHAKRISHNA PRAKASHAN PVT. LTD., New Delhi ✆ 23266498, 23276379, Fax: 91-11-23278144	info@radhakrishanprakashan.com
RADICA INFORMATICS, New Delhi ✆ 22196636	gku_1@yahoo.com
RADICAL BOOKS PVT. LTD., New Delhi ✆ 23283639, Fax: 91-121-2521607	ck@radicalbooks.co.in
RAHUL FOUNDATION, Lucknow ✆ 2383928	rahulfoundation@rediffmail.com
RAHUL FOUNDATION, Gorakhpur ✆ 2241922, Fax: 3096414	rahulfoundation@rediffmail.com
RAINBOW BOOK PUBLISHERS, Chengannur ✆ 2426427	nomarainbow@sify.com
RAINBOW PUBLISHERS LTD., Noida ✆ 91-24584977, 011-22724314, 23951378 ▮ 9810579302, Fax: 23940154	rainbow_p@vsnl.net, yaten@nda.vsnl.net.in
RAJ BOOK CENTRE, Delhi ✆ 27454933, 27652926, Fax: 27444926	jatin159@yahoo.com, jain159@rediffmail.com
RAJ KAMAL PRAKASHAN PVT. LTD., New Delhi ✆ 23274463, 23288769, Fax: 23278144	rajkamalprakashan@email.com
RAJKIRAN BOOK AGENCY, Delhi ✆ 91-11-27613386	rajkiranbooks@yahoo.co.uk
RAJ PUBLISHING HOUSE, Jaipur ✆ 2622141, 2650410	rajpublishing@satyam.net.in
RAJA LAXMI BOOK HOUSE, Hyderabad ✆ 23402835, 55585883, Fax: 55363209	rlbhpra2002@yahoo.com
RAJA POCKET BOOKS, Delhi ✆ 27611410, 27612036, 23251092, 23251109 Fax: 27611227	sales@rajcomics.com

RAJASTHAN ADULT EDUCATION ASSOCIATION, Jaipur
✆ 2517464, 2510912, Fax: 2517464 — rajadult@jp1.dot.net.in

RAJASTHAN HINDI GRANTH AKADEMI, Jaipur
✆ 2711129, Fax: 91-141-2710341 — hindgranth@indiatimes.com

RAJASTHAN PATRIKA PVT. LTD., Jaipur
✆ 39404142, Fax: 91-141-2566011 — info@rajasthanpatrika.com

RAJASTHANI GRANTHAGAR, Jodhpur
✆ (O) 2623933 (R) 2432567, Fax: 2611555 — rgranthagar@satyam.net.in

RAJAT BOOK CORNER, Amritsar
✆ (O) 2223055 (R) 2212747 — happyrajan@rediffmail.com

RAJBHASHA VIBHAG, New Delhi
✆ 24617695, 24698054, 24617807, Fax: 24611031 — nicdol@alpha.nic.in

RAJESH JAIN & CO., Delhi
✆ 91-11-23868005 — rajeshjain@india.com

RAJESH PUBLICATIONS, New Delhi
✆ 91-11-23274550 — rajeshpublications@rediffmail.com

RAJESHWAR BOOKS PVT. LTD., New Delhi
✆ 26177569, Fax: 91-11-26183871 — rajeshwarbooks@gmail.com

RAJESHWAR BOOKS PVT. LTD., New Delhi
✆ 26108016, 26177569, Fax: 26108016 — rajeshwarbooks@vsnl.com

RAJHANS PRAKASHAN, Pune
✆ (O) 022-24473459, 24465063
(R) 25435113, 25442113, Fax: 24473459 — rajhans1@pn2.vsnl.net.in

RAJHAUNS VITARAN, Goa
✆ 2220320, 2232177 — rdbhide@goacom.com

RAJKAMAL PRAKASHAN (P) LTD., New Delhi
✆ 23274463, 23288769, Fax: 23278144, 23251803 — info@rajkamalprakashan.com

RAJPAL & SONS, Delhi
✆ 23865483, 23869812, Fax: 91-11-23867791 — mail@rajpalsons.com

RAJUSHA PUBLICATION, Delhi
✆ 22175255, 31049485, Fax: 22968809 — rajushapublication@msn.com

RAJYA SABHA SECRETARIAT, New Delhi
✆ 23034160, Fax: 91-11-23013917 — rssa@sansad.nic.in

RAM ADVANI BOOKSELLERS, Lucknow
✆ 0522-2224057, Fax: 0522-2223511 — radvani@sancharnet.in

RAM CHANDER & SONS, New Delhi
✆ 23412065, 23416276, Fax: 23411484 — sundra@mantraonline.com

RAMPUR RAZA LIBRARY, Rampur
✆ 2325045, 2327244, Fax: 91-595-2340548 — whsiddiqui@rediffmail.com

RAMA BROTHERS INDIA PVT. LTD., New Delhi
✆ (O) 25727313, 25815936 (R) 25875288
▮ 9811026021, Fax: 25815936 — ramabrothers@mantraonline.com, naval_passi@mantraonline.com

RAMAKRISHNA MATH, Hyderabad
✆ 27633937, Fax: 27633936 — rkmath@hd2.dot.net.in

RAMAKRISHNA MISSION, New Delhi
✆ 23587110, 23583023, Fax: 23580848 — rkndlh@ndf.vsnl.net.in, ashram@rkmissiondel.org, rkmissiondelhi@vsnl.com

RAMAKRISHNA NEWS AGENCIES, Hyderabad
✆ 24614641, 24602491, Fax: 24614346 — rknewsagencies@rediffmail.com

RAMAN MEDIA NETWORK, New Delhi
✆ 26975809 ▮ 9810319059 — rmnindia@yahoo.com

RAMASHRAYA BOOK DEPOT, Dharwar
✆ (O) 2442487 (R) 2740515, 2740998 — ramashraya_pub@yahoo.com

RAMESH BOOK DEPOT, Jaipur
✆ 2220742, Fax: 91-141-2220742 — sumeetchandok@hotmail.com

RAMESH BOOK DEPOT, New Delhi
✆ 51637730-2, Fax: 51637730 — sumeetchandak@hotmail.com

RAMESH PUBLISHING HOUSE, New Delhi
✆ 23275124, Fax: 91-11-23275224 — rphbooks@nda.vsnl.net.in

RAMNIKA FOUNDATION, New Delhi
✆ 24658368 — shilpayan@mantramail.com

RANDOM HOUSE GROUP, New Delhi
✆ 29818663, Fax: 29818663 — randomhouse@vsnl.net

RANDOM HOUSE PUBLISHERS INDIA PVT. LTD. (THE), Noida
✆ 4607500, Fax: 91-120-4607518 — contact@randomhouse.co.in

RANDOM HOUSE PUBLISHERS INDIA PVT. LTD., New Delhi
✆ 41528305-06, Fax: 91-11-41528307 — nskrishna@randomhouse.co.in

RANEE PUBLICATIONS, New Delhi
✆ 23251502, Fax: 23276025 — raneepublications@vsnl.com

RANG PRAKASHAN/JAINSON BOOK SHOP, Indore
✆ 2538787, Fax: 91-731-2469627 — info@jainsonbookworld.com

RANI PUBLICATIONS, Chennai
✆ 25324771 — rani.chen@gems.vsnl.net.in

RANJAN PUBLICATIONS, New Delhi
✆ 23278835, 23282998, Fax: 23275124 — ranjanpublications@rediffmail.com

RASHMIC BANSAL, New Delhi
✆ 26928653, 26928658, Fax: 26919528 — bansal@vastushastri.com

RASHTRIYA SANSKRIT SANSTHAN, New Delhi
✆ 28524993, 28524995, 28520976, 28520977
Fax: 91-11-28521948 — rsks@nda.vsnl.net.in

RASHTRIYA SANSKRIT SANSTHAN, Allahabad
✆ 91-11-25540976 — rsks@nda.vsnl.net.in

RASHTRIYA SANSKRIT VIDYAPEETH, Tirupathi
✆ 2286799, Fax: 81-877-2287809 — registrar_rsvp@yahoo.co.in

RASIK ANTARBHARATI, Pune
✆ 91-20-24440730 — rasikantarbharati@vsnl.net

RASTOGI PUBLICATIONS, Meerut
✆ 2510688, 2516080, Fax: 22521545 — info@rastogipublications.com

RATAN PRAKASHAN MANDIR, Agra
✆ 91-562-2520019, 2527465, Fax: 2527463 — sales@ratanprakashan.com

RATAN SUBSCRIPTION SERVICES, New Delhi
✆ 30125002, Fax: 91-11-23240195 — ratansubscription@hotmail.com

RATIONAL BUSINESS CORPORATION, New Delhi
✆ 27462300, 27462700, Fax: 22915357 — ashish@desmat.com

RATNA SAGAR PVT. LTD., Delhi
✆ 27654095-99, 47038000 — rsagar@nda.vsnl.net.in
Fax: 91-11-27650787, 47038099

RAVE MEDIA, New Delhi
✆ 26340503, Fax: 91-11-26349902 — niha@ravemedia.in

RAVI BOOKS, Delhi
✆ 22914588 ▮ 9810554502 — ravibooksdelhi@rediffmail.com

RAVI POCKET BOOKS, Meerut
✆ 91-121-2531011, 2521067 — a2zcomputerbooks@yahoo.co.in

RAVINDER SINGH & SONS, Jalandhar
✆ 91-181-2461681 — arundhi99@hotmail.com

RAWAT BOOKSELLERS, Jaipur
✆ 2651748, 2657006, Fax: 2651748 — rawatbooks@pinkline.net, rawatpublication@hotmail.com

RAWAT PUBLICATIONS, Jaipur
✆ 2651748, 2657006, Fax: 2651748 — info@rawatbooks.com

READ BOOKS, New Delhi
✆ 40529050, Fax: 91-11-40529050 — readbooks@gmail.com

READERS CORNER, Patna
✆ 0612-2225958, Fax: 2221099 — readerscorner1969@rediffmail.com

READERS PUBLICATIONS, Thiruvalla
✆ (O) 0473-2636395 (R) 2619416, Fax: 0473-2631308 — readers@md4.vsnl.net.in

READWELL PUBLICATIONS, New Delhi
✆ 25712649, Fax: 91-11-25812385 — readwell@sify.com

READWORTHY PUBLICATIONS PVT. LTD., New Delhi
✆ 25371324, Fax: 91-11-25371323 — info@readworthypub.com

RED INK LITERARY AGENCY, New Delhi
✆ 24694610, Fax: 91-11-24618637 — anuj.redink@gmail.com

REGENCY PUBLICATIONS, New Delhi
✆ 25883539, 25884571 ▮ 9811011264 — regency@satyam.net.in

REGENERATIONS, New Delhi
✆ 23255799, 23287589, Fax: 91-11-23270385 — aryanbooks@vsnl.com

REKHA BOOK DISTRIBUTORS, Chennai
✆ 28141665 — rekhabhs@md5.vsnl.net.in

REKHA PRAKASHAN, New Delhi
✆ (O) 23279904, 23279907 (R) 26321783 — bnaryan@satyam.net.in
Fax: 91-11-2321783

REKHA PRINTERS PVT. LTD., Delhi
✆ 26830401, 26829337, Fax: 26852280 — krishan@nde.vsnl.net.in

RELIANCE PUBLISHING HOUSE, New Delhi
✆ 25842605, 25842748, 25847377, Fax: 25842605 — reliance@indianbooksindustry.com, rphbooks@indiatimes.com

REM DISTRIBUTORS INDIA, New Delhi
✆ 26535929, 25500998, Fax: 26969159, 26117058 — dkginfo@bol.net.in

REMADHAV PUBLICATIONS PVT. LTD., Ghaziabad
✆ 2754228, Fax: 91-120-2702672 — contace@remadhav.com

RESEARCH FOUNDATION, Mumbai
resfaxexports@indiatimes.com

RESEARCH FOUNDATION FOR SCIENCE TECHNOLOGY AND ECOLOGY, New Delhi
✆ 26968077, 26863772, Fax: 91-11-26856795 — vshiva@vsnl.com

RESEARCH INDIA PRESS, New Delhi
✆ 91-11-26047013 — researchindiapress@yahoo.co.in

RESEARCH INDIA PUBLICATIONS, Delhi
✆ 65394240, Fax: 91-11-27297815 — info@ripublication.com, subscription@ripublication.com, services@ripublication.com

RESEARCH PRESS, New Delhi
✆ 23284894, 23281819, Fax: 91-11-23281819 — researchpress@vsnl.com

RESEARCH TRENDS, Trivandrum
✆ 344424, Fax: 344423 — rtrends@md2.vsnl.net.in

RESEARCHCO BOOK CENTRE, New Delhi
✆ 23240257, Fax: 91-11-23240273 — akjain@del2.vsnl.net.in

RESPONSE BOOKS, New Delhi
✆ 40539222, Fax: 91-11-40539234 — info@sagepub.in

RESPONSE BOOKS, New Delhi
✆ 26491290, Fax: 26491290 — responsebooks@indiasage.com

RGTI BOOK DIVISION, Chennai
✆ 91-44-24335238, 24335272, 32660278 — vijay.k@rgtitech.com

RICHA PRAKASHAN, New Delhi
✆ 24640153, Fax: 24634935 — ragupta@ndb.vsnl.net.in

RICHARDCARSWELL.COM, Delhi
9310260022, Fax: 91-11-23911057 — kaushalgoyal@yahoo.com

RIFCON SAT SAHATIYA KENDRA, Jodhpur
✆ 308155 — rathisuresh@hotmal.com, suresh@sureshrathiindia.com

RISHI EXPORTS, Mumbai
✆ 24925651, 24927383, 24942538
Fax: 022-24950392, 22048163 — ibhpba@vsnl.com

RITANA BOOKS, New Delhi
✆ 24617278, Fax: 24636063 — ritana@vsnl.com

RITWIK PRAKASHAN, New Delhi
✆ 23725470, 23514862
Fax: 23558613, 23542142 — tarunvijay@vsnl.com

RIVERSTONE PRESS, Delhi
✆ 55151448, Fax: 27345935 — riverstonepress@vsnl.net

RIYAZ IMPEX, Mumbai
✆ 23460577, 23473257, Fax: 23471803 — riyazimp@vsnl.com

ROHAN BOOK COMPANY, Delhi
✆ 22303898, Fax: 91-11-22309396 — rohanbooks@gmail.com

ROLI BOOKS (P) LTD., New Delhi
✆ 29212271, 29212782, 40682000
Fax: 91-11-29217185 — info@rolibooks.com, editorial@rolibooks.com

ROMIL PUBLISHERS (P) LTD., Delhi
✆ (O) 22211154, 22436849 (R) 22421652, 22217558
Fax: 011-22212435, 22048017 — romilpub@ndf.vsnl.net.in

ROOPAL BOOK STALL, Nadiad
✆ 02692-235353 — and_roopalbook@rediffmail.com

ROSHANI PRAKASHAN, West Bengal
✆ 91-33-25850249 — roshnaiprakashan@sify.com

ROUTLEDGE (TAYLOR AND FRANCIS GROUP), New Delhi
✆ 23712131, 23351453, Fax: 23712123 — routledge@satyam.net.in

ROY PUBLICATIONS, Patna
✆ 2672544, 2663343, Fax: 2669954 — roy60@sify.com

ROYAL BIBLIOMAN, Bangalore
✆ 080-6615209, 6694074, Fax: 6615209 — bkdas@pacific.net.in

ROYAL BOOK DEPOT, Bhilai
✆ 431093, Fax: 0788-392386 — royalboosks@rediff.com

ROYAL EDUCATIONAL STORES, New Delhi
✆ 27034400, Fax: 91-11-27034832 — info@royaleducationbooks.com

ROYAL PUBLISHERS (PVT.) LTD., New Delhi
✆ (O) 23253648, 23244667 (R) 22821397
Fax: 23250591 — royalpublishers2002@yahoo.co.in

RUPA & CO., Kolkata
✆ 22416597, 22410691, Fax: 22410691 — info@rupabooks.com

S

S.B.D. SUBSCRIPTION SERVICES (SUDARSHAN BOOK DISTRIBUTORS), New Delhi
✆ 25723138, 55450350
Fax: 91-11-25817268 — spdbooks@gmail.com

S. CHAND & COMPANY LTD., New Delhi
✆ 23672080-81-82, Fax: 91-11-23677446 — schand@vsnl.com

S. CHAND TECHNOLOGIES PVT. LTD., New Delhi
✆ 26326022-23, Fax: 26326024 — sctech@vsnl.net

S. DINESH & CO., Jalandhar
✆ 2280208, 2892393, 250979
Fax: 91-181-281980 — dinesh97@jha.vsnl.net.in

S. DINESH & COMPANY, New Delhi
✆ 23250628, 2328260-76, Fax: 0181-2281980 — dinesh97@jla.vsnl.net.in

S.K. KATARIA & SONS, New Delhi
✆ 91-11-23243489 — katariabooks@yahoo.com

S. KARGER (INDIA), New Delhi
✆ 26109931, Fax: 2606504 — fmunshi_unixl@yahoo.co.uk

S. VISWANATHAN (PRINTERS & PUBLISHERS) PVT. LTD., Chennai
✆ (O) 28265623, 28265633 (R) 28263359
Fax: 28256002 — svprint@md2.vsnl.net.in

S.B.P. CONSULTANTS & ENGINEERS PVT. LTD., New Delhi
✆ 23243075, 23284212, Fax: 23243078 — sbpcon@ndf.vsnl.net.in, salls@sbpprojectfinder.com, sbpindia@hotmail.com

S.B.S. PUBLISHERS DISTRIBUTORS, Bangalore
✆ 2262815, 2266088, Fax: 2269648 — sales@sbpprojectfinder.com, sapua@giasbg1.vsnl.net.in

S.E.I. TECHNOLOGIES PVT. LTD., New Delhi
✆ 25755920, 25762725, 25762726
Fax: 011-25766775, 25755000 — seitech@pobox.com

S.K. EDUCATIONALS PVT. LTD., New Delhi
✆ 27158461-63, Fax: 91-11-27158460 — heights@bol.net.in

S.M. BOOK DISTRIBUTORS, New Delhi
✆ (O) & (R) 25751562 ▮ 9810154719, Fax: 25854388 — vipian@rediffmail.com

S.R.C. PUBLISHERS (PVT.) LTD., Hyderabad
✆ 23241033, Fax: 23249722 — srcpublishers@hotmail.com

S.S. EDUCATIONAL (AIDS) STORES, Delhi
✆ 27053526, 27056395 — s.seducationalaids@hotmail.com

S.T. REDDIAR & SONS (QUILON) PVT. LTD., Quilon
✆ 278778, 275140, 277921 — estiar@md4.vsnl.net.in

S.V.S. BOOKS DISTRIBUTORS, Bangalore
✆ 26696039, Fax: 26696039 — svsbooks@gjiasbga.vsnl.net.in

SAAROL HEALTH AND RESEARCH FOUNDATION, New Delhi
✆ 26235168, Fax: 26212016 — info@saaol.com

SABDA, Pondicherry
✆ (O) 2334980, 2223328 (R) 2223367, 2334958
Fax: 2223328 — sabda@sriaurobindoashram.org

SABHARWAL BOOK WHOLESELLERS, New Delhi
✆ (O) 55390704, 23250586 (R) 25764304
▮ 9811220876, Fax: 23279603 — varun.book@yahoo.co.in

SACHI PRAKASHAN, Ghaziabad
✆ 2880329, Fax: 91-120-2880324 — screenindia@gmail.com

SADANA PUBLISHERS & DISTRIBUTORS, Ghaziabad
✆ 2750356 ▮ 9810130829, Fax: 2750356 — vijaysadana@hotmail.com

SAFDAR HASHMI MEMORIAL TRUST (SAHMAT), New Delhi
✆ 23711276, 23323077, Fax: 23351424 — sahmat@nde.vsnl.net.in

SAGAR PUBLICATIONS, New Delhi
✆ 23320648, 23328245, Fax: 24632222 — sagarpub@vsnl.net.in

SAGAR PUBLISHERS & DISTRIBUTORS, Nagpur
✆ 527134, 452735, Fax: 544093 — tcraft@ipindia.com

SAGE PUBLICATIONS INDIA (P) LTD., New Delhi
✆ 40539222, Fax: 91-11-40529234 — info@sagepub.in

SAGE PUBLICATIONS INDIA (P) LTD., New Delhi
✆ 26485884, 26444958, 26453915, Fax: 26472426 — sageind@nda.vsnl.net.in

SAHAJA EXPORTS INTERNATIONAL, Kolkata
✆ 2190466, 2414003, Fax: 033-24192338 — sahityam@cal2.vsnl.net.in

SAHITYA AKADEMI, New Delhi
✆ 23386626-28, Fax: 91-11-23382428 — ecy@ndn.vsnl.net.in, sahityaakademisales@vsnl.net

SAHITYA AMRIT, New Delhi
✆ 23289555, Fax: 91-11-23289666 — info@prabhatbooks.com

SAHITYA BHARTI, Delhi
✆ 22002274, Fax: 91-11-22099764, 22054604 — sahityabharti@yahoo.com, sb@mailz.net

SAHITYA BHAWAN PUBLICATIONS, Agra
✆ 2531013, Fax: 91-562-2531351 — rsvbansal@hotmail.com

SAHITYA BHAWAN PUBLISHERS & DISTRIBUTORS PVT. LTD., Agra
✆ 2523369 Mobile: 9412258080, 9412258081
Fax: 91-562-2858183 — sahityabhawan@dataone.in

SAHITYA PRAKASHAN, Delhi
✆ 22790165 — yogendrapalsahitya@yahoo.com

SAHITYA SADAN, Gaya
✆ 2220500, Fax: 2220600 — sahityasadan@rediffmail.com

SAHITYA UPKRAM, Karnal
Mobile: 9354762343 — sahitya_upkram@yahoo.co.in

SAHITYA VITHI PRAKASHAN, Delhi
Mobile: 9811280634 — drpradeep@mantraonline.com

SAHITYIKA, Kolkata
✆ 28700222, Fax: 24642494 — chitrabhanucomp@vsnl.net

SAHNI PUBLICATIONS, Delhi
✆ 23822006, 23820751, Fax: 91-11-23914283 — sahni@sahnipublications.com

SAHNI PUBLISHERS & DISTRIBUTORS, Gwalior
✆ 0751-540717 — kapilpustaksadan@rediffmail.com

SAI BABA EDUCATIONAL AIDS, Delhi
✆ 22041749, 31054660 Mobile: 9810883413 — saibabaeducationalaids@yahoo.co.in

SAI EARLY LEARNERS PVT. LTD., New Delhi
✆ 26386165, 26387070, Fax: 26383788 — ghai@nde.vsnl.net.in, sterlin.gpvb@axcess.net.in

SAI EDUCATION INTERNATIONAL PUBLISHING CENTRE, Noida
✆ 120-2512116, Fax: 2513226 — humilityseries@rediffmail.com, humilityseries@indiatimes.com

SAI ENTERPRISES, Agra
✆ 2331325, 2330270, 2232021
Fax: 91-562-2310433, 2330270 — rdaultani@hotmail.com

SAI TOWERS PUBLISHING, Bangalore
✆ 28455758, 28451648, Fax: 28451649 — bangalore@saitower@vsnl.com

SAKSHI PRAKASHAN, Delhi
✆ 22324833, Fax: 91-11-22324833 — goelbooks@rediffmail.com

SALONI PUBLISHING HOUSE, New Delhi
✆ (O) 30912396, 33059560 (R) 30915583
Mobile: 9811142321, Fax: 23280611 — salonipublishinghouse@yahoo.com

SAMAY PRAKASHAN, New Delhi
✆ 23272145, 23270889, Fax: 23270889 — samayprakashan@yahoo.co.in

SAMAYANTAR PRAKASHAN, Delhi
✆ 91-11-22744598 — samayantar@yahoo.com

SAMAYIK PRAKASHAN, Delhi
✆ (O) 23282733, 23270715, 23270716
(R) 22175472, 22262499, Fax: 23270715
samayikprakashan@rediffmail.com

SAMI PUBLICATIONS PVT. LTD., New Delhi
✆ 23253514, 23277913, Fax: 23277913
ibsdelhi@del2.vsnl.net.in

SAMSKAR, Delhi
✆ 22541930, Fax: 22512980
madhulika-ag@hotmail

SAMSKRITI, New Delhi
✆ 26137390, 26473482, Fax: 26473482
samskriti@vsnl.com

SAMVAD SAHITYA PRASAR, Meerut
✆ 91-121-2764866
samvadindia@vsnl.net

SAMYAK PRAKASHAN, New Delhi
✆ 65706888, 25216147 ▮ 9810161823, 9810249452
budhdharam@bol.net.in

SANDEEP PUBLISHERS AND DISTRIBUTORS, Delhi
▮ 9868853420
sandeep_publishers_distributors@yahoo.com

SANDHAN, Delhi
✆ 27296030
subhanjali@rediffmail.com

SANGAM BOOK DEPOT, New Delhi
✆ 23272106, 23289417, Fax: 23289417
sbd@bol.net.in

SANGAM PUBLISHERS & DISTRIBUTORS, New Delhi
✆ 23518802, Fax: 23610700
sangampublishers@rediffmail.com

SANGAT PRINTERS PVT. LTD., New Delhi
✆ 41411217, Fax: 41412032
tulipchildrenbooks@gmail.com

SANGEET NATAK ADKADEMI, New Delhi
✆ 23387246, Fax: 23385715
sangeetnatak@bol.net.in

SANGEETA SCIENTIFIC HOUSE, New Delhi
✆ (O) 23255012 (R) 52351024 ▮ 9810050340
Fax: 91-11-23282127
sshjbs@yahoo.com

SANJAY & COMPANY, Mumbai
✆ 020-24968068/69, Fax: 24965876
sanjay@tarladalal.com

SANJAY ENTERPRISES, New Delhi
✆ 25727696, 26663600
sundaram@bom2.vsnl.net.in

SANJAY PRAKASHAN, New Delhi
✆ 23245808, 51045808
sanjay-prakashan@yahoo.com

SANKEERTHANAM PUBLICATIONS, Kollam
✆ 0474-3207700
sankeerthanamklm@yahoo.co.in

SANKHLA PRINTERS, Bikaner
✆ 2200955, Fax: 2204100
vagdevi_jpi@sancharnet.in

SANSKAR, Delhi
✆ 22541930
samskar_culp@hotmail.com

SANSKAR BHARTI PRAKASHAN, New Delhi
✆ 23552350, 23628160, 23512733
Fax: 23628160, 23552350
sbharti@vsnl.com,
vishalarora@mantraonline.com

SANSKRITI PRAKASHAN, Wasai
✆ 0250-2462469
samvadindia@vsnl.net

SANTHAM BOOK (P) LTD., Chennai
✆ 24354622, 24354655
santhambooks@mantramail.com

SAPNA BOOK HOUSE, Bangalore
✆ 22266088, 22261871, 22262815, 22269448 — sapnabooks@vsnl.com,
Fax: 91-80-22269648 — sapna@giasbgrl.vsnl.net.in

SAPPHIRE (INDIA) PUBLISHERS PVT. LTD., New Delhi
✆ 45567067, 28114044, Fax: 28114045 — schoolbks@yahoo.co.in

SAPRA & SAPRA PUBLISHERS DISTRIBUTORS PVT. LTD., New Delhi
✆ 26837040, Fax: 26322498 — psapra@ndf.vsnl.net.in

SARA BOOKS PVT. LTD., New Delhi
✆ 23266107, Fax: 23266102 — sarabooks@eth.net

SARAS BOOKS, New Delhi
✆ (O) 23283800, 23256861 (R) 25812682 — cuckoo@ndf.vsnl.net.in
9810124244, Fax: 011-23264765

SARASWATI HOUSE (P) LTD., New Delhi
✆ 23281022, 23283022, 23243022, 23244022 — delhi@saraswatihouse.com
Fax: 23245011, 23243519

SARASWATI VIHAR, New Delhi
✆ 24620063, Fax: 24645795 — fullcircle@vsnl.com

SARAT BOOK HOUSE, Kolkata
✆ (O) 033-22418389, 22418060, 22413700 — sarat@cal2.vsnl.net.in
(R) 22461059, 22468069, Fax: 033-22418060

SARJANA, Bikaner
✆ 2260830 — vagdevibooks@gmail

SAROJ PRAKASHAN, Allahabad
✆ (O) 0532-2608334 (R) 2641566 — sarojprakashan@rediffmail.com

SARUP & SONS, New Delhi
✆ 23281029, 23244664, Fax: 23277098 — sarupandsonsin@hotmail.com

SASTA SAHITYA MANDAL, New Delhi
✆ 23310505, 41523565, Fax: 41523565 — manager@sastasahityamandal.org

SAT VICHAR DARSHAN, Mumbai
✆ 23864919, 23866986, Fax: 23866435 — ddsat@giasbm01.vsnl.net.in

SATHIAPRAKASHINI BIBLE PUBLISHING COMPANY, Angamalli
✆ 452499, 453083 — daniel@giasmd01.vsnl.net.in

SATISH SERIAL PUBLICATIONS, Delhi
✆ 27672852, 27672469, Fax: 27672046 — info@satishserial.com

SATNAM ENTERPRISES, New Delhi
✆ 41563911, 23289119 — mail@sbspublishers.com,
satnamenterprises@indiatimes.com

SATYA DHARMA BODH MISSION, Hardwar
✆ 01332-27100 — arorafmc@utr.ernet.in

SATYA DHARMA BODH MISSION, Surat
✆ 2322639 — satyadharm2002@yahoo.co.in

SATYAM BOOKS, New Delhi
✆ (O) 23245698, 23242686 (R) 22459334 — satyambooks@hotmail.com
Fax: 23267131

SATYAM PUBLISHING HOUSE, New Delhi
✆ 25358640 — satyampub_2006@yahoo.com

SATYAVIR GOEL, New Delhi
✆ 27021789, Fax: 23521027 — infor@battingperfectsix.com

SAUHARDA BOOK STORE, Mysore
✆ 424394 — yajiv@bgl.vsnl.net.in, rajiv@dgl.vsnl.net.in

SAUJANYA BOOKS, Delhi
✆ 22923541, Fax: 22919007 — saujanya@del3.vsnl.net.in

SAURABH BOOKS & EDUCATIONAL SERVICE, Delhi
✆ 27471067, 27477867, Fax: 27471067 — anoop_sareen@rediffmail.com

SAURABH PUBLISHING (P) LTD., New Delhi
✆ 25509668 — deepak_saurabh@yahoo.com

SAURABH: THE READERS BOOK SHOP, Bhagalpur
✆ 421108 — shreeman8@yahoo.com

SAVAN BOOKS, Chennai
✆ (O) 24454500, 24421229 (R) 24413792
Fax: 91-044-24910910 — asis56@md3.vsnl.net.in, assisbi@md3.vsnl.net.in

SCHOLAR PUBLISHING HOUSE (P) LTD., New Delhi
✆ 23541299, 2362303, Fax: 23676565 — scholar@vsnl.com, scholar@del2.vsnl.net.in

SCHOLARS HUB, New Delhi
✆ 24310049, 41720543 ▮ 9811170218 — vipinscholarshub@yahoo.co.in

SCHOLASTIC INDIA (P) LTD., Gurgaon
✆ 0124-4068940 (6 Lines), Fax: 0124-4068946 — clubs.del@scholastic.co.in

SCHOOL-FELLOW, New Delhi
✆ 55692662 — schoolfellow@sify.com

SCI-TECH MEDIA, Delhi
✆ 22719192, 22715313, 35349254 — scitech_media@yahoo.com, bookjunction@hotmail.com

SCIENCE DIRECT, New Delhi
✆ & Fax: 26447164 — esindia@vsnl.net

SCIENCE PRESS, New Delhi
✆ 23258579, 23259263, Fax: 23258934, 23243225 — narosa@ndc.vsnl.net.in

SCIENTIFIC AND TECHNICAL BOOKS, New Delhi
✆ 25713604 ▮ 9810234957, Fax: 25819143 — stb@vsnl.net

SCIENTIFIC BOOK CENTRE, Guwahati
✆ (O) 0361-2266846 (R) 0361-2221273 — sbcbook@sify.com

SCIENTIFIC BOOK DEPOT, Cuttack
✆ 0671-614183 — ctk_scbkdpt@sancharnet.in

SCIENTIFIC BOOKS & PERIODICALS, Mumbai
✆ 22071227, 2582287, Fax: 22070396 — scpdcals@vsnl.com

SCIENTIFIC BOOKS SUPPLIERS, Delhi
✆ & Fax: 27341616 — sciencebooks@rediffmail.com, jlejain@satyam.net.in, jb_jain@satyam.net.in

SCIENTIFIC INTERNATIONAL PVT. LTD., New Delhi
✆ (O) 23287580 (R) 22461388
▮ 9811016553, Fax: 23286096 — sipldlhi@vsnl.net

SCIENTIFIC PUBLISHERS (INDIA), Jodhpur
✆ 2433323, 2624154, Fax: 2512580, 2512712 — info@scientificpub.com, amrish@jpl.vsnl.net.in, atrans@jp1.dot.net.in

SCIENTIFIC SERVICES, Hyderabad
✆ 27611708, 26501483 — scientific_services@rediffmail.com

SCITECH PUBLICATIONS (INDIA) PVT. LTD., Chennai
✆ 044-22238403 — scitechcorp@yahoo.co.in

SCREEN WORLD PUBLICATION, Mumbai
✆ (O) 28908039 (R) 28692244 — swpub@bom3.vsnl.net.in, screenworldndia.com

SEAGULL BOOKS, Kolkata
✆ 033-22873737, 22877942, Fax: 033-22805143 — seagullfoundation@vsnl.com

SEGMENT BOOK DISTRIBUTORS, New Delhi
✆ 41631191, Fax: 41563498 — segment@vsnl.net

SELECT BOOK POINT, Hyderabad
✆ (O) 040-55628895, 55628896, 55730858
(R) 24330931, Fax: 55730858 — sbp_book@yahoo.com

SELECT BOOK SERVICE SYNDICATE, New Delhi
✆ 23247795, 33102624, Fax: 23278271 — sbs.sushil@airtelbroadband.in

SELECT BOOK SHOP, Bangalore
✆ 080-23386880, 5580770; Fax: 080-25711129 — selectobookshop@hotmail.com

SELECTIVE & SCIENTIFIC BOOKS, Delhi
✆ 22484131, 23352438 ▮ 9810766022
Fax: 23736679 — ssbooks@rediffmail.com

SELF-EMPLOYMENT BUREAU (PUBLICATION), Kolkatta
✆ 25460304 — sebpcal@vsnl.net

SELINA PUBLISHERS, New Delhi
✆ (O) 23280711, 23277230, 23927688
(R) 23911185, Fax: 23277230 — selina@vsnl.com

SELVI BOOK SHOP, Madurai
✆ 0452-345169, 343510 — selvibooks_mdu@sify.com

SERIALS PUBLICATIONS, New Delhi
✆ 23245225, Fax: 23272135 — serials@satyam.net.in

SETH & COMPANY, New Delhi
✆ (O) 23387578, 23387579, 23387479, 23956081
(R) 26221555, Fax: 26221555, 23387479 — sethair60@hotmail

SEVAK PUBLICATIONS, Mumbai
✆ 24120747, 24131198, Fax: 24168612 — sevak@bom2.vsnl.net.in

SHABDASANDHAN PRAKASHAN, New Delhi
✆ 25268341, Fax: 25268341 — shabdasandhan@yahoo.com

SHAHEED BHAGAT SINGH YADGARI PRAKASHAN, Ludhiana
▮ 9888025102 — sbyp@gmail.com

SHAILAJA PRAKASHAN, Delhi
✆ 22320798 — shailjaprakashan@rediffmail.com

SHAILMA.COM PVT. LTD., New Delhi
✆ 24441818 ▮ 9810423528, Fax: 24441818 — shailma@vsnl.com

SHAKUNTALA KALA NIKETAN, Delhi
✆ 27113945, 27117366 — shakuntlakalaniketan@yahoo.com

SHANKAR'S BOOK AGENCY PVT. LTD., New Delhi
✆ 23279967, 23257771, 65381560
Fax: 91-11-23285534 — sbapld@vsnl.com, sbapld@gmail.com

SHANTHA PUBLISHERS, Chennai
✆ 28115618, 28265618, 28266018 — admin@shanthapublishers.com
Fax: 28116018, 28266018

SHANTI PRAKASHAN, Delhi
✆ 27753568, 27753200 — shantisarwar@eth.net

SHANTI PUBLICATIONS, Delhi
✆ 22307950 — info@shantipublications.com

SHARADA PUBLISHING HOUSE, Delhi
✆ 32921560, 27552102 — bansal-sph@rediffmail.com

SHARAN BOOK DEPOT, Jaipur
✆ 601801, 320680 — parampsj@detainfosys.net

SHARDA BOOK DEPOT, Dhanbad
✆ 0326-2253950, Fax: 0326-2251445 — shardabookssin@yahoo.com

SHARDA PRAKASHAN, New Delhi
✆ 23279853, 23280234, Fax: 23280234, 23279853 — jhari@ndb.vsnl.net.in

SHEIKH JAVEED AHMAD, Kashmir
✆ 2478288, Fax: 2470158 — citybookcener@yahoo.com

SHEIKH MOHD USMAN AND SONS (REGD.), Kashmir
✆ (O) 2491291 (R) 2477287, Fax: 2477287 — sh_usman@rediffmail.com

SHERIDEN BOOK COMPANY, New Delhi
✆ 23260511, 23287423, 23281705 — contact@sheridenbooks.com
Fax: 91-11-23287423

SHETH PUBLISHING HOUSE, Mumbai
✆ 25774200, 25773707-08, Fax: 25774200 — sph@bom5.vsnl.net.in

SHIKSHA VIBHAG, RAJASTHAN, Bikaner
✆ 2528875, Fax: 2201861 — diridu@raj.raj.nic.in

SHILALEKH PUBLISHERS, Delhi
✆ 22303184 ▮ 9868049123 — shilalekhbooks@indiabookfair.com, info@shilalekhbooks.com
Fax: 22155926

SHILPAYAN, Delhi
✆ 22821174, 22827190 — shilpayan2005@yahoo.co.in
Fax: 22821174, 22827190

SHIPRA LIBRARY SERVICES & SHIPRA PUBLICATIONS, Delhi
✆ (O) 65277210, 22500954, 22458662 — info@shiprapublications.com
(R) 22017531, Fax: 22458662

SHISHU SAHITYA SAMSAD (P) LTD., Kolkata
✆ (O) 23507669, 23503195 (R) 24644864, 24642929 — samsad@cal3.vsnl.net.in
Fax: 23603508

SHIV KHERA, New Delhi
✆ 26148804, Fax: 26145626 — shivkhera@shivkhera.com

SHIV OM WORLD, New Delhi
✆ 29941296 — urmil95@yahoo.co.in

SHIV SHAKTI BOOKS TRADERS, New Delhi
✆ 25215082, 25935082, Fax: 011-25211682 — ssbt@forensicbooksworld.com

SHIVALAYA ENTERPRISES, Delhi
✆ (O) & (R) 22445526 ▮ 9811892244 — books@indianacademicpublisher.com

SHIVALIK PRAKASHAN, Delhi
✆ 42351161, Fax: 23842641 — shivalikprakashan@yahoo.com

SHIVANI BOOK DISTRIBUTORS, New Delhi
✆ (O) & (R) 25267568, Fax: 011-25251557 — shiv_distributors@yahoo.co.in
9818436910

SHIVANI BOOKS, New Delhi
9350870414, Fax: 011-23281244 — shivanibooks@hotmail.com

SHIVNERI PUBLISHERS & DISTRIBUTORS, Amravati
✆ 0721-2660860 9422856777 — ujjwaladeshmukh@rediffmail.com

SHREE ALMORA BOOK DEPOT, Almora
✆ (O) 230148, 22113, 23561 (R) 233043, 234113 — shyam2@nde.vsnl.net.in
Fax: 234113

SHREE BOOKS, Trivanandapuram
✆ 0471-2466169 — nomarainbow@sify.com

SHREE BOOK SQUARE, Hyderabad
✆ 27566820 — shreebooksquare@yahoo.com

SHREE GREEN BOOK HOUSE, Dehradun
✆ 0135-2621932, Fax: 0135-22621141 — sgbhdon@yahoo.co.in

SHREE KABIR GYAN PRAKASHAN KENDRA, Giridih
✆ 06532-223393 — kabirgyanmandir@yahoo.com

SHREE NAV JEEVAN AGENCY, Pune
✆ 91-20-4020662, Telefax: 91-20-4477804 — snja9@hotmail.com

SHREE NIWAS PUBLICATIONS, Jaipur
✆ 0141-2353254, Fax: 91-175-2353254 — shreniwas300800@gmail.com

SHREE PARAMHANS SWAMI ADGADANANDJI ASHRAM TRUST, Mumbai
✆ 56303811, 56349000, Fax: 23643109 — suneja@bom7.vsnl.net.in, contact@yatharthgeeta.com

SHREE PRABHA EDUCATIONAL AIDS, Delhi
✆ 27106652 — shreeprabhaeducationalaids@gmail.com

SHREE PUBLISHERS & DISTRIBUTORS, New Delhi
✆ 23273027 9212015603 — shreebook@yahoo.co.in

SHREYA PUBLICATIONS, Kolkata
✆ 033-23439310, Fax: 033-22465756 — shreyapublications@yahoo.co.in

SHRI JAINENDRA PRESS, New Delhi
✆ 25795180, Fax: 011-25797221 — sjp@mlbd.com

SHRI PRANNATH MISSION, Delhi
✆ 27658111, Fax: 011-27658111 — prannathmission@gmail.com

SHRI SAI PRINTORGRAPHERS, Delhi
✆ (O) 27654826 (R) 27659446, Fax: 27654827 — frienpub@ndf.vsnl.net.in

SHRIYANS PUBLICATIONS LTD., Jaipur
✆ 2325795, 2320713, Fax: 2323606 — preeti78@datainfosys.net

SHROFF PUBLISHERS & DISTRIBUTORS PVT. LTD., Mumbai
✆ 022-27634290, 27689126 — spdorders@shroffpublishers.com, spdinfo@shroffpublishers.com
Fax: 022-27683337

SHUBHI PUBLICATIONS, Gurgaon
✆ 0124-4088499, Fax: 0124-4375200 — shubhipublications@yahoo.co.in

SHYAM PUSTAK BHANDAR, Rampur
✆ (O) 2324671 (R) 2351515 — 98371-80333@escotelmobile.com

SIDDHARTH BROTHERS, Hyderabad
✆ 24412408 — siddharthchalksnboards@rediffmail.com

SIDDHARTHA SOFT SERVICES, Secunderabad
✆ 27806308, 27806466 — softservices@rediffmail.com

SIDHARTH PUBLICATIONS, New Delhi
✆ 51613753/54, Fax: 2638805/06 — arpl@id.eth.net

SIKH BOOKS, Amritsar
sukhdev_2000@yahoo.com

SIKKAS GROUP, New Delhi
✆ 25654257-59, Fax: 25654256 — sales@sikkas.com

SIKSHA SANGHA, Kolkata
✆ 22190526, 22417396 — siksha@vsnl.net

SIMRO BOOK AGENCY, New Delhi
✆ 25167495 ▮ 9868344917 — nd-simro@rediffmail.com

SINGA ROHINI TRADING COMPANY, Chennai
✆ 044-22266117 — singarohini@yahoo.co.in

SINGH BROTHERS, Amritsar
✆ 2545787, 2550739, Fax: 2543965 — info@singhbrothers.com, singhbro@vsnl.com

SINHAND PUBLICATIONS, Nagpur
✆ 642003, 646474, Fax: 643994 — nagaloka@nagpur.dot.net.in

SITA BOOKS & PERIODICALS PVT. LTD., Mumbai
✆ 55973281, 55973282, 55973283
Fax: 55973284 — ssrao@bom5.vsnl.net.in, sitabook@bom7.vsnl.net.in

SIXTH DIMENSION MULTIMEDIA PVT. LTD., New Delhi
✆ 26224301, 26237785, 26547785
Fax: 91-11-26237785 — sixthdimension@vsnl.com

SMRITI BOOKS, New Delhi
✆ 26816142, 26844615, Fax: 24458269 — sunitapb@hotmail.com, sunitapb@usa.net

SNAB PUBLISHERS PVT. LTD., New Delhi
✆ (O) 23250091, 29214011, 30921147
(R) 26214011, 26238727, Fax: 23252948 — nitamehta@nitamehta.com

SOBHAGYA DEEP PRAKASHAN, New Delhi
✆ 29840051 — sobhagyadep@yahoo.co.in

SOBHAGYA DEEP PRAKASHAN, New Delhi
✆ 26262699, 26262605, Fax: 26264534 — sobhagya@vsnl.net

SOCIETY FOR CREATIVE INTELLIGENCE, Gurgaon
✆ 26580220, 26138805 — cosmicbeam@vsnl.com

SOCIETY FOR INTEGRATED DEVELOPMENT OF HIMALAYAS, Mussorie
✆ 2631304, 2632904 — sidhsri@sancharnet.in

SOFTMAX SOFTWARE SOLUTION, Delhi
✆ 65250328, 42444652 — softmax_education@yahoo.com

SOGANI BOOK HOUSE, Indore
✆ 2545130, 2546928, Fax: 2544597 — sbh@bom4.vsnl.net.in

SOM SUDHA PRAKASHAN, New Delhi
✆ 27057070, 27058080, Fax: 27041515 — somsudha@eth.net

SOMAIYA PUBLICATIONS (P) LTD., New Delhi
✆ 23723351, 23324929, Fax: 23723351 — somaiya@ndf.vsnl.net.in

SONA PRODUCTS PVT. LTD., New Delhi
✆ 26811313-21, Fax: 26811317 — business@sonaproducts.com

SONA OVERSEAS, New Delhi
overseas@sonaproducts.com

SONA PRODUCTS PRIVATE LTD., New Delhi
business@sonaproducts.com

SONAL BOOK ENTERPRISES, Jammu
✆ (O) 2463522 (R) 9419195660, Fax: 0191-2454119 — ranjeev81@rediffmail.com

SONALI PUBLICATIONS, New Delhi
✆ (O) 23279245, 23253475 (R) 22414930 — dphtemt@indiatimes.com

SONI PUBLICATIONS (P) LTD., New Delhi
✆ 23628831, 23535454, Fax: 23612870 — sonipub@ndf.vsnl.net.in

SOURCE PUBLISHERS (P) LTD., Mumbai
✆ 26465741, 26001558, Fax: 26002060 — source@bom2.vsnl.net.in

SOUTH ASIA DISTRIBUTORS & PUBLISHERS, New Delhi
✆ 26494077, 26490267 — sadp@nda.vsnl.net.in
Fax: 91-11-26491482, 29955643

SOUTH ASIAN PUBLISHERS (P) LTD., New Delhi
✆ 26345315, 26345713 — sapub@ndb.net.in

SOUTHERN BOOK STAR, Delhi
✆ (O) 27100223, 27381363 (R) 27109260 — sbookstar@satyam.net.in

SOUVENIR PUBLISHERS, Delhi
✆ (O) 23515437, 55155020, 23681500 — souvenir@hotmail.com, sovenirpublishers@hotmail.com
(R) 23627138, Fax: 91-11-23670004

SPARDHA PRAKASHAN, Jamshedpur
✆ 0657-2487423, Fax: 0657-2487423 — priya_spardha@sify.com

SPECTRUM BOOKS PVT. LTD., New Delhi
✆ 25623501, 25507922, Fax: 25611640 — spectrumindia@vsnl.com

SPECTRUM PUBLICATIONS, Guwahati
✆ (O) 0361-2638435 (R) 0361-2546244, 2520361 — unipub@bsnl.in
Fax: 0361-2638434

SPIDER BOOKS, Chennai
✆ 91-44-42171048 — spider@spiderbooks.net

SPIRE MEDIA PVT. LTD., New Delhi
✆ 26282025, Fax: 91-11-26282026 — injoespire.co.in, contact@spire.co.in

SPIRITUAL QUEST, Kolkata
✆ 22355366, Fax: 22351386 — ranjit@8877.com

SPORTS PUBLICATIONS, New Delhi
✆ 65749511, Fax: 23240261 — lakshythani@hotmail.com

SPRING TIME SOFTWARE, New Delhi
✆ 45091750, Fax: 91-11-45091750 — info@springtimesoftware.net

SPRINGER-VERLAG GMBH & CO. KG, New Delhi
✆ 23358590, Fax: 23358716 — svdel@nde.vsnl.net.in

SQUARE PRINT SERVICES, New Delhi
✆ 40511986 — sps-ajay@rediffmail.com

SREE RAMA PUBLISHERS, Hyderabad
✆ 24743514, 55825299 — sreeramapublishers@yahoo.com

SRI ARAVIND CHETANA SAMAJ, Delhi
📱 9310052647, Fax: 23556005 — satm@satm.net

SRI ARAVIND CHETANA SAMAJ, Delhi
✆ 23674147, 33044906, Fax: 30904335 — sachetas@satm.net

SRI AUROBINDO BOOKS DISTRIBUTION AGENCY, Pondicherry
✆ 2333154, 2334458, Fax: 2330682 — saapress@auroville.org.in

SRI ESWAR ENTERPRISES, Chennai
✆ (O) 24345902, 24323659, 24339591
(R) 22244431, Fax: 24339590 — yempeges@md3.vsnl.net.in

SRI GANESH AGENCY, Delhi
✆ 22717685/6669, Fax: 22716669 — gopalun@yahoo.com

SRI GAYATRI PRINTOGRAPHS, New Delhi
✆ 23286757, 23274874, Fax: 23273335 — info@hindibook.com

SRI GIRI TRADING AGENCY, Chennai
✆ 24943551, Fax: 044-24953821 — akshayaa@md2.vsnl.net.in

SRI JAGANNATH RESEARCH CENTRE, Puri
✆ 22462 — sjrcpuri@hotmail.com

SRI MARIAMMAN STORES, Virudhunagar
✆ (O) 245417 (R) 280793, Fax: 245417 — sunder@virudhunagaronline.com

SRI RAMAKRISHNA MATH, Chennai
✆ 24941231, 24941959, Fax: 24943955 — srkmath@giasmd01.vsnl.net.in

SRI SAI BOOKLINKS, Hyderabad
✆ 27564391 — allani@safy.com

SRI SANGEETHA VANI, Chennai
✆ 24981196 — tambi@md2.vsnl.net.in

SRI SATHYA SAI RAM EDUCATIONAL BOOKS, New Delhi
✆ 25507375 📱 9810900937 — sssreb@yahoo.co.in

SRI SATHYA SAI TOWERS HOTELS PVT. LTD., Andhra Pradesh
✆ 08555-287270, 287327, Fax: 287302 — prasanthi@saitowers.com

SRI SRI RADHA PARTHASARATHY TRUST, New Delhi
✆ 26235133-37, Fax: 26215421 — mahamantra.gkg@pambo.net

SRI VANI STORES, Anantpur
✆ (O) 08554-240114 (R) 08554-232114 — srivani38@hotmail.com

SRIJAN SOLUTIONS PVT. LTD., New Delhi
✆ 25727253, 25727254, Fax: 25721592 — info@srijansolutions.com

SRIKUNJ SADBHAVANA MANCH, New Delhi
✆ 25466019, 25453975, Fax: 25465926 — contact@srikunj.com

ST. PAUL INTERNATIONAL BOOK CENTRE, New Delhi
✆ 23320381, 51513127 — spi6@debol.net.in

ST. PAUL PUBLICATIONS, Mumbai
✆ 26510023, 26400126, Fax: 26454425 — stpauls@vsnl.com

STANDARD BOOK AGENCY, New Delhi
✆ 23279440, Fax: 23252583 — stanbook@vsnl.net

STANDARD BOOK COMPANY, New Delhi
✆ 23414447, 23413899, Fax: 23413828 — sales@sbcindia.com

STANDARD LITERATURE CO. PVT. LTD. (THE), New Delhi
✆ 26176546, 41656254, Fax: 41656019 — standlit@airtalbroadband.in, newdelhi@standlitbooks.com

STANDARD NETWORK SERVICES, New Delhi
✆ 24601325, 31082327 ▮ 9891158484 — infostd@bol.net.in, sns1@bol.net.in

STANDARD PUBLISHERS DISTRIBUTORS, Delhi
✆ 23262700, 23285798, 23257220
Fax: 23243180, 23273335 — stpub@vsnl.com

STANDARD PUBLISHERS (INDIA), New Delhi
✆ (O) 25415043, 25435043 (R) 25014181
Fax: 25374397 — srallbooks3@bol.net.in

STAR BOOK SERVICE, Pune
✆ 4486093, Fax: 4024752 — mahesh_pashte@yahoo.com

STAR BOOKS DISTRIBUTOR, New Delhi
✆ 41562819, 23264462, Fax: 23264451 — sales@star-bk.com

STAR PUBLICATIONS PVT. LTD., New Delhi
✆ (O) 23261696, 23286757, 23257220, 23274874
(R) 26410363, 26427181, Fax: 23273335, 26481565 — starpub@satyam.net.in, hbc@satyam.net.in

STATESMAN LTD. (THE), New Delhi
✆ 23315911, Fax: 23353055, 23315295 — sman@nde.vsnl.net.in

STELLAR INDUSTIRES PVT. LTD., New Delhi
✆ 26833520, 26828769, Fax: 26316201 — stellarpp@vsnl.com

STERLING BOOK HOUSE, Mumbai
✆ 22612521, 22659599, Fax: 22623551 — sbh@vsnl.com, sterling@bom5.vsnl.net.in

STERLING PUBLISHERS PRIVATE LIMITED, New Delhi
✆ (O) 26387070, 26386209, 26386165, 26385677
(R) 26162422, 26162426, Fax: 26383788 — mail@sterlingpublishers.com, info@sterlingpublishers.com, sterlingpublishers@airtelmail.in

STONE HILL FOUNDATION PUBLISHING PVT. LTD., Kochi
✆ 0484-2321513, 4012517, Fax: 91-484-2321778 — editionindia@asianetindia.com

STONE TECHNOLOGY CENTRE, Jaipur
✆ 0141-2376171, 2379653, Fax: 2365232 — stonetec@sancharnet.in, vikram97@hotmail.com

STORY OF LIFE (THE), Muzaffarnagar
pksharma@nda.vsnl.net.in

STRAND BOOK STALL, Mumbai
✆ 22661994, 22661719, 22614613
Fax: 022-22051754, 22630154 — strandbookstall@vsnl.com

STRAWBERRY STOP/S.S. EDUCATIONAL (AIDS) STORES, Delhi
✆ 27053526, 27056395 ▮ 9811059403, 9810021148 — sseducationalaids@hotmail.com

STREE, Kolkata
✆ 24660812, Fax: 24664614, 24666677 — stree@cal2.vsnl.net.in

STUDENT AID PUBLICATIONS, Delhi
✆ 27557146, Telefax: 27557146 — stuaid@nda.vsnl.net.in, editoral@studentaidpublications.in

STUDENTS' AGENCIES (I) PVT. LTD., Mumbai
✆ 022-23513334/5/6/7, Fax: 23514212 — students@vsnl.com, students@bom3.vsnl.net.in

STUDENTS CORNER, Dhanbad
✆ 0326-251516, Fax: 0326-251445
✉ scbooks@rediffmail.com, studentscorner@libraryservicemail.com

STUDENTS FRIENDS, Patna
✉ shiv_frinds@yahoo.com

STUDENTS STORES PVT. LTD., Delhi
✆ 23928377, 23965726, 23951867
Fax: 23936758
✉ devra@vsnl.com

STUFUN DOT COM. PVT. LTD., Mumbai
✆ 28862529, Fax: 28541370
✉ info@stufun.com

SUBHA BOOK CENTRE, New Delhi
✆ 23632679
✉ subha_books@rediffmail.com

SUBHASH BROTHERS, Delhi
✆ (O) 23261011, 23283733 (R) 25748440
▮ 9810004034, Fax: 23261011
✉ info@subhashbrothers.com

SUBODH GRANTHMALA KARYALAY, Ranchi
✆ 0651-202858, 200819
✉ suboh12@dte.vsnl.net.in

SUBODH POCKET BOOKS, New Delhi
✆ 23274513, 23278858
✉ anilkumar@subodhbooks.com, subodhbooks@vsnl.net

SUCCESS SYSTEMS INFOTECH, Delhi
✆ 27187227, 27105555
✉ vaid@giasd01.vsnl.net.in

SUDARSHAN BOOK DISTRIBUTORS, New Delhi
✆ 28714138, 28714238, Fax: 91-11-28712268
✉ sbdbooks@gmail.com

SUDARSHAN PUBLICATIONS (P) LTD., New Delhi
✆ 51520717, 51520718, Fax: 51520718
✉ sudarshanpublication@hotmail.com

SUDHA PUBLICATIONS PVT. LTD., New Delhi
✆ 25718495, 25712898, Fax: 25754647
✉ csrindia@mantraonline.com

SUGAT BOOK DEPOT, Nagpur
✆ (O) 2640413 (R) 2640142
✉ sugatbookdepot@sify.com

SULEKHA ADVERTSING PVT. LTD., Patna
✆ 220648, 220647, Fax: 230347
✉ poppycool@hotmail.com

SULTAN CHAND & SONS (P) LTD., New Delhi
✆ 23251727, 23272532, 23243939
Fax: 011-23254295
✉ scs@del2.vsnl.net.in, nbcnd@mdb.vsnl.net.in

SUMAIYAH DISTRIBUTORS PVT. LTD., New Delhi
✆ 23244148, 23285674, Fax: 23244133
✉ sumaiyah@vsnl.net, sumaiyahbook@yahoo.com

SUMAN PRAKASHAN, New Delhi
✆ 25760759, 51596090, Fax: 25754739
✉ info@sumanprakashan.com

SUMEET PUBLICATIONS, Delhi
✆ 23281704
✉ ca.sumeetgupta@yahoo.com

SUMSAC INTERNATIONAL & GYAN DEEP, New Delhi
✆ 23358398, 23842930, 23328669
▮ 9810154549, 9312352191
✉ sumsac@satyam.net.in

SUNDEEP PRAKASHAN, Delhi
✆ 27382430, 27382530, Fax: 91-11-27382430
✉ books@vsnl.com, info@sundeepbooks.com

SUNDERDAS GIANCHAND, Mumbai
✆ 22080518, 22088151, Fax: 22055444 — ramshe@bom5.vsnl.net.in

SUNIL BOOK SERVICE, New Delhi
✆ 23618426, Fax: 91-11-23638444
▮ 9818568722, 9871078971 — jain_bros@hotmail.com

SUNRISE PUBLICATIONS, Delhi
✆ 22025199 — sunprisepublication@front.ru

SUNRISE PUBLISHERS, Delhi
✆ & Fax: 22469733 — sunrisepub@rediffmail.com

SUNRISE PUBLISHERS, Delhi
✆ 22307415, Fax: 91-11-22307414 ▮ 9810237091 — sunrisepub@rediffmail.com

SUNRISE PUBLISHING HOUSE, New Delhi
✆ 26286781 ▮ 9818442310, Fax: 51620812 — m_c_sharma@yahoo.com

SUNSHINE BOOKS, New Delhi
✆ 26646773, 26641833, 26640619, Fax: 26641833 — info@sunshine-books.com

SUNSHINE BOOKS, New Delhi
✆ 41564077 ▮ 9312229307, Fax: 011-41564077 — info@sunshine-books.com

SUPER BOOK HOUSE, Mumbai
✆ 22830446, 22020106, Fax: 228330751 — superbh@vsnl.com

SUPER DISTRIBUTORS, New Delhi
✆ 25727696, Fax: 25854747 — sundaram@bom2.vsnl.net.in

SUPERNOVA PUBLISHERS & DISTRIBUTORS PVT. LTD., New Delhi
✆ 29239349, 29238285, Fax: 91-11-29239249 — info@supernovapublishers.com, snpd_india@yahoo.co.in

SUPREME BOOKS (REGD.), Delhi
✆ 27605404, 27650514, 23256606, 23275451
Fax: 27650514, 27654141 — supremebooksr@hotmail.com

SURA BOOKS (P) LTD., Chennai
✆ 26162173, 26161090, 26161099
Fax: 26162173 — surabooks@eth.net, enquiry@surabooks.com

SURBHI BOOK DISTRIBUTOR, New Delhi
✆ 25525999, Fax: 25525999 — soodanil@yahoo.com

SURBHI ENTERPRISES, Delhi
✆ 25257319 — surabhis@bol.net.in

SURESH & COMPANY, Delhi
✆ 23828315, 23826812 — mapchart@now-india.net.in

SURJEET PUBLICATIONS, Delhi
✆ (O) 23914746, 23914174, 23982395
(R) 27453842, Fax: 23918475 — surpub@del3.vsnl.net.in

SURJYA HAZARIKA EDUCATIONAL TRUST, Guwahati
✆ 91-361-2458807, Fax: 91-361-2529094 — surjyahazarika@rediffmail.com

SURUCHI PRAKASHAN, New Delhi
✆ 23514672, 23679996, Fax: 23679914 — suruchiprakashan@vsnl.net

SURVEY OF INDIA PERIODICALS, New Delhi
✆ 30919843, 32325775, Fax: 91-11-23722122 — sipsurvey@rediffmail.com, sipsurvey@indiatimes.com

SURYAPRABHA PRAKASHAN, New Delhi
✆ 23285915, 25477805 ▮ 9871814577 — suryaprabhap@yahoo.co.in

SURYASTRA COMMUNICATIONS PVT. LTD., New Delhi
✆ 26520479 — info@suryastra.com

SURYAM SCIENTIFIC SURGICO (REGD.), Delhi
✆ 23911254, 23974378, Fax: 23923568 — shivscientific@vsnl.net

SURYASTRA COMMUNICATIONS PVT. LTD., New Delhi
✆ 26520479 — info@suryastra.com

SUVARTHA BHAVAN, Thiruvalla
✆ (O) 2640334 (R) 2604016, Fax: 0473-2630503 — jins@giasmd01.vsnl.net.in, suvarthabhava@rediffmail.com

SUVIDHA DISCOUNT MART PVT. LTD., New Delhi
✆ 23350335 — database@satyam.net.in

SUVIDHA LAW HOUSE PVT. LTD., Bhopal
✆ 2551597, 2559586, Fax: 2559586 — law@satyam.net.in

SUYOGYA PRAKASHAN, New Delhi
✆ 29234190, 29244159, Fax: 91-11-23973082 — atmaram_books@hotmail.com

SWADESH PRAKASHAN PVT. LTD., New Delhi
✆ 23516869, 23624858, Fax: 23551489 — sppl@yahoo.com

SWAMI JYOTIRMAYANANDA ASHRAM, Ghaziabad
✆ 91-120-2600237 — iys@vsnl.com, iys@ndf.vsnl.net.in

SWAMI RAMA CENTRE, Dehradun
✆ 2412068, Fax: 2412008 — hitsrc@sancharnet.in

SWAMI RAMA TIRTHA MISSION, New Delhi
✆ 23528302, 23559350 — sstmissiondelhi@yahoo.co.in

SWAMY LAW HOUSE, Ernakulam
✆ (O) 2361341, 2366285 (R) 2431236
Fax: 2366285 — swamylawhouse@spectrum.net.in

SWARAJ PRAKASHAN, New Delhi
✆ 23289915 ▮ 9350544790 — swaraj_prakashan@yahoo.co.in

T

T.B.H. PUBLISHERS & DISTRIBUTORS, Chennai
✆ 25390150, 25387156, 25362305, 2852457
28663168, Fax: 044-25392754, 28587710 — tbhpd@md4.vsnl.net.in

T.B.I. PUBLISHERS DISTRIBUTORS, New Delhi
✆ 24632903, 24690513, 24693257
Fax: 24610576, 23325247 — tbi@del3.vsnl.net.in, tbidelhi@dartmail.dart.net.com

T.B.S. PUBLISHERS & DISTRIBUTORS, Calicut
✆ (O) 0495-2720085/86, 2720086
(R) 2721160, Fax: 0495-2721414 — tbsbook@vsnl.com

T.F.Y. TECHNICAL PUBLICATIONS, Delhi
✆ 23919914, 27211146, Fax: 27137530 — ✉ mukat@vsnl.com

T.R. PUBLICATIONS PRIVATE LTD., Chennai
✆ 24340765, 24322920, Fax.: 2348837 — ✉ trpubs@md5.vsnl.net.in

TAJ COMPANY, Delhi
✆ (O) 23230630 (R) 23222128, Fax: 23237241 — ✉ taj@ndf.vsnl.net.in

TAKBEER PUBLICATIONS (P) LTD., Srinagar
✆ (O) 0194-2473818 (R) 01933-213354
Fax: 0194-2473818 — ✉ ehsan04@sancharnet.in

TAKHLEEQKAR PUBLISHERS, Delhi
✆ 22442572 — ✉ qissey@rediffmail.com

TAKSHASHILA PRAKASHAN, New Delhi
✆ 23258802, 22513959, Fax: 23258767 — ✉ takshila_prakashan@indiatimes.com

TAMIL NADU BOOK HOUSE, Chennai
✆ 2832984, 28441043, 28443381 — ✉ pillai12@vsnl.net

TAMIL NADU BOOKSELLERS & DISTRIBUTORS ASSOCIATION, Chennai
✆ 28111790, Fax: 28111806 — ✉ tamilnadubooksellers@gmail.com

TAMILARASI PATHIPPAGAM, Chennai
✆ 28241865, 28264046 — ✉ thambi@md2.vsnl.net.in

TARA PUBLISHING, Chennai
✆ 91-44-24401696, Fax: 91-44-24453658 — ✉ mail@tarabooks.com

TARAKSHEEL SOCIETY BHARAT, Barnala
✆ 233244, 241744, Fax: 241744 — ✉ taraksheel@yahoo.com, amitter@ch1.dot.net.in

TARU-BOOKS & JOURNALS, New Delhi
✆ 25580534, 25575166, Fax: 25585397 — ✉ taru@poboxes.com

TATA ENERGY RESEARCH INSTITUTE, New Delhi
✆ 24682100, 24682111, Fax: 4682144, 4682145 — ✉ mailbox@teri.res.in

TATA INFOMEDIA LIMITED, New Delhi
✆ 23327880-82, 23730037-39, 55303278-80
Fax: 23327884 — ✉ tildelhi@vsnl.net

TATA INFORMEDIA LIMITED, Mumbai
✆ 24300941, Fax: 022-24302707 — ✉ brightsparks@tatainfomedia.com

TATA MCGRAW-HILL PUBLISHING CO. LTD., New Delhi
✆ (O) 25882743-6, 25882918 (R) 26444797
Fax: 25885154, 25883902 — ✉ info_india@mcgraw-hill.com, marketing_india@mcgraw-hill.com

TAUSCO BOOK DISTRIBUTORS, New Delhi
✆ (O) 26890397 (R) & Fax: 26136821 — ✉ tausco@nde.vsnl.net.in

TAXMANN PUBLICATIONS PVT. LTD., New Delhi
✆ (O) 28712352, 25743662, 25743692
(R) 25195502, 25435691, Fax: 28715041 — ✉ mitra_pal@taxmann.com

TAXSHILA PRAKASHAN, New Delhi
✆ 30128802, 23258802, Fax: 23258802 — ✉ taxshila_prakashan@indiatimes.com

TAYLOR & FRANCIS BOOKS INDIA PVT. LTD., New Delhi
✆ 23712131, Fax: 91-11-23712132 — ✉ tandfindia@airtelbroadband.in

TECHMEDIA, New Delhi
✆ (O) 23267741, 23272329, 23254990, 23254991
(R) 23969355, Fax: 23262008 — ✉ tm@vsnl.com

TECHNICAL BOOK BUREAU (INDIA), New Delhi
✆ 26955317 ▮ 9810990700 — tech_book_bureau_india@yahoo.com

TECHNICAL BOOK SOURCE, New Delhi
✆ 23289038 ▮ 9891324324, Fax: 23275357 — technicalbook2000@yahoo.co.in

TECHNICAL BUREAU INDIA (P) LTD., Delhi
✆ 23649501, 23648477 ▮ 9811589130
Fax: 011-23648477 — ahuja_gaurav@satyam.net.in, technical_bureau@yahoo.com, techbureau@safy.com

TECHNICAL PUBLICATIONS, Pune
✆ 91-20-24495496, Fax: 91-20-24495497 — technical@vtubooks.com

TECHNIZ BOOKS INTERNATIONAL, New Delhi
✆ 26284790-91, 26486911, 26414791
▮ 9810510602, 9811072381, Fax: 26473611 — info@technizbooks.com, abitechbooks@vsnl.net

TECHNOBOOKS.COM, New Delhi
✆ 51606573, 26281273, Fax: 26473611 — info@technobooks.com

TECHNOLOGY INFORMATION FORECASTING AND ASSESSMENT COUNCIL (TIFAC), New Delhi
✆ 26862331, Fax: 26863866 — publication@tifac.org.in, ghosh@tifac.ernet.in

TECHNOMECH BOOKS INTERNATIONAL, Delhi
✆ 22513724 ▮ 9891652475, Fax: 011-51642947 — tbibooks@indiatimes.com

TEKSONS BOOK SHOP, New Delhi
✆ 24617030, 24640649, Fax: 24617238 — taksons@del3.vsnl.net.in

THAKKAR STATIONERS, Mahuva
✆ 02844-222141, 225141 ▮ 9426272294 — thakkarstat@yahoo.co.in

THANU FOUNDATION, Chennai
✆ 26260882, Fax: 044-26214494 — thanufound@mailcity.com

THE AATMIC SCIENCE FOUNDATION, Allahabad
✆ 91-532-2461303 — editor.sos@gmail.com

THE ASIASTIC SOCIETY, Kolkata
✆ 22290779, 22297251, 22497250, Fax: 22172355 — aslibcal@vsnl.net.in

THE BEST BOOK SHOP, New Delhi
✆ 51601086 — bestbooks@india.com

THE BOOK LINE, New Delhi
✆ (O) 23242009 (R) 25283394, Fax: 91-011-23242009 — sales@thebooklineonline.co.in

THE BOOK MARK, New Delhi
✆ 24693216, 24644071, Fax: 24634935 — ragupta@del2.vsnl.net.in

THE BOOK SHOPPE, Bangalore
✆ (O) 25084623, 25716993,
Fax: 91-80-25716993, 25533022 — bcipub@blr.vsnl.net.in

THE CHILDREN'S KNOWLEDGE CENTRE, Faridabad
✆ 91-129-2273712 — libresource@gmail.com

THE ENERGY AND RESOURCES INSTITUTE, New Delhi
✆ 24682100, 41504900, Fax: 91-11-24682144-45 — teripress@teri.res.in

THE ENGLISH BOOK STORE, New Delhi
✆ 23417126, 23415031, 23417936
Fax: 91-11-23417731 — ebs@vsnl.com

THE FAMILY INDIA, New Delhi
▮ 9810188578 — contact@thefamilyindia.org

THE FOUNDATION FOR RESEARCH IN COMMUNITY HEALTH, Pune
✆ 25887020, Fax: 25881308 — frchpune@giaspn01.vsnl.net.in

THE HINDU, Chennai
✆ 91-44-28589060, Fax: 91-44-28545703 — marketing@thehindu.co.in

THE INFOWARE HOUSE, Ahmedabad
✆ 6460896, 31015889, Fax: 91-78-2133292 — is@vsnl.com, infowarehouse_2000@yahoo.com

THE INTERNATIONAL BOOK SERVICE, Pune
✆ (O) 25677405 (R) 25678060 — interbhs@pn3.vsnl.net.in

THE LIFE ETERNAL TRUST, New Delhi
✆ 26178156, Fax: 26866801 — kalrajesh@rediffmail.com

THE LIVING TREASURE (REGD.), New Delhi
✆ 32950633 ▮ 9811655321, Fax: 91-11-25440685 — contact@thelivingtreasure.com

THE SELF-EMPLOYMENT BUREAU (PUBLICATION), Kolkata
✆ 91-33-25460304 — scbpcal@vsnl.net

THE STANDARD BOOK COMPANY, Bangalore
✆ 25535522, 25535544, 25535588, Fax: 25536323 — standard@vsnl.com

THE THEOSOPHICAL PUBLISHING HOUSE, Chennai
✆ 24911338, 24466613, Fax: 91-44-24901399 — tphindia@vsnl.com, theos.soc@gems.vsnl.net.in

THE TIMES OF INDIA, Hyderabad
✆ 23355335, Fax: 23355302 — rajesh.kondru@timesgroup.com

THE UNITED BOOK HOUSE, New Delhi
✆ 91-11-27323798 ▮ 9811211139 — rajiv_ubh_delhi2000@yahoo.com

THE VARIETY BOOK DEPOT, New Delhi
✆ (O) 23417175, 23412567, 23415030 (R) 24602032 24624028, Fax: 91-11-23415335, 51517201 — varietybookdepot@rediffmail.com

THE VIVEKA FOUNDATION, New Delhi
✆ 26492473 — viveka4@vsnl.com

THE WALT DISNEY CO. (INDIA) PVT. LTD., Mumbai
✆ 91-22-66516618, 56637752 Fax: 91-33-66541709 — naveen.chopra@disney.com

THE WISE OWL, New Delhi
✆ 41721050, 29813206, Fax: 91-11-41721050 — thewiseowl@bol.net.in

THE WORLD BANK, New Delhi
✆ 41479465, 24617241, Fax: 91-11-24619393 — balasubramanian@worldbank.org

THIEME MEDICAL AND SCIENTIFIC PUBLISHERS (P) LTD., New Delhi
✆ 23263522, Fax: 91-11-23263522 — thieme-santosh@gmail.com

THINK/GOODWORD BOOKS, New Delhi
✆ 24697971, Fax: 24697333 — skhan@vsnl.com

THINK INCORPORATED, New Delhi
✆ 24356464, 24359898, 24354253 Fax: 24357980 — thinkinc@vsnl.com

THIRUMAGAL NILAYAM, Chennai
✆ 24342899, 24327696, 24337428 Fax: 44-24341559 — thirumagal@intamm.com

THOMAS INTERNATIONAL PUBLISHING COMPANY INDIA PVT. LTD., New Delhi
✆ 23359130, 23359167, Fax: 23359170 — trim@vsnl.com

THOMAS NELSON & SONS LTD., New Delhi
✆ 24346244, 24346266 — germanbk@vsnl.com

THOMSON ASIA (PTE) LTD. INDIA, Mumbai
✆ 26453960, Fax: 26453907 — sunil.patki@thomsonlearning.com.sg

THOMSON INFORMATION SOUTH ASIA PVT. LTD., New Delhi
✆ 26209428, 26209419, Fax: 91-11-26209422 — ambika.nair@thomson.com

THOMSON PRESS (INDIA) LTD., Noida
✆ 24562925, 24562949, 24562049, Fax: 24562969 — amanocha@thomsonpress.com

THOMSON PRESS (INDIA) LTD., Faridabad
✆ 91-129-2285520-21, 91-11-51616080
Fax: 91-129-2284511, 91-11-26818670-75 — kraina@thomsonpress.com

THREE STAR PUBLICATIONS (P) LTD., Delhi
✆ 23236758, 23237209, Fax: 91-11-23235438 — tspbooks@bol.net.in

TIME BOOKS, Mumbai
✆ 23885563, 23887801 — bombay@readnbuy.net

TIMELY BOOKS CENTRE, Kolkata
✆ 22376794, 22366794, Fax: 22374149 — timely@vsnl.net

TINY TOT PUBLICATIONS, Delhi
✆ 22163582, 22167314, Fax: 22143023 — tinytotpub@hotmail.com

TIRUMALA SOFTWARE, New Delhi
✆ 26444341, Fax: 91-11-26473611 — tirumala@email.com

TODAY TOMORROWS PRINTERS & PUBLISHERS, New Delhi
✆ 23241021, 23242621, Fax: 23242621 — ttpp@vsnl.com

TOP JOURNALS & TRADE SERVICE, New Delhi
✆ (O) 26832913 (R) 26832913
Fax: 91-11-26832913 — mmseigell@yahoo.com

TOTAL LIBRARY SOLUTION (I) PVT. LTD., New Delhi
✆ 25832289, 25836593, 25833253
Fax: 25831179 — tls@del3.vsnl.net.in, tls@vsnl.com

TOUHA ENTERPRISES, Srinagar
✆ 2453417 — tahapub.2003@yahoo.com

TOWARDS FREEDOM, Kolkata
✆ 91-33-23212902, 23591529, 31030579 — towardsfreedom@vsnl.net

TOWER PERIODICAL SUBSCRIPTION AGENCY, Chennai
✆ 8472305 — prhpn@yahoo.com

TRAFFICO ENGINEERS, New Delhi
✆ 26831100, 26921100 — traffico@ndf.vsnl.net.in

TRANS-INDIA BOOK DISTRIBUTORS, New Delhi
9899214093 — transindiabooks@indiatimes.com

TRANSWORLD BOOK SERVICES, New Delhi
✆ (O) 24624055, 24652250 (R) 24535043
9810004985, Fax: 28535043 — twbs@del3.vsnl.net.in

TRANSWORLD SUBSCRIPTION AGENCY, Secunderabad
✆ 270772216, Fax: 27075614 — transhyd@hd1.vsnl.net.in

TREECRAFT COMMUNICATIONS, Jaipur
✆ 0141-2340333 — treecrft@jp1.dot.in

TRIPATHGA PRAKASHAN (P) LTD., Delhi
✆ 91-11-22026541 — tripathga@hotmail.com

TRIPATHGA PRAKASHAN (P) LTD., Bhopal
✆ 91-755-5283460, 91-11-22026541 — tripathga@hotmail.com

TRIPATHI BOOK DISTRIBUTORS, Allahabad
✆ 91-532-2561162, Fax: 91-532-2560866 — tbxalld@sancharnet.in

TRIRATNA GRANTHAMALYA, Nagpur
✆ 642003, 646474 — nagaloka@nagpr.dot.net.in

TRISHUL PUBLICATIONS, Noida
✆ (O) 011-33338285 (R) 3097662 — integral@del3.vsnl.net.in

TRUEMAN BOOK COMPANY, New Delhi
✆ 23242482, 23242483, Fax: 91-11-23242483 — trueman@satyam.net.in

TRUMP & GATES, New Delhi
✆ 23367497, 23367498, Fax: 91-11-23367687 — info@trumpandgates.com

TULIKA BOOKS, New Delhi
✆ 26491448, 26491625, Fax: 26497999 — tulika@ndf.vsnl.net.in

TULIKA PUBLISHERS, Chennai
✆ (O) 24981639, 24671117 (R) 24991176
Fax: 24671113 — kaka@tulikabooks.com, tulbooks@md4.vsnl.net.in

TULSI BOOK CENTRE, Madurai
✆ 0452-749928 — tulsibookmdu@yahoo.com

TURNING POINT: A BOOK SHOP, Madurai
✆ (O) 0452-2347398, 5370937 (R) 5377558
Fax: 738382 — bookplaza@rediffmail.com

TUSHAR PUBLICATIONS, New Delhi
✆ (O) 23671520, 23556407 (R) 26145330
26148870, Fax: 23610394 — subhashgoel_13@sify.com

U

U.B.S. PUBLISHERS' DISTRIBUTORS LTD., New Delhi
✆ 23273601, 23266645-46
Fax: 91-11-23276593, 23274261 — ubspd@gobookshopping.com, ubspd@ubspd.com

U.D.H. PUBLISHERS AND DISTRIBUTORS (P) LTD., New Delhi
✆ 23258449, 23246533, 41562623, 41562603
65499654, Fax: 23258474 — udhpd@vsnl.net, udhpd@airtelbroadband.net.in

UJJAL BOOK STORES, Kolkata
✆ 23515515, 22416258 — itbpc@gems.vsnl.net.in

UNICATE PUBLISHERS & DISTRIBUTORS, Pune
✆ 6631067, 6631894, Fax: 6631067 — unicate@vsnl.com

UNICORN BOOK SERVICE, Delhi
✆ 22720284, 22724183, 22723713, Fax: 22720284 — unicornbooks@yahoo.com

UNICORN BOOKS PVT. LTD., New Delhi
✆ (O) 23272783-84, 23276539 (R) 23969846
Fax: 23257790, 23260518 — unicornbooks@vsnl.com

UNIMO PUBLICATIONS/UNIVERSAL MEDIA ORGANISATION, New Delhi
✆ 25884680 — @ unimo@unito-world.org

UNIQUE BOOK AGENCY, Ahmedabad
✆ 079-6747453, 6742878, Fax: 079-6750417 — @ ljbca@wilnetonline.net, ljcc@wilnetonline.net

UNIQUE PUBLICATIONS, New Delhi
✆ 29833520, Fax: 29831694 — @ unique@hotmail.com

UNIQUE PUBLISHERS, New Delhi
✆ 41564400-11, Fax: 91-11-41564422 — @ uniquepublishersindia@gmail.com

UNIQUE SELLERS, New Delhi
✆ 23245444, 23245111, Fax: 23245111 — @ uniqueselr@hotmail.com

UNISTAR BOOKS PVT. LTD., Chandigarh
✆ 5077427-8, Fax: 5089761 — @ pcis@rediffmail.com

UNITED BOOK TRADERS, Jodhpur
✆ 0291-2624154 — @ scienti@sancharnet.in

UNITED BOOKS & PERIODICALS, Mumbai
✆ 26116909, 26105852, Fax: 91-22-26105852 — @ gavakar@bom4.vsnl.net.in, unitedbooks@vsnl.com

UNITED CHILDREN'S MOVEMENT REGD., New Delhi
✆ (O) & (R) 25722830 ▮ 9899435248, Fax: 25781744 — @ darshan@unitedchild.org

UNITED MAP CO., Delhi
✆ 23657395, 23650165, Fax: 23650165 — @ unimapco@bharatconnect.com

UNITED NATIONS EDUCATIONAL, SCIENTIFIC AND CULTURAL ORGANIZATION, New Delhi
✆ 26713000, Fax: 26713001-02 — @ newdelhi@unesco.org, unesco.delhi@unesco.org

UNITED PUBLICATION, Delhi
✆ 23657395, 23650165, Fax: 23650165 — @ unimapco@bharatconnect.com

UNITED PUBLISHERS, Guwahati
✆ 2517059, Fax: 2544791 — @ unipub@sancharnet.in

UNIVERSAL BOOK CORPORATION, Mumbai
✆ 22061159, 22016122, 22050629, 22078096
Fax: 22014080, 22062404 — @ unibooks@vsnl.com

UNIVERSAL BOOK DISTRIBUTING CO., Lucknow
✆ 2374909, 2333401, Fax: 2374909 — @ ubdco@sancharnel.in, ubdco@lw1.vsnl.net.in

UNIVERSAL BOOKSELLERS, Lucknow
✆ 2225894, 2224135, 2238398, Fax: 2218547 — @ universal@lwl.vsnl.net.in

UNIVERSAL BOOK SERVICE, Jabalpur
✆ 2310591, 2314961, Fax: 2313843 — @ manish_batheja@yahoo.com

UNIVERSAL BOOK SERVICE, Pune
✆ 4455188 — @ universalbooks@eth.net

UNIVERSAL BOOK SHOP, New Delhi
✆ (O) 26101076, 26103896 (R) 26186743, Fax: 26103896 — @ ubsbookshop@yahoo.com

UNIVERSAL BOOK STALL, Delhi
✆ (O) 23261903, 23250653, 23273601
(R) 25787112, Fax: 011-23272595, 23250653 — @ ubsns@bol.net.in

UNIVERSAL BOOK STALL, New Delhi
✆ 23273601, 23266646, Fax: 23274261, 23276593 — @ ubspd@upspd.com

UNIVERSAL BOOK TRADERS, Delhi
✆ 23911966, 23990487, 23961288, Fax: 23924152 — unilaw@vsnl.com

UNIVERSAL LAW PUBLISHING CO. PVT. LTD., Delhi
✆ (O) 27215334, 27438103, 27458529 — unilaw@vsnl.com
(R) 27459020, 27234101, 27459023, Fax: 27459022

UNIVERSAL SUBSCRIPTION AGENCY (P) LTD., Gurgaon
✆ 0124-5001410-13, Fax: 5052913 — gistdel@gistglobal.com

UNIVERSITIES PRESS (INDIA) LTD., Hyderabad
✆ 27662849/50, Fax: 27645046 — hyd2_upilco@sancharnet.in, upilcoend@dot.net.in

UNIVERSITY BOOK HOUSE PVT. LTD., Jaipur
✆ 2311466, 2313382, Fax: 91-141-4013697 — uni_bookhouse@yahoo.com

UNIVERSITY OF KASHMIR, Srinagar
✆ 91-194-2427448, Fax: 91-194-2427448 — rufai@kashmiruniversity.net

UPKAR PRAKASHAN, Agra
✆ (O) 91-562-2530966, 3208693 ▮ 9837050002 — info@upkarprakashan.com
(R) 2531313, 2530390, Fax: 91-562-2531940

UPPAL PUBLISHING HOUSE/UPPAL BOOK STORE, New Delhi
✆ (O) 23273756 (R) 22083884, Fax: 23286571 — uph@mantraonline.com

UPPER INDIA TECHNOLOGIES (E-DIKSHA.COM), New Delhi
✆ 25993861, 25912191, 25912205 ▮ 9810475590 — ediksha@bol.net.in
Fax: 91-11-25993861

UPVAN GRANTHALAYA, Jodhpur
✆ 2748488, 2747931, Fax: 5120509 — upvangranthalaya@sify.com

URDU ACADEMY, Delhi
✆ 23863697, 23830635/36/37/38, Fax: 23863773 — urduacademydelhi@yahoo.co.in

URDU BOOK REVIEW, New Delhi
✆ 23266347 — artifiqbalubr@yahoo.co.in

URDU SCIENCE, New Delhi
✆ 26924366, Fax: 26924366 — parvaiz@ndf.vsnl.net.in

URVISH BOOK STORES, Surat
✆ (O) 2475102, 2470405 (R) 2473302 — urvishstores@yahoo.com

USBORNE PUBLISHING, New Delhi
✆ 26169147 — overleaf@vsnl.net

USEFUL BOOK SERVICE, Lucknow
✆ 2380063, 2346805, 2769345, Fax: 2388535 — useful@id.eth.net, useful@satyam.net.in

UTKARSH BOOKS DISTRIBUTORS, New Delhi
✆ 26496964 — utkarshbd@rediffmail.com

UTKARSH PUBLICATIONS, New Delhi
✆ 25533689, Fax: 25533897 — kokchalovebug@rediffmail.com

UTPAL PUBLICATIONS, Delhi
✆ (O) 22464458 (R) 26493456 ▮ 9818447636 — utpalbooks@rediffmail.com

UTTAR PRADESH HINDI SANSTHAN, Lucknow
✆ 3048205-06, Fax: 91-522-3048205 — director@hindisansthan.in

UTTAR PRADESH URDU AKADEMI, Lucknow
✆ 2720683, Fax: 2720683 — upuacc@avadh.net

V

V. PUBLICATION BOOK STALL, Kottayam
✆ 0481-2567470/71, 2302980 — info@vpublishers.com

V.K. (INDIA) ENTERPRISES, New Delhi
✆ 23250105, 23250106, Fax: 23250141 — trjain@vsnl.com, delhi@vkpublications.com

V.K. PUBLICATIONS, New Delhi
✆ 23290105, Fax: 91-11-23290141 — trijain@vsnl.com

V.K.G. BOOKS INTERNATIONAL, New Delhi
✆ 26480970, 26421114, Fax: 26486287 — vkgboks@ndb.vsnl.net.in

V.P.H. SUBSCRIPTION SERVICES, Kolkata
Fax: 23588297 — vijoyaph@cal2.vsnl.net.in

V.R. ENTERPRISES, Delhi
✆ 27565562, Fax: 27865139 — vrenterprises@mantraonline.com

VAARAANTARI RANI (RANI WEEKLY), Chennai
✆ 25324771 — rani.chen@gems.vsnl.net.in

VAASTU-FENGSHUI-HOME DECORS, New Delhi
✆ 25701836 — wondervision@hotmail.com

VAGDEVI PRAKASHAN, Bikaner
✆ (O) & (R) 2200955, 2521200, Fax: 2204100 — vagdevi_jp1@sancharnet.in

VAGYOGA CHETANA PUBLICATION, Varanasi
✆ 2311706, Fax: 0542-2314615 — Vagyoga@hotmail.com

VAIBHAV LITCO, Delhi
✆ 38108989, 20043308 ▮ 9810425755
Telefax: 23646564 — vaibhavlitco@rediffmail.com

VAK (THE SPIRITUAL BOOKSHOP), Pondicherry
✆ 234908, 234542 — himatsingka@auroville.org.in

VAKILS FEFFER AND SUMENS LTD., Mumbai
✆ (O) 22619121, 22611221 (R) 22631977
Fax: 22610432 — bimal@vakilsonline.com

VALLEY BOOK HOUSE, Srinagar
✆ 2428526, Fax: 2427537 — telehamid1@rediffmail.com

VALUE BOOKS PVT. LTD., New Delhi
▮ 9810507555, 9811528900, Fax: 91-11-25860888 — galoswal@yahoo.com

VANI PRAKASHAN, New Delhi
✆ (O) 23273167, 23275710 (R) 22286292, 22110879
Fax: 23275710 — vaniprakashan@gmail.com, vani_prakashan@mantraonline.com

VANS INFORMATION AND INVESTOR SERVICES LTD., New Delhi
✆ 23279201, 23279202, Fax: 23279203 — vansdel@nda.vsnl.net.in

VARDHMAN BOOKS, Delhi
▮ (O) 9811287652 (R) 32367515 — vardhmanbooks@indiatimes.com

VARDHMAN PUBLICATIONS, Delhi
✆ 22141122, 35201206 — vardhmanmaps@yahoo.com

VARIETY BOOK DEPOT (THE), New Delhi
✆ (O) 23412567, 23417175, 23415030
(R) 24602032, 24624028, Fax: 23415335, 51517201
@ varietybookdepot@rediffmail.com

VARIETY BOOK STORE, Chandigarh
✆ 2702241, Fax: 0172-2710894
@ vbs_69@yahoo.com

VARMA BOOK DISTRIBUTORS, Pune
✆ 24450595, 24456525, Fax: 24450148
@ guest@biointu.ernet.in, varma@vsnl.com

VARSHA BOOK DISTRIBUTORS, Hyderabad
✆ 27632126
@ varshabooks@usa.net

VARTIKA PRAKASHAN, New Delhi
✆ 29230181
@ anil@bol.net.in

VARUN BOOKS INTERNATIONAL, New Delhi
✆ 23250586, 23255747, 55390704
▮ 9811220876, Telefax: 23279603
@ varunbooks@rediffmail.com, varunbooks@yahoo.co.in

VARUN EXPORTS, New Delhi
✆ 23289259, 23271632, 23286096
Fax: 91-11-23286096
@ varunex@vsnl.net

VASAN BOOK COMPANY, New Delhi
✆ 23245666, 23283078, Fax: 91-11-41563666
@ info@harisai.com, vasan@harisai.com

VASAN BOOK DEPOT, Bangalore
✆ 6705679, 2264709, Fax: 6705107
@ vasanbks@bgl.vsnl.net.in

VASAN PUBLICATIONS, Bangalore
✆ 080-26705679, 080-26705107, Fax: 26705107
@ info@mastermindbooks.com

VASANTHA BOOK STALL, Kollam
✆ 2748572, Fax: 2743311
@ vasanthabooks@rediffmail.com

VASUNDHARA PRAKASHAN PVT. LTD., Mumbai
✆ 56960587, 25705857, Fax: 25705291
@ envirotekindia@vsnl.net

VATSAL PRAKASHAN, Bikaner
✆ 91-151-2206452
@ vagdevibooks@gmail.com

VAYU BOOK SHOPPING.COM, New Delhi
✆ 65235268, Fax: 91-11-41564445
@ vayubookshopping@yahoo.com

VEDA-SANSTHANA, New Delhi
✆ 25102316
@ vedic_science@yahoo.co.in

VEE KUMAR PUBLICATIONS PVT. LTD., New Delhi
✆ 25720718, 25760718, Fax: 25711718
@ kumarpublications@rediffmail.com

VEENA BOOK CENTRE, Bangalore
✆ 23469183, 2876706, 2265077
Fax: 23469359, 2261132
@ vbc@bgl.vsnl.net.in

VENDRAME INSTITUTE PUBLICATIONS, Shillong
✆ (O) 0364-2250141 (R) 2250577
@ mathias@sancharnet.in

VIBHA BOOKS INTERNATIONAL, New Delhi
▮ 9868525200
@ vibhabooks@hotmail.com

VICTORY GRAPHIK, Hyderabad
✆ 91-40-24613753, Fax: 91-49-24613731
@ victorygraphik@yahoo.co.in

VIDYA BOOKS, New Delhi
✆ 25707396 ▮ 9811387853, Fax: 25707396
@ vidyabooks97@rediffmail.com

VIDYA CHITR PRAKASHAN, New Delhi ✆ 23262667, 23271400, Fax: 23271400	vidyachitr@indiatimes.com, vcp@vsnl.com
VIDYA PRAKASHAN MANDIR, Meerut ✆ (O) 2516012, 2510830 (R) 2511192, 2513783 Fax: 2512755	info@vidyaprakashan.com
VIDYA PRAKASHAN MANDIR LTD., Meerut ✆ 2510830, 2513845, Fax: 2512755	info@vidyaprak.com
VIDYA VIHAR, New Delhi ✆ 23257555, Fax: 91-11-23253233	prabhatbooks@id.eth.net
VIDYAPURI, Cuttack ✆ (O) 2620637 (R) 2617260	ctk-vpuri@sancharnet.in
VIDYARAMBHAM PUBLISHERS, Alappuzha ✆ 0477-2251259, 2261151, Fax: 2254658	vidyarambham@sancharnet.in
VIDYARTHI KENDRA, Varanasi ✆ 2329888, 2320730, Fax: 2391322	vidyarti@nde_vsnl.net.in
VIDYARTHI PRAKASHAN (P) LTD., Saharanpur ✆ (O) 2726724, 2726298 (R) 2725179, 2726245 Fax: 0132-2727104	vidyarthipark@rediffmail.com
VIDYARTHI SALES AGENCIES, Mumbai ✆ 23829330, 23867279, 23851416 ▮ 9821770062 Fax: 23895661	vidyarthi@rolta.net
VIGYAN PRASAR, Noida ✆ 0120-2404430/31/35/36 (R) 26175242 Fax: 91-120-2404437	vigyan@hub.nic.in
VIJ BOOK STORE, New Delhi ✆ 011-43596460, 65449971, Telefax: 011-43596460	vijbooks@rediffmail.com
VIJAY BOOK SERVICE, Delhi ✆ 27316172	mehta-76@hotmail.com
VIJAY GOEL, Delhi ✆ 22324833, Fax: 91-11-22324833	goelbooks@rediffmail.com
VIJAY PRAKASHAN, New Delhi ✆ 25462580, 25422580, Fax: 25422580	galaxy10@vsnl.com
VIJAY STORES, Ahmedabad ✆ 079-25356479, 25331321, Fax: 2403492, 25356479	vijay_magazine@indiatimes.com, pkamdarad1@sancharnet.in
VIJAYA PRAKASHAN, Ahmedabad ✆ 6924003, Fax: 26764765	shevadepd@yahoo.co.uk, vijpr@yahoo.com
VIJAYA STORES, Chennai ✆ 2494007, 24954932	vijayastores@vsnl.net.in
VIJAYA VIHAARAM, Secunderabad ✆ 27007053, Fax: 27002240	vijayavihaaram@rediffmail.com
VIJAYAWADA BOOK FESTIVAL SOCIETY, Vijayawada ✆ 0866-2570843, 2573354	bookfestvj@sancharnet.in
VIJAYKUMAR GOVINDRAM HASANAND, Delhi ✆ 23914945, 23977216, Fax: 23911057	ajayarya@vsnl.com
VIKAS BOOK DISTRIBUTORS, Delhi ✆ 22098340	vikas_book@yahoo.com

VIKAS BOOKS LTD., New Delhi
✆ 32445202, 23287224, Fax: 91-565-2601537 — atuljain@vikasbooksltd.com

VIKAS LAW HOUSE, Delhi
✆ 22410091, 22230491 — vikas_law@rediffmail.com

VIKAS PAPERBACKS, Delhi
✆ 32932084, Fax: 91-11-23281244 — vikaspaperbacks@yahoo.com

VIKAS PUBLISHING HOUSE PVT. LTD., Noida
✆ 0120-4078900, Fax: 0120-4078999 — helpline@vikaspublishing.com

VIKMANS MULTIMEDIA (INDIA) PVT. LTD., New Delhi
✆ 26429547, 26212325, Fax: 11-26429547 — skaur@del12.net.in

VINAYAKA AGENCIES, Bangalore
✆ 23307022, 23303142, Fax: 23381559 — kpn_pacemaker@usa.net

VINOD PUSTAK MANDIR, Agra
✆ (O) 2155179, 2155187 (R) 2524532
Fax: 0562-2519090 — vpm@agr.dot.net.in, vpm@sancharnet.in

VINTAGE BOOKS, New Delhi
✆ 26867595, 26567709 — vinbooks@bol.net.in, vintage_books@yahoo.com

VINTAGE MEDIA, Delhi
✆ 27241674, 27135299 — vinmedia@bol.net.in

VISALA ANDHRA PUBLISHING HOUSE, Hyderabad
✆ 24744580, 24735905, 24602946
Fax: 91-40-24735905 — visalaandhraph@yahoo.com

VISHAL BOOK CENTRE, Kolkata
✆ 033-22527816, 22523709, Fax: 033-22523564 — vishal@cal.vsnl.net.in

VISHAL PRAKASHAN MANDIR, Meerut
✆ 0121-2648776, 2642596, 2519897
Fax: 91-121-2668118 — info@vishalprakashanmandir.com

VISHAL PUBLICATION CO., Jalandhar
✆ 0181-2232294, Fax: 91-181-5005403 — vishalpubco@rediffmail.com

VISHV GRANTH MALA, Thane
9970016684 — samvadindia@vsnl.net

VISHV VIJAY PVT. LTD., New Delhi
✆ 23321313, Fax: 51540714, 23625020 — mybooks@vishvbooks.com

VISHVA BHARATI RESEARCH INSTITUTE/VISHVA BHARATI BOOK AGENCY, Bhadohi
✆ 05414-251045, Fax: 91-5414-251045 — drbdvivedi@hotmail.com

VISHVAS PUBLICATIONS PVT. LTD., Chandigarh
✆ 2653139, 2641778, 2385649, Fax: 2641778 — vishvas@glide.net.in

VISHWA BHARATI YOGA SANSTHAN, Delhi
✆ 22525818, Fax: 22547253 — prembhatia_vbys@yahoo.com

VISHWA VIDYALAYA PRAKASHAN, Varanasi
✆ (O) 0542-2413741, 2413082
(R) 2436349, 2311423, Fax: 2413082 — sales@vvpbooks.com

VISION BOOKS PVT. LTD., New Delhi
✆ (O) 23278877 (R) 23972062, Fax: 91-11-23278879 — mail@orientpaperbacks

VISION WORLD WIDE, New Delhi
✆ 25767207, 25729468, Fax: 25767205 — gbajaj@hotmail.com

VISTA INTERNATIONAL PUBLISHING HOUSE, Delhi
✆ 22921212, 65126093 — viph-vista@hotmail.com

VITASTA PUBLISHING PRIVATE LIMITED, New Delhi
✆ 23283024, Fax: 91-11-23263522 — renu@vitastapublishing.com

VIVA BOOKS PVT. LTD./VIVA MARKETING, New Delhi
✆ 42242200, 42242214, Fax: 91-11-23267224 — viva@mantraonline.com, viva@vivagroupindia.net, vivamarketing@vivagroupindia.net

VIVEK PRAKASHAN, Delhi
✆ (O) 23854014, 23944465 (R) 26948198, 27651104 Fax: 23944014 — vivek.prakashan@rediffmail.com

VIVEKANAND YOGASHRAM, Delhi
✆ 22502142, Fax: 22424057 — healing@bol.net.in

VOLUNTARY HEALTH ASSOCIATION OF INDIA, New Delhi
✆ 26518071-72, 26515018, Fax: 26853708 — vhai@vsnl.com, vhai@del2.vsnl.net.in

VORA MEDICAL PUBLICATIONS, Mumbai
✆ 23754161, 23704053, Fax: 23704053 — voramedpub@yahoo.co.in

VRINDA PUBLICATIONS (P) LTD., Delhi
✆ 22755315-16, Fax: 22757220, 22795949 — vrinda@ndf.vsnl.net.in

■ ■ ■

W

W.P. PUBLISHERS & DISTRIBUTORS PVT. LTD., Bangalore
✆ 32721980, 5273536, 5273207 Fax: 91-80-41642688 — murali@wppublishers.com, mail@wpublishers.com

W.R. GOYAL PUBLISHERS & DISTRIBUTORS, Delhi
✆ 23852986, Fax: 91-11-23850961 — goyal@vsnl.com

WWW.E-DIKSHA.COM, New Delhi
✆ 25912191, 25912205, Fax: 25912205 — uitratra@bol.net.in

WADHWA & COMPANY, New Delhi
✆ 26482756, 26232344, Fax: 26228898 — wadhwa@wadhwain.com

WALDEN BOOKS, Hyderabad
✆ 23313434, Fax: 23393344 — walden@hd1.vsnl.net.in

WATTAN PUBLICATIONS, Srinagar
✆ (O) 0194-2458436, 2458794 (R) 2451722 — wattan_publications@yahoo.com

WEBNOTIONS BOOKS INDIA PVT. LTD., New Delhi
9899868109 — shinug@a1bookd.com

WELLWORTH BOOKS INTERNATIONAL, New Delhi
✆ 25521743, Fax: 91-11-25524078 — wellworthbooks@yahoo.co.in

WESTERN BOOK DEPOT, Nagpur
✆ (O) 2524659 (R) 2532544, Fax: 0712-2537896 — westernbookdejul@hotmail.com

WESTLAND BOOK PVT. LTD., Bangalore ✆ 26606048, 26612243	@ ewbbir@dg1.vsnl.net.in
WESTVILLE PUBLISHING HOUSE, New Delhi ✆ 25284742, 25267469, Fax: 25267469	@ westville_2002@yahoo.co.in
WILCO INTERNATIONAL/WILCO PUBLISHING HOUSE, Mumbai ✆ 22842574, 22041420, Fax: 91-22-22041429	@ wilco@bom2.vsnl.net.in, wilcos@vsnl.com, wexports@bom5.vsnl.net.in
WILEY-DREANTECH INDIA (P) LTD., New Delhi ✆ 23260877, 23270877, Fax: 23275895	@ ldgbooks@vsnl.com, wdt@vsnl.net
WILEY INDIA (P) LTD., New Delhi ✆ 43630000, 23260877, 23270877 Fax: 91-11-23275895	@ csupport@wileyindia.com, wdt@vsnl.net
WINDOM PUBLISHING PVT. LTD., Chennai ✆ 23743062, 23745826	@ pkmadhu@md3.vsnl.net.in
WINGS PUBLICATIONS, Bangalore ✆ (O) 26637244, 2649002 (R) 26722861	@ wings@theoffice.net
WINLAND BOOKS, Kerala ✆ 0478-2872886 ▮ 9846192611	@ nishadebrahim@hotmail.com
WINNERZ TRACK, Delhi ✆ 22619775	@ winnerztrack@gmail.com
WINSAR PUBLISHING CO., Dehradun ✆ 91-135-3294463	@ info@uttarakhandyearbook.com
WINSOME BOOKS INDIA, Delhi ✆ 43026937, Fax: 91-11-65845445	@ windsomebooks@rediffmail.com
WISDOM BOOKS PVT. LTD., Kolkata ✆ (O) 33-24764311/4313, Fax: 24764313	@ admin@wisdombooks.com
WISDOM PUBLICATIONS, Delhi ✆ 65289229, Fax: 91-11-22157646	@ wisdompublications@rediffmail.com
WISDOM TREE, New Delhi ✆ 23247966-7, Fax: 91-11-23247966	@ wisdomtree@vsnl.com
WITNESS BOOKS, Goa ✆ 0832-2463050 ▮ 9823026348, Fax: 2463050	@ witnessbooks@rediffmail.com
WOLTERS KLUWER ACADEMIC PUBLISHERS, New Delhi ✆ 26520175, Fax: 26520176	@ kluwer@nde.vsnl.net.in
WOLTERS KLUWER ACADEMIC PUBLISHERS, New Delhi ✆ 46530300, Fax: 91-11-46530399	@ vinay.singh@wolterskluwer.com
WONDERLAND PUBLISHERS, Delhi ✆ 27102745	@ wonderlands@mantraonline.com
WONDERVISION, New Delhi ▮ 9810094519	@ wondervision@rediffmail.com
WORDSPEAK INC., New Delhi ✆ 23255799, 23287589, Fax: 91-11-23270385	@ aryanbooks@vsnl.com
WORLD ASSEMBLY OF MUSLIM YOUTH, New Delhi ✆ 26929354, Fax: 23282834	@ wamy@satyam.net.in
WORLD BOOK, Kolkata ✆ 2192328	@ worldbook@sify.com

WORLD BOOK ENTERPRISES, New Delhi
✆ 23273025 — worldbook@mantraonline.com

WORLD BOOK HOUSE, Guwahati
tnsatyal@yahoo.co.in

WORLD BOOK INC. INDIGO, Mumbai
✆ 22040477 — indigoedu.vsnl.net

WORLD BOOK SERVICE, Mumbai
✆ 25222240, Fax: 25294971 — hsk@giasbm01.vsnl.net.in

WORLD BOOKS, Bangalore
✆ (O) 56996472 ▮ 9845698062 — pmjoyworlds@yahoo.com.in

WORLD HEALTH ORGANIZATION, New Delhi
✆ 23370804, 23318607, Fax: 91-11-23370809 — publications@searo.who.int

WORLD SCIENTIFIC PUBLISHING CO. PTE. LTD., Bangalore
✆ 22863744, 22865189, 22229351
Fax: 22863744, 23344593 — wspcind@blr.vsnl.net.in

WORLD SCIENTIFIC PUBLISHING CO. PVT. LTD., Chennai
✆ 22773551 — jnangia@wspc.com

WORLD WIDE FUND FOR NATURE INDIA (WWF-INDIA) BOOK SHOP, New Delhi
✆ 41504802, Fax: 91-11-41504779 — marketing@wwfindia.net

WORLDVIEW PUBLICATIONS, Delhi
✆ 23918974, Fax: 23919045 — worldview@vsnl.com

WORLDWIDE BOOK TRADERS, Delhi
✆ (O) 22448456 (R) 22485269, 33186318, 33189529 — diwan-96@hotmail.com

WRITER'S PUBLISHING HOUSE, Bhopal
✆ 2485444, 2481101 — wphbhopal@yahoo.co.in

WROX INDIA PVT. LTD., Mumbai
✆ 28251811, 28252563, Fax: 28309533 — support@wrox.co.in

X

XACT GROUP, Delhi
✆ 91-11-27228802, 27442268, Fax: 91-11-47091120 — info@xactstudio.com

Y

YAK BOOK CHANNEL, Jammu Tawi
✆ 0191-248909, 2549919, 2578909 ✉ rajiv1@nde.vsnl.net.in
Fax: 247885, 2547862

YAQOOB BROTHERS, Srinagar
✆ (O) 0091-194-2425880 (R) 2421578 ✉ yaqoob@nde.vsnl.net.in
Fax: 2427537

YASH PUBLISHING HOUSE, Bikaner
✆ 0151-2207587 ✉ yash_pub@yahoo.com

YASHDEEP PRAKASHAN, Faridabad
✆ 91-129-4074957, Fax: 91-129-4074957 ✉ vikeshbeniwal@yahoo.com

YATIN PUBLICATIONS (REGD.), Delhi
✆ 23285501, 23260329, Fax: 23285501 ✉ info@brilliantbooksindia.com

YODA PRESS, New Delhi
✆ 43582770, 23324096 ✉ parul@yodapress.com

YOGA CONSCIOUSNESS TRUST, Vizianagaram
✆ 91-8966-278680 ✉ kiranvsr@yahoo.com

YOGA PUBLISHING HOUSE, Delhi
✆ 91-11-22376155 ✉ girikripa@vsnl.com

YOGA PUBLICATIONS TRUST, Munger
✆ 06344-222430, Fax: 220169 ✉ ypt@yogavision.net

YOGA SOCIETY, Ghaziabad
✆ 4600237 ✉ iys@ndf.vsnl.net.in

YOGODA SATSANGA DHYANA KENDRA, Hyderabad
✆ 27767261, 23358331, Fax: 23746671 ✉ ipshah@nomus.net.in

YOGODA SATSANGA SAKHA KENDRA, Delhi
✆ 91-11-23346271, 23362948 ✉ yssdelhikendra@gmail.com
Fax: 91-11-23362948

YOGODA SATSANGA SOCIETY OF INDIA, Ranchi
✆ 91-651-2460071 ✉ info@yogoda.in

YOGSON INTERNATIONAL, New Delhi
✆ 23541299, 23628303, Fax: 23676565 ✉ scholar@vsnl.com

YOUNG ANGELS, New Delhi
✆ 91-11-45044727 ✉ youngangels01@gmail.com

YUG KALYAN, Gorakhpur
✆ 91-551-2333030, Fax: 91-551-2336997 ✉ manager@gitapress.org

YUG NIRMAN YOJNA, Mathura
✆ 91-565-2530128, Fax: 91-565-2530200 ✉ ajsansthan@awgp.org

Z

ZENITH GLOBAL CONSULTANT LTD., Mumbai
✆ 22046094-95, Fax: 22041844 — @ zenglobe@bom3.vsnl.net.in

ZOOLOGICAL SURVEY OF INDIA, Kolkata
✆ 22875463, Fax: 24006893 — @ rrr-ppozsi@yahoo.com

ZOOLOGICAL SURVEY OF INDIA, Kolkata
✆ 22475463, Fax: 24008595 — @ ratis-raj@hotmail.com, dirzsi@wb.nic.in

ZUBAAN, New Delhi
✆ 26494617, 26494618, Telefax: 26494613 — @ zubaanwbooks@vsnl.net, zubaan@gmail.com

JOSEPH CONRAD

...... Heart of Darkness	60.00
...... Lord Jim	60.00
...... The Nigger of the 'Narcissus'	60.00
...... The Secret Agent	70.00

LEWIS CARROLL

...... Alice's Adventures in Wonderland & Through the Looking-Glass	60.00

MARK TWAIN

...... The Adventures of Tom Sawyer and the Adventures of Huckleberry Finn	95.00

MARY SHELLEY

...... Frankenstein	75.00

NATHANIEL HAWTHORNE

...... The Scarlet Letter	70.00

ROBERT LOUIS STEVENSON

...... Treasure Island	60.00

RUDYARD KIPLING

...... The Jungle Books	85.00

SIR WALTER SCOTT

...... Ivanhoe	85.00

THOMAS HARDY

...... Far from the Madding Crowd	80.00
...... Jude the Obscure	80.00
...... The Mayor of Casterbridge	75.00
...... The Return of the Native	85.00
...... Tess of the D'Urbervilles	85.00

VIRGINIA WOOLF

...... Mrs Dalloway	60.00
...... Orlando	85.00
...... To the Lighthouse	60.00
...... The Waves	60.00

WILLIAM SHAKESPEARE

...... Antony and Cleopatra	60.00
...... As You Like It	60.00
...... Hamlet	60.00
...... Henry IV Part One	60.00
...... Henry V	60.00
...... Julius Caesar	60.00
...... King Lear	60.00
...... Macbeth	60.00
...... Measure for Measure	60.00
...... The Merchant of Venice	60.00
...... A Midsummer Night's Dream	60.00
...... Much Ado About Nothing	60.00
...... Othello	60.00
...... Romeo and Juliet	60.00
...... The Tempest	60.00
...... Twelfth Night	60.00

PEACOCK BOOKS

AN IMPRINT OF ATLANTIC PUBLISHERS & DISTRIBUTORS (P) LTD.

Please send your orders to

ATLANTIC

PUBLISHERS & DISTRIBUTORS (P) LTD

Showroom & Sales: 7/22, Ansari Road, Darya Ganj, New Delhi-110 002
Tel: +91-11-4077 5252, 2327 3880, 2327 5880, 2328 0451, 3090 3641
Fax: +91-11-2328 5873 • E-mail: info@atlanticbooks.com
Chennai Branch: 5, Nallathambi Street, Wallajah Road, Chennai-600 002
Tel.: +91-44-6461 1085, 3241 3319, Mobile: 099406 84835 • E-mail: chennai@atlanticbooks.com